START BY BELIEVING

START BY BELIEVING

LARRY NASSAR'S CRIMES,
THE INSTITUTIONS THAT ENABLED HIM,
AND THE BRAVE WOMEN
WHO STOPPED A MONSTER

JOHN BARR
& DAN MURPHY

hachette
BOOKS

NEW YORK   BOSTON

Hachette Books
Hachette Book Group
1290 Avenue of the Americas
New York, NY 10104

HachetteBooks.com

Twitter.com/HachetteBooks

Instagram.com/HachetteBooks

First Edition: January 2020

Hachette Books is a division of Hachette Book Group, Inc.

The Hachette Books name and logo are trademarks of Hachette Book Group, Inc.

The publisher is not responsible for websites (or their content) that are not owned by the publisher.

The Hachette Speakers Bureau provides a wide range of authors for speaking events. To find out more, go to www.hachettespeakersbureau.com or call (866) 376-6591.

Print book interior design by Six Red Marbles, Inc.

Library of Congress Cataloging-in-Publication Data
Names: Barr, John (Sportswriter), author. | Murphy, Dan (Sportswriter), author.
Title: Start by believing: Larry Nassar's crimes, the institutions that enabled him, and the brave women who stopped a monster / John Barr & Dan Murphy.
Description: First edition. | New York, NY: Hachette Books, 2020. | Includes index.
Identifiers: LCCN 2019031505 (print) | LCCN 2019031506 (ebook) | ISBN 9780316532150 (hardcover) | ISBN 9780316532136 (ebook)
Subjects: LCSH: Nassar, Larry. | Women athletes—Abuse of—United States. | Child sexual abuse—United States. | Child molesters—United States. | Sex crimes—United States. | Sexual abuse victims—United States. | Sports—Corrupt practices—United States. | Universities and colleges—Corrupt practices—United States.
Classification: LCC HV6570.2 .B34 2020 (print) | LCC HV6570.2 (ebook) | DDC 364.15/3092—dc23
LC record available at https://lccn.loc.gov/2019031505
LC ebook record available at https://lccn.loc.gov/2019031506

ISBNs: 978-0-316-53215-0 (hardcover), 978-0-316-53213-6 (ebook)

Printed in the United States of America

LSC-C

10 9 8 7 6 5 4 3 2 1

For the survivors

Contents

Contents

Part III
THE WRONG ARMY

This is what it looks like when the adults in authority do not respond properly to disclosures of sexual assault.... *This is what it looks like.*

It looks like a courtroom full of survivors who carry deep wounds.

—RACHAEL DENHOLLANDER

Authors' Note

Before there were hundreds, there were two. On August 29, 2016, Rachael Denhollander, a thirty-one-year-old former gymnast, filed a report with the Michigan State University police department, telling a detective she had been sexually assaulted sixteen years earlier by her doctor, Larry Nassar, during medical examinations. Ten days later, Jamie Dantzscher, under the name "Jane JD Doe," filed the first civil lawsuit against Nassar, USA Gymnastics, and its top officials, revealing how Nassar sexually assaulted her for years. The following week, the stories of both women appeared in the *Indianapolis Star*, the newspaper whose dogged reporters first brought the decades-long scandal to the public's attention.

It was around that time that we began our own reporting on the Nassar case. At the time, we didn't have any idea where the story would lead us. Nobody did. The world—strangers, close friends, and even some of his victims—did not yet understand how Nassar created a career that allowed him to prey on hundreds of girls and young women or how the environment that produced the largest sexual abuse scandal in the history of sports fostered his crimes.

What became clear early in our reporting is that Nassar's crimes weren't limited to a few women like Rachael Denhollander and Jamie Dantzscher in the distant past. He was a master manipulator who for decades groomed and sexually abused his patients, a group that included some of America's biggest Olympic stars, including some who had just weeks earlier won gold medals in Brazil. While many of these women weren't yet ready to share their stories with the public, we learned the scope of Nassar's crimes would be enough to shock the nation if eventually revealed in full. Our reporting raised pressing questions about how many others were suffering in silence and how he was able to hide his actions for so long while operating so close to the spotlight.

The pursuit of answers led us to a deeper understanding of the trauma experienced by sexual assault victims and the courage needed to publicly reveal abuse. It also led us into the highly dysfunctional world of club and elite-level gymnastics, a world where emotional and physical abuse is normalized, where young girls are conditioned not to question authority and to remain silent as they are used and broken. This is the world in which Nassar hid in plain sight for more than a quarter century.

Understanding how Nassar gained unfettered access to thousands of young girls, despite repeated warning signs, meant confronting an uncomfortable truth: he didn't gain that access alone. Nassar was surrounded by a complex web of enablers, a group that included coaches of club, collegiate, and elite-level gymnasts; the USA Gymnastics organization and its top administrators and coaches; and medical professionals, administrators, and coaches at Michigan State University.

The material in these pages is the result of more than two and a half years of reporting. We've interviewed sources from dozens of states. We've reviewed thousands of pages of documents, including public court records, police reports, Title IX reports, and other documents obtained from Michigan State University through public records requests. We also drew on newspaper reports, social media posts, and the personal materials of those involved.

Authors' Note

While more than 150 sources spoke with us, many did so under the condition that they remain unnamed. Others declined to be interviewed for the book or didn't respond to interview requests. Most notable among those who chose not to be interviewed: Larry Nassar, who did not speak to any reporters during the time between his arrest and the publishing of this book. We did our best to provide everyone mentioned in the story that follows an opportunity to participate and share their perspective.

As our research gave us a deeper insight into Nassar and his actions, we came to understand this as a story about power and control. In the beginning, Nassar and the systems at USA Gymnastics and Michigan State University that enabled him exercised total control over the lives of the young women and girls he sexually assaulted. In the end, this remarkable group of survivors took back control, spoke truth to power, toppled the leadership of both institutions, and, in so doing, empowered countless others.

Our decision to focus this version of events on certain women involved should in no way diminish the importance of those not mentioned. Each survivor's story matters. It is our hope that the accounts we chose reflect the strength and courage exhibited by the collective group. We have extensively checked events via interviews and through documents and other primary sources. We have sought to include a full range of perspectives in a fluid, unfolding story.

We also wrestled with the question of surnames. We've decided to forego the journalistic practice of referring to certain women, like Jamie Dantzscher and Rachael Denhollander, whom you'll meet in just a few pages, by their surnames upon second reference. The same applies to Kyle Stephens, whom you'll meet later in the book. For the sake of consistency and clarity—and because the reader will follow these three women through many stages of life—we chose to use their first names throughout the book. While on occasion we'll use first names of others for the purpose of clarity, we'll generally use surnames for all other subjects.

Telling these stories properly means including sensitive events and difficult information of a nature that may be a trigger for survivors of sexual assault or others impacted by other types of sexual misconduct. After consulting with experts, we felt it was important to provide a fact-based account of Nassar's crimes that avoided minimizing his actions or making the events unclear by relying on euphemisms. We hope readers will approach this story with that cautionary note in mind and also keep in mind resources like the National Sexual Assault Hotline (800-656-HOPE) and the National Child Abuse Hotline (800-422-4453).

Prologue

More than anything, she remembers the fear. As Jamie Dantzscher walked briskly through the executive air terminal of the Oakland airport she was gripped by a familiar churning in the pit of her stomach. It was the same feeling she experienced years earlier at every practice, competition, and trip to the ranch.

By the summer of 2016, Jamie thought she was on her way to putting gymnastics in her past. She'd recently earned her real estate license. She hoped it would be her ticket away from the gymnastics camps and coaching that served as a source of income but that were also a constant reminder of her own career in a leotard. She even avoided watching gymnastics on television. The thought of hearing praise for Bela and Marta Karolyi, the legendary coaching couple who steered Jamie and her teammates to a bronze medal at the 2000 Sydney Olympics, made her feel sick.

Jamie never felt proud of her decorated, elite gymnastics career. The memories of physically abusive training, eating disorders, and suicidal thoughts would forever outweigh the stacks of awards and honors she collected. The best day she experienced in the sport, she often told people, was the day she quit.

At thirty-four, Jamie was finally poised to put that part of her life behind her when a conversation with another gymnast unearthed the darkest and most repressed of her gymnastics memories. It was something she'd never shared with anyone. She consulted with a former teammate before fully accepting the truth: she was a victim of sexual assault. Jamie's former teammate Dominique Moceanu had then connected her to a woman named Katherine Starr, a former Olympian and sexual abuse survivor in Southern California, who worked as a legal consultant on child sex abuse cases.

Starr made the ninety-minute flight to Oakland that morning on the Beechcraft King Air twin turboprop owned by the man she wanted Jamie to meet. John Manly had never heard of Jamie before their August 12, 2016, meeting was scheduled. Never laid eyes on her until she was walking through the terminal. The Irvine, California–based attorney had met with hundreds of victims of child sex abuse through the years and represented more than two thousand of them. He had never heard a story like the one Jamie would begin to unravel.

Inside the meeting room, John Manly sipped a soft drink and squinted as he peered through the miniblinds and watched Jamie draw closer.

"Boy, she's tiny," he thought to himself as the former gymnast came into focus.

The room was a tight fit. Housed in what looked from the outside like a portable classroom, it was no more than eight-by-eight feet and felt even smaller when Manly closed the blinds. Jamie, dressed in yoga pants and a T-shirt, her brunette hair pulled back in a ponytail, settled into her seat and fixed her brown eyes on the attorney. She'd just come from coaching a practice.

Manly started, as he always did, with an apology. He told Jamie what happened to her was not her fault and that she displayed courage by making it to the airport hangar that morning. Jamie steeled herself and, for the first time, started to tell these virtual strangers about her former doctor.

"He was my buddy," she began, as she recounted her time on the US national team.

She explained that the doctor told her to call him by his first name, snuck her candy when she was weak from hunger, and comforted her with hugs after particularly hard training sessions. He was so kind that she never thought twice about his unsupervised visits to her hotel rooms. He sat on the edge of her bed at training camps and told her he was treating her injuries while he slipped his hands over her breasts and inside her vagina. Manly and Starr listened quietly while looking at Jamie. Her eyes held a "thousand-yard stare," the demeanor of someone describing a near-death experience.

Jamie was not the stereotypical high achiever filled with bubbly energy, the gymnastics personality of television broadcasts and Olympic competitions. Manly was struck by a dark sadness in her face as she described her time as one of America's best young athletes. It was a look he knew well. He ticked through his list of standard questions he asks at the start of a sexual assault case. "Have you ever been married? Do you have trouble keeping jobs? Do you have trust issues with men?"

Jamie's answers confirmed what Manly and Starr believed when they agreed to make the trip to Oakland. He locked eyes with Jamie from across the conference table.

"I believe you were sexually assaulted," Manly told her. "I want to take your case."

My case? What case? Jamie thought to herself. She hadn't come to the meeting prepared to file a lawsuit. She thought the meeting was a step in the process of reporting a man who'd molested her while she was pursuing her Olympic dream.

"Nobody's going to believe me, and they're going to come after me," she told Manly.

"Yes, they will," he assured her. "Because you're telling the truth."

Jamie managed to hold back the tears until she left the conference room. They were streaming down her face by the time she got back to her car. She'd dealt with the people who wielded power in the world of elite gymnastics for so long, dealt with the control they exercised over every aspect of her life. She criticized the sport before and wanted no part of the people and responses that would follow if she spoke up again.

The thought of returning to that lonely place filled her with a sense of dread. The reality that she was a victim of sexual assault was only now starting to take shape in her mind. As she drove away, her first instinct was to tell her mother about what had happened in her meeting with Manly, and that's when the full weight of it came down on her.

What the fuck is going on with my life?

The skies were cloudy on the first day of the fall semester in East Lansing, Michigan. A cool breeze swept through the campus of Michigan State University. Groups of young men and women walked and rode bikes along the banks of the Red Cedar River, mapping out new schedules and morning routines. A few blocks south, a line snaked out the front door of the university police department headquarters. Students lingered outside the squat, utilitarian building, chatting excitedly about their summers and the year ahead as they waited to collect their campus parking passes.

Rachael and Jacob Denhollander steered their silver minivan around the students and into the small parking lot outside the station. Jacob cut the engine. They sat side by side staring through the windshield, and together they prayed.

The night before, the Denhollanders and their three young children drove from their home in Louisville, Kentucky, to the house where Rachael was raised in Kalamazoo, Michigan. The kids stayed with her parents, who were happy for the distraction. They tried to keep their minds from replaying the stories Rachael was about to tell the police.

Neither Rachael nor Jacob was looking forward to what lay ahead. Truthfully, they had no idea what would come of their trip to East Lansing. The previous few weeks had been a nerve-racking, sleep-deprived whirlwind. On August 4, Rachael had come across an article on the *Indianapolis Star*'s website, an in-depth investigation of the way USA Gymnastics—the national governing body for the sport—had for years mishandled sexual misconduct cases by failing to alert authorities to multiple allegations of sexual abuse made against coaches. To Rachael, the trio of reporters whose names appeared at the top of the page seemed to be thorough, fair, and knowledgeable on a subject that other outlets had struggled to cover in the past. A spark of hope flitted inside her. Perhaps, she thought, the opportunity she spent half her life waiting for had finally come.

Rachael fired off an email to the newspaper's investigative team to ask if, in their reporting, they had come across any complaints about a particular prominent Olympic physician. After eleven anxious nights, a reply arrived in her inbox from reporter Mark Alesia. He wanted to talk. Someone else, Alesia explained, was asking questions about the same doctor. Alesia told Rachael he couldn't share much about the other tipster, only that it was an attorney based in California, someone who had also come across their article when he was doing his own research on sexual assault in elite gymnastics.

For years, Rachael and her parents had wondered if she was the only one who was violated in the exam room at the end of the hallway at the MSU Sports Medicine Clinic. Her mother sat in the room for several appointments and harbored misgivings after a couple of them, uneasy feelings that Rachael eventually confirmed were warranted.

Surely there were others, they thought. They wondered if anyone else had raised concerns about the doctor's methods and been waved off. Perhaps someone had spoken up and nothing came of it. They coped together, never sharing the full story with anyone in a position of authority. Rachael didn't see the point in battling a powerful community figure when she didn't feel there was a chance to stop him. She promised herself, however, that if a window ever opened, if the opportunity for justice ever arrived, she would be ready to leap through it.

"You cannot imagine," she replied to Alesia, "what it means to hear there is someone else who mentioned him."

It was time to leap. Rachael agreed to share her story with the *Star* reporters in the hope that it would convince others to come forward. She went to work gathering any shred of information she could find to prove she was telling the truth. She collected old medical records and notes compiled from years of trying to understand what happened to her. She called medical experts and lawyers to get their opinions on her case. One of them surprised her by letting her know that it was not too late to file a police report.

After weeks of phone conversations and late-night research, Rachael scheduled a trip to East Lansing to meet with a detective. She compiled all her evidence and typed out a cover letter to summarize what happened to her. She kept the inches-thick stack of paper inside a manila folder, which now rested on her lap inside the minivan parked outside the university's police station. She and Jacob finished their prayer and unclipped their seatbelts.

"Well, this is it," Jacob said. She nodded, and they made their way to the front of the building.

Rachael told the cadet seated behind the glass partition at the reception desk that she was a few minutes early for an appointment with Detective Andrea Munford. They sat on a wooden bench and waited, Rachael in a long skirt and professional blouse, Jacob in a blazer and khakis. They watched as a parade of flip-flopped, bed-headed college students shuffled past.

Rachael gripped her husband's hand and held it tightly to one side of her body. On the other side, she kept the thick manila folder tucked snugly against her ribs. She tried to bury her concerns about what they were about to do and the even bigger concerns about where she had to do it. The MSU police chief, she knew, reported to the same university president who sat at the top of the chain for the medical school where her abuser had worked for nearly twenty years. He was a beloved man and an asset to a prestigious academic program and athletic department. Rachael's mind was filled with all the obvious reasons why Michigan State might want to make her and the problem she was about to present go away quietly. That was not her plan.

Munford, the leader of the department's special victims unit who joined the force shortly after graduating from Michigan State nearly two decades earlier, met the Denhollanders in the lobby and walked them back to a small, sparse interview room in a quiet part of the building. The short, dark-haired detective greeted them with a firm handshake. Rachael tried with little success to get a read on what preconceived notions the exceedingly professional, no-nonsense woman might hold about her case. She took a seat next to Jacob on a sofa built for two inside the cozy interview room. Munford sat in a comfortable chair on the other side of the table. A mini-fridge hummed in the corner. The lone box of tissues beside the Denhollanders went untouched.

Rachael's folder lay open on the coffee table. Piece by piece, she worked her way through the documents she had collected as she outlined for Munford a technical, matter-of-fact version of her story. She told Munford about participating in gymnastics as a young girl. She explained that she loved the sport despite the toll it took on her long, spindly body—a frame not built for gymnastics. She pulled old medical records out of her manila folder and showed the detective her different ailments and where she went to have them treated. Munford nodded along and scribbled notes on the pad in her lap.

Rachael told her that as a teenager her gymnastics coach had helped her get an appointment with a famed physician who worked with Olympians and some of Michigan State's top athletes on campus in East Lansing. She explained how the doctor groped her and put two of his fingers inside of her vagina while telling her that his "treatments" would fix her back problems. She told Munford that both she and her mother saw that the doctor appeared to be aroused after one of her final appointments. She pointed out that the records in front of them on the coffee table made no mention of internal treatments.

With the confidence of an expert witness testifying in court, Rachael then flipped to a series of articles from prominent medical journals and walked Munford through the science of pelvic floor adjustments. The articles described how physicians can manipulate muscles near a patient's groin to help solve some types of hip and back issues. The authors explained the value of a treatment that could be uncomfortable for obvious reasons. They also drew clear distinctions about when and how it was appropriate to use the technique.

Munford leaned over the table and asked questions as Rachael highlighted certain passages. This, Rachael told her, was how the doctor would try to justify the way he touched her if Munford questioned him. She suggested a few ways that Munford might challenge those assertions if the police decided this was a case worth pursuing.

She started to explain to Munford why she was only now in East Lansing talking about her experiences more than a decade after her last appointment. Munford assured her that waiting to report wasn't abnormal. Even so, Rachael wanted to prove that she was trustworthy. She pulled a letter out of her folder from a Michigan prosecutor, an old family friend who helped Rachael prepare for their meeting, vouching for her character. She had several similar letters from other community members confirming they believed Rachael to be smart, well-intentioned, and honest.

Rachael pulled out copies of case law and legislative history that would be key to determining if her sixteen-year-old case was within the limits of what could still be prosecuted. She showed Munford the *Indianapolis Star*'s exposé on the gymnastics world. She told her she had contacted reporters at the newspaper and that they said she wasn't the only one who had mentioned the doctor's name.

Munford nodded. The veteran investigator continued to play her cards close to the vest. She didn't mention that she already knew that Rachael wasn't alone.

The previous week, after speaking to Rachael on the phone to set up her appointment and go over the basic information of her complaint, Munford walked down the hallway and poked her head into the office of her boss, the department's assistant chief, Captain Valerie O'Brien. The name Rachael mentioned on the phone had sounded oddly familiar.

"Hey," Munford asked. "What was the name of the doctor you investigated for sexual assault a couple years back?"

O'Brien didn't take long to answer. "Larry Nassar," she said.

Munford thanked her. That's what she had thought.

Days later, as Rachael finished showing Munford the contents of her folder in the interview room, the detective held on to her stoic expression. Munford knew Nassar had talked his way out of at least one complaint in the past. His medical credentials and the long line of supporters willing to attest to his kindhearted, devoted personality were convincing. She knew sexual assault cases were hard to prosecute even when they involved perpetrators with far seedier reputations. But Rachael's story was convincing too, and Munford could tell the couple in front of her was braced for a long, painful process. The odds were stacked against them, but Munford saw a battle worth fighting.

She thanked the Denhollanders for their time and said she would follow up with them soon while she walked them back to the front door. She kept Rachael's contact information by her desk on a small, rectangular, white piece of paper. The slip of paper would stay there for years, long after their fight reached a conclusion that seemed impossible, unthinkable even, in the late summer of 2016. It served as a reminder of how a world-changing moment begins. Three bold words are printed across the top: **Start by Believing**.

Part I

THE BANALITY OF EVIL

Chapter 1

The Awkward Introvert

Larry Nassar wanted to be a runner.

Fred Nassar, Larry's father, was a runner. Fred set records in the 440-yard dash at his high school in Dearborn, Michigan, a blue-collar town on the outskirts of Detroit. Fred grew up to be an engineer. He married a woman named Mary, and they moved a short distance north to start a family. They had five children and named the youngest, born in 1963, Lawrence Gerard Nassar.

Larry was a quiet boy. He joined his junior high school's track team and planned to continue running at North Farmington High School when he arrived in 1977. But like many younger siblings, Larry wanted the company and approval of his big brother. Mike Nassar, two years older, had found a different role in the North Farmington High athletic department. He was the school's first student athletic trainer.

Sports medicine and athletic training remained a fledgling field in the 1970s. Most college and professional sports teams had a credentialed trainer, but they were virtually nonexistent at the high school level. It was common for coaches or even a student volunteer to assume those responsibilities.

Mike persuaded Larry to follow him into the field. Larry gave up on running and became the high school's next student athletic trainer. By the time he started taping ankles and stretching hamstrings for North Farmington High School athletes, Larry had grown to be a trim teenager with a big mop of dark hair above thick, aviator-style eyeglasses.

Mike and Larry were self-taught. They developed their skills by reading books on athletic training and through experience. Larry worked with the football team, the basketball team, and many other student-athletes in the novel role his brother carved for him. Before long, his list of responsibilities included the girls' gymnastics team at North Farmington. The gymnasts kept him busy during the winter of his senior year. The school's yearbook summarizes their season as one hampered by injuries. He earned a varsity letter for the amount of time he spent working with the team.

The Nassar siblings, in letters submitted to a federal judge decades later, recalled Larry as a diligent worker, oftentimes showing up late to family dinners in high school due to his training duties.

Larry tinkered. He once tried to find a way to design a football helmet that was easier to remove in the event of a head or neck injury. His oldest sister, Lin, twelve years his senior, invited the boys along to the classical dance classes she taught. Larry studied the ballerinas as they warmed up at the beginning of their classes and took note of how the dancers kept their ankles, knees, and hips limber and healthy. He took what he learned back to school and taught the same stretches to the athletes he was treating.

Larry Nassar's interest in gymnastics never waned once he was introduced to the sport. He decided to attend the University of Michigan, where he majored in kinesiology, the study of how bodies move and a common stepping-stone to a career in what was the still-burgeoning field of athletic training. He continued to work with athletes—gymnasts and others—on campus in Ann Arbor. He completed his degree in 1985 and moved back toward Detroit to start work on a master's program in athletic training at Wayne State University. There he sought out a volunteer role working with future

Hall of Fame coach Steve Whitlock and his nearby troupe of young gymnasts known as the Acronauts. Whitlock remembers Nassar first approaching him at his gym inside a Bloomfield Hills, Michigan, strip mall when Nassar was still in high school and eager to learn about the types of medical care gymnasts required.

While many high schools offered gymnastics as a sport, the most talented and competitive gymnasts are products of club gyms. Unlike in most other sports, a typical female gymnast hits the prime of her career in her teenage years. Most gyms hold introductory classes for children as young as three or four years old, and the cream of the crop separates itself quickly. By the time they reach junior high, the competitive gymnasts put in long hours at least six days a week. Many are fueled by aspirations of winning medals at national and international meets or earning a college scholarship.

Well-connected club coaches become power brokers, gatekeepers who decide which gymnasts get the time and opportunities to continue climbing. As a skilled gymnast matriculates through the levels of competition with good performances at local, regional, and eventually national competitions, the pool of peers grows smaller, and the community becomes more insular and tightly knit. Gyms and coaches can launch themselves into these elite circles with a single great gymnast. One success story can build a reputation that attracts more top-end talent.

Steve Whitlock had one of the best gyms in Michigan when Nassar joined him during his graduate studies. He connected Nassar with Jack Rockwell, the US national team trainer, and suggested that the motivated young man would be a good fit to help care for athletes at regional and national events. At that time, in a sport that can be particularly hard on the body, it often fell on coaches to tape their gymnasts or assess whether injuries were serious enough to merit a doctor's visit. Whitlock recognized Nassar's apparent passion for the sport and thought it could be a great asset for the country's top gymnasts.

Nassar jumped at the opportunity. He was spending a good deal of his free time dreaming up small inventions to be tested at the gym. He built a contraption that cooled the chalk that the girls used for their grip. Cooler chalk stuck to the hands better and added a little extra relief to palms torn open by endless repetitions on the uneven bars. Nassar also tried to fashion patches of synthetic skin into grips the gymnasts could use to prevent some tearing in the first place. He focused on the ankles, too, developing a set of braces that would lessen the wear and tear of stiff dismounts and hard landings on the joint. He called his braces the "Nassar System" and eventually found enough business to take out full-page advertisements in popular gymnastics magazines. The ads featured elite coaches of Olympic gymnastics touting his product as "the best ankle brace I have ever used for training."

Now in his mid-twenties, the awkward introvert started to become a familiar face at gymnastics events around the Midwest. He drove to Indianapolis to help out at the Pan-American Games in the summer of 1987. A year later, he flew to Salt Lake City for the 1988 US Gymnastics Olympic Trials. For four long days in early August, he bounced around the Salt Palace Convention Center wearing a red cross on his shirt while working on gymnasts and trying to pick the brains of Olympic doctors.

The coaches in Utah were happy to see Nassar. It was rare to find a medical professional who understood their sport well enough to know how to treat its most common problems. More importantly, he didn't cost a dime. Nassar volunteered his time and paid his own way to the events, filling up credit cards to attend. He told the coaches and doctors he met that he was eager to learn and gain experience.

Nassar returned to Michigan with a world of potential in front of him. He was now a known entity at the top levels of the gymnastics community and certain he wanted to make a career out of treating injuries of young athletes with a hands-on approach. He had applied earlier that year to medical schools with programs in osteopathy, a branch of medicine that focuses on treating problems by manually manipulating and massaging the body. He stayed close to home. Michigan State's College of Osteopathic Medicine—one of the top programs in the country—accepted Nassar as part of its incoming class in the fall of 1988. He promptly ended his master's degree training at Wayne State and made plans to move a little more than an hour down the road to East Lansing.

Classes started less than a month after Nassar returned from his trip to Utah. In that time, he packed his belongings in Detroit; settled into his new place; and connected with an ambitious, young coach, a man who was well on his way to building a gymnastics juggernaut just a few miles away from the Michigan State campus.

John Geddert's star was just starting to rise in the 1980s, but it was already clear to those who knew him well that the brash alpha male with a hard-set jaw and piercing eyes was going to be a force in gymnastics. Geddert's start as a gymnast came during high school in Alpena, Michigan, a small town in the state's northeastern corner along the shores of a small scoop of Lake Huron known as Thunder Bay.

He and his high school girlfriend, Kathryn, were standout athletes and decided to attend Central Michigan University together. They married in 1977, after their freshman year. Geddert, who specialized in the horizontal bars, went on to win three letters for the Chippewas before graduating with a degree in health and physical education. Gary Anderson, a coach from the US national team, offered Geddert an entry-level coaching job at MarVaTeens Gymnastics, his gym in Maryland.

Geddert made $150 a week coaching at the private club while trying to lay the groundwork for a career in gymnastics. After four years in Maryland, the Gedderts moved back to Michigan in 1984 where both were offered coaching positions at Great Lakes Gymnastics Club in Lansing. Paula and Don Hartwick started the club a few years earlier in hopes of creating a place where their daughters and other children could enjoy an inclusive, fun-focused gymnastics experience. Geddert's focus was on winning.

The setting was a humble one when they first arrived. Geddert ran the practices, which were held inside a converted metal warehouse with almost no windows or ventilation. A couple years later, the Hartwicks found a new space down the street that would better accommodate their growing club in a recently vacated school building.

The Walter French School was housed in a three-story, pre–Depression era brick building perched at the corner of Cedar Street and Mt. Hope Avenue until it closed its doors in 1981. Five years later, Great Lakes Gymnastics moved into a small gym on an upper floor, and a cast of coaches under Geddert's direction went to work building a powerhouse.

By the summer of 1988, the black leotards with red and yellow piping worn by all Great Lakes gymnasts turned heads and intimidated competitors as soon as they appeared at an event. The girls marched into events together, precise and deliberate from the moment they walked through the door. They almost always left with medals around their necks or trophies in hand. Geddert's demanding coaching style would, over time, produce dozens of state champions and college scholarship offers.

Interest in the sport, and in their club specifically, had grown enough that the gym moved to a bigger space inside the otherwise vacant building. Other entrances to the former school were boarded up with plywood. The neighborhood was not the safest area in Lansing. But inside their corner of the old Walter French Academy, the gym had grown into a formidable operation with top-of-the-line training equipment. And now, thanks to the arrival of a spirited, young medical student looking to build some more experience in treating athletes, Great Lakes was going to be able to offer something no other gym in the area could offer. Larry Nassar, a certified athletic trainer, would be available to the gymnasts on a daily basis to keep them healthy.

Once again, Nassar agreed to work as a volunteer. The coaches at Great Lakes found a space for him to set up his training table in what was once part of a hallway just outside the gym's walls. A large, metal-grated security gate separated the space from the rest of the abandoned hallway, enclosing the makeshift room. An exit door against the back wall was boarded up to prevent people from breaking into the school. That left only one way in and out of the area—through two sets of heavy, brown doors with loud, clanging push-bars and long, skinny slivers of glass for windows.

The brown doors hung in the back corner of the Great Lakes gym. Nassar walked through the gym's main entrance each afternoon shouldering a large trainer's bag stuffed with tapes, lotions, and bottles of pills. He strode past the small viewing gallery with its PVC pipe railing and folding chairs set up for parents, across the floor routine mat, around the edges of the balance beams, and through the vault strip to reach his domain.

Despite the demands of being a first-semester medical student, Nassar, now twenty-five, averaged twenty hours a week in his improvised office at Great Lakes. He told the girls to call him Larry. He waited in his room most weekday afternoons for any gymnast who hurt herself in practice or needed some help dealing with the general wear and tear that comes from long hours of training. Occasionally, he walked the floor of the gym to help with endurance-training circuits. He often could be found with a camera around his neck, snapping pictures of the girls in their leotards or close-up shots of visible injuries. He wanted to document what he saw, he told everyone, to help with his studies.

Schoolwork, even his exams, took a back seat to gymnastics during Nassar's first semester at medical school in the fall of 1988. When the US and Soviet national teams joined forces in early December for a post-Olympic tour through several large American cities, the organizers invited Nassar to come along to help care for the athletes. The tour visited eight cities in ten whirlwind days and surprised the reporters who covered some of the events with a lightheartedness not usually seen at the sport's top level. International stars choreographed unique coed routines to the delight of the crowds and at night played pranks on each other. Soviet star Elena Shushunova elated American fans by flashing something she had not shown during her all-around gold medal performance in Seoul months earlier—a smile.

Nassar soaked in the experience while his classmates were back in snowy Michigan taking their final exams. He had convinced all but one of his professors to allow him to take his tests before heading out on the road. Only one—a dreaded biochemistry exam—waited for him on the day he returned to Michigan. After all the fun and long days on tour, he didn't do well enough for a passing score. He would have to repeat biochemistry the next semester.

If the failed exam was a sign that Nassar was spending too much time with gymnasts, he didn't heed its warning. During the spring semester of 1989, he continued to spend his afternoons lingering behind the heavy, brown doors at Great Lakes and his weekends helping out at competitions and meets in various cities and towns throughout the Midwest. When it came time for professors to submit final grades, Nassar came up short in biochemistry again.

At the end of the semester, a faculty panel of professors and doctors informed him there would be no spot for him as a second-year student the following school year. He was flunking out of medical school. He explained to the panel that his grades suffered because of the time he dedicated to his work as an athletic trainer. He suggested that he could switch from a four-year plan to a five-year plan, leaving time to continue his work outside the classroom. They told him he didn't have the priorities or the proper focus to be a student at Michigan State.

Nassar appealed to the dean of the medical school, but his visit to the office of Dean Myron S. Magen was brief. Dr. Magen, who was coming to the end of a long tenure running the program, agreed with his colleagues. Nassar's plan to become an osteopathic doctor had hit an impasse.

All but out of options, Nassar turned to his friends in the gymnastics community for help. Geddert agreed to write a letter to Magen on his athletic trainer's behalf. He promised the dean he would keep Nassar out of the old Walter French Academy building until the day he showed up with a diploma from medical school. Nassar drummed up more support from Jack Rockwell, the national team athletic trainer who helped Nassar get a foot in the door and served as one of his early mentors. Rockwell promised the dean that Nassar would also be kept away from all gymnastics events until he finished his coursework. Magen was convinced. It seemed Nassar's intentions were set back on the right course. He would be allowed to continue taking classes at Michigan State.

Nassar knew what he wanted by the summer of 1989. And now, he had allies who were willing to help him get it. He kept the promises his friends made on his behalf for about a month before returning to the Great Lakes gym. Gymnastics was booming in the United States as the 1980s came to a close. There was no way he was going to stay away.

Chapter 2

The Absolute Monarch

Larry Nassar's early years in the club gymnastics world came during a period of unprecedented popularity for the sport in America. The three years that followed the 1984 Olympics in Los Angeles featured the largest recorded period of growth for USA Gymnastics since the organization started tracking membership numbers—from 40,542 in 1984 to 63,485 in 1987. That three-year stretch remains the largest percentage increase, year over year, in the sport's history in the United States.

For decades gymnastics in America had been an afterthought. The sport was more art than science, not yet predicated on skills that required power and intensity. In the early to mid-1960s, not a single club or college on US soil owned a full Olympic-sized floor exercise mat. In the Soviet Union, by contrast, gymnastics was taught in schools, and roughly eight hundred thousand people were active in the sport.

Growing up behind the Iron Curtain in Romania, Bela Karolyi was a hulking hammer thrower and boxing champion. Born in 1942, he enrolled in the Romania College of Physical Education in Bucharest, where he struggled to pass a proficiency skills test in gymnastics. Stubborn from the start, Karolyi threw himself into the sport and ended up coaching the women's collegiate team during his final year of college. He grew close to the team's star, Marta Eross. They married shortly after graduation, in 1963, the same year Larry

Nassar was born, and moved to a growing coal-mining town to teach elementary school.

Years later, while running a gymnastics program in the small mountain town of Oneşti, as Bela Karolyi would later detail in his book about that period of his life, he noticed a six-year-old gracefully flipping cartwheels at recess. He invited her to join his new training school, where he was pushing students beyond their limits in hopes of creating "a new kind of gymnast" that he would describe years later in a book he cowrote as "very athletic, aggressive and powerful, and doing difficult skills."

Within a decade and with the help of the Karolyis' coaching, that little girl, Nadia Comăneci, was ready to revolutionize the sport. Prior to 1976, no gymnast had recorded a perfect score of ten during Olympic competition. During the Montreal Olympic games that year, Comăneci recorded seven flawless "perfect 10" performances en route to three gold medals in a performance that propelled the Romanian team to dominance on the world stage. In a country of 21 million citizens that was accustomed to being a satellite state of the Soviet Union, Comăneci and Karolyi became instant celebrities. After Comăneci's historic performance in Montreal, she was viewed as a national treasure, and Karolyi—a man who never had trouble attracting attention in a variety of ways—was watched closely by the country's most powerful men.

Four years later at the 1980 Moscow Olympics, when Comăneci failed to win gold in the all-around competition, settling instead for silver behind Russia's Elena Davydova, Karolyi's protest caused a temporary disruption at the games. Karolyi's embarrassing outbursts and criticism of the judges delayed the games for forty minutes. His behavior in Moscow caused him to fall out of favor with the Romanian Communist Party, and he was reprimanded upon his return home.

By then, Karolyi had already clashed with the Communist Romanian dictator Nicolae Ceauşescu over the way Ceauşescu had used Comăneci and his national team as propaganda tools. In 1981, with their status within Romania suddenly in question, the Karolyis and their longtime choreographer, Geza Pozsar, defected to the United States while on an international gymnastics tour.

The trio stayed up all night in a New York City hotel room weighing their decision hours before their team was due to fly back to Romania. In the morning, Karolyi said goodbye to Comăneci and told her, according to his book, "If you appreciate everything I did for you, you shut up and don't say a word. Go, now please, and call the other girls down to the reception area." Then the Karolyis and Pozsar slipped away to hide out in the apartment of one of Marta's relatives who had emigrated years earlier.

The powerhouse program Bela and Marta Karolyi developed in Romania was forged with the pain and suffering of the young girls in their care. Pozsar, who worked with them from 1974 to 2002 and would go on to run his own club in California, considers some of the things he witnessed inside the couple's Romanian training centers to be "atrocities."

"Bela was an absolute Monarch," Pozsar said. "He was like Louis XIV of France. He was a dictator. In Romania he had absolute power."

Pozsar said he witnessed Karolyi verbally but never physically abusing his star gymnast. Comăneci has never accused Karolyi of being physically abusive and won't speak about her time with the Karolyis. Other former Romanian gymnasts, however, have gone public in recent years, saying it was commonplace for the Karolyis to hit them, deny them food, and push them past the point of exhaustion while they lived and trained at the Karolyis' gym. In the centralized system that existed in Romania at the time, gymnasts and their parents were given little choice about where and when athletes would train.

Trudi Kollar remembers taking the train through the night in 1976 as a twelve-year-old. She and her mother traveled the 260 miles from their hometown of Arad, Romania, to Oneşti, Comăneci's hometown and the place where Romania's elite gymnasts were sent to train with the Karolyis. Back then, Kollar went by the name Emilia Eberle. She says she recalls she and her mother were greeted by a smiling Bela Karolyi the morning after their train ride at the training center and how Karolyi showed them to her new dorm room. Concerned her daughter hadn't eaten enough on the long train ride, Eberle's mother took a roll of bread from her bag in front of Karolyi and left it in a drawer for her to eat later. After her mother left (parents were not allowed to be with their children during training), Eberle said Karolyi returned to her room, took the bread, and struck her so hard with an open hand that he knocked her off her feet onto the bed.

"If I ever see anything like this again, I'm going to beat you to death," she said he hollered at her. That was her first encounter with the man who would train her for the next six years.

Pozsar remembers Karolyi hitting Eberle so hard during practices with his large and powerful hands in her back and on her sides that the sound of the blows echoed through the gym. The Karolyis demanded perfection, and if the gymnasts failed to achieve it during their routines, they would often be slapped in the face or on the backs of their heads or have their hair pulled. Eberle recalls an almost daily routine of physical and emotional abuse.

"It was mostly Marta who would hit us," Eberle said, recalling how the ring on Marta's finger and her fingernails frequently left marks and scratches and caused bleeding.

Gymnasts were weighed twice daily, once before the 8:00 a.m. practice and again prior to the afternoon practice. "We were always called fat pigs and cows," said Eberle, who weighed sixty-six pounds as a fourteen-year-old.

During one training session on the uneven bars, the blisters on Eberle's hands started to bleed so badly she fell and hit her head.

"Oh look, Bela, she is fat as a pig—maybe she should go on a diet," Eberle recalls Marta Karolyi saying to her husband at the time.

Pozsar, the choreographer, said he once saw Bela Karolyi strike another gymnast so hard with his open hand after she failed to execute a vault that the girl collapsed to the floor and urinated in her leotard. When Karolyi saw that the young gymnast had soiled the floor, he kicked her, Pozsar said.

In 1978, Gabriela Geiculescu was a national champion gymnast in Romania. She trained with a physically abusive coach in Bucharest who once struck her so hard in the back during a practice she remembers struggling to breathe. As violent as her situation was, she had heard horror stories from other gymnasts who were sent to train with the Karolyis and was terrified when she found out she was being sent to their training center, which by then had moved to the Transylvanian city of Deva.

Geiculescu said she was never physically abused by the Karolyis, but she remembers being so deprived of food she would occasionally eat toothpaste just to have the sensation of flavor in her mouth. She plucked apples from the trash cans on the streets of Deva and would sneak food into her dorm room in a jar, submerging it in the water tank of a toilet in order to hide it from Bela Karolyi's random searches of her room.

Until recent years, a thin, prepubescent body had long been considered the ideal form for a gymnast to impress the judges at competitions and to execute physically demanding routines. The Karolyis, however, took it to extremes, Pozsar said, going so far as to deny gymnasts food to stave off the onset of puberty.

"[When] they start to get into puberty, they begin to think and to become more conservative," Karolyi wrote in his book years later. "'Wait,' the teenage girl tells herself. 'I am cute. What for I am falling on my face and bending my nose?' But until that point they are going freely.... We discovered that you cannot overwork young children."

Breakfast for the gymnasts consisted of a few crackers with jam, lunch a piece of chicken with greens, and dinner a small sandwich, not even close to enough nourishment to sustain gymnasts, who routinely trained eight hours or more a day.

The gymnasts were also given handfuls of what they were told were "vitamins," pills that often left Geiculescu so disoriented she struggled to execute routines. She remembers the gnawing hunger and being so "out of her body" from the pills that at one practice she sprinted full speed into the horse during a failed vault attempt and collapsed on the mat.

"I was twelve or thirteen and thinking God doesn't exist," she said. "Because if God existed, he wouldn't let this happen to children."

Pozsar would sneak gymnasts chocolate and said he has "huge remorse" he was "part of a system so brutal." The Karolyis, through their attorney, declined to comment for this book, but, in April 2018, the couple addressed past allegations of physical abuse in an interview with NBC News correspondent Savannah Guthrie:

GUTHRIE: "Did you ever hit a gymnast?"
MARTA KAROLYI: "No."
BELA KAROLYI: "Probably, over fifty years ago in Romania when even slapping or spanking was a common procedure, yes."

The Karolyis denied ever hitting gymnasts during their time as coaches in the United States, with Bela saying "if anybody comes up with that one, that's a dirty lie."

Two years after skipping their New York City flight and defecting from Romania, the Karolyis had settled in Houston, Texas, and were running a small training center for budding American gymnasts. One day, Karolyi received a phone call from a man named John Traetta, whom he had met in the late 1970s shortly after Comăneci's dazzling performance in Montreal.

Traetta had come off a remarkable run of success coaching boys' gymnastics for a decade at DeWitt Clinton High School in the Bronx, winning ten straight New York City championships. He had stopped coaching and turned to producing made-for-television gymnastics events in the 1980s for broadcast networks and cable outlets such as HBO and USA Network.

Traetta was organizing a gymnastics invitational to be broadcast the following spring from Caesars Palace in Las Vegas. On the phone, he told Karolyi he was in search of up-and-coming stars to add to the program. Traetta was offering $2,000 college scholarships to each gymnast who attended.

"You're going to want to invite one of my athletes," Karolyi told him. "She's the best athlete I've ever coached in the United States." Traetta asked for her name. "Mary Lou Retton," Karolyi responded.

A four-foot-nine, ninety-four-pound dynamo from West Virginia with a million-watt smile, Retton first approached Karolyi about training with him in the summer of 1982. She was compact and explosive, a great fit for the more powerful brand of gymnastics Karolyi brought to the sport. As the only elite gymnast in her home state, though, she needed better competition and better coaching to push her to greater heights. Karolyi told Retton's parents their daughter had the potential to be an Olympic medalist, but time to perfect her skills was running short. She arrived in Houston on New Year's Day 1983 and immediately got to work with her new coach. Her goal wasn't just to make the Olympics when the summer games returned to American soil the following year but to make an impact when they did. Karolyi's job was to help her get there.

Retton's performance at the 1984 Los Angeles Summer Olympics catapulted her to stardom and further cemented the reputation of Karolyi as the coach who molded Olympic champions. Retton was the first American woman to ever win gold in gymnastics and instantly became the most popular athlete to emerge from the summer games.

The games themselves were a huge financial success. The Olympic organizing committee, headed by successful travel executive Peter Ueberroth, sold the television rights to ABC for $225 million. Unlike other Olympic hosts that went into massive debt building stadiums and infrastructure, Los Angeles turned the event into a financial windfall. The first city to host a privately financed Olympics was able to manage costs largely by using existing structures such as the LA Coliseum, which played host to the opening and closing ceremonies, and by selling corporate sponsorships. The 1984 summer games ended with a $232 million surplus. Ueberroth was named *Time*'s Man of the Year, and of all the athletes who cashed in after the games, none had the earning potential of Retton.

Three weeks after the Olympic games, Traetta met with Retton and her parents in Houston to sign a one-page agreement allowing him to serve as Retton's agent. Along with her brother and Karolyi, Traetta managed Retton's career for the better part of the next six years. He brokered a book deal and endorsement contracts with

Wheaties (Retton was the first woman to appear on the front of the brand's cereal boxes), McDonald's, Energizer batteries, and other sponsors. During his time as her agent, from 1984 to 1989, Traetta says Retton made more than $6 million, "an astronomical amount at that time for an athlete."

Retton's enduring popularity brought hordes of new athletes to gymnastics in the aftermath of the Los Angeles games, and the sport continued to grow for decades to come. In 1980, more than 30,500 athletes were registered with USA Gymnastics. That number more than doubled by 1994, and by 2019, the organization boasted more than two hundred thousand members (athletes, coaches, and instructors) competing and working out of more than thirty-four hundred registered gyms. An estimated total of 4.8 million children and teens participated in gymnastics in the United States in 2018, with the vast majority of them not sanctioned by the sport's national governing body, USA Gymnastics.

By 1989, the time Traetta's contract ended with Retton, others in the gymnastics hierarchy had taken notice of her star power and its financial implications. Mike Jacki, the former president of USA Gymnastics' precursor, the United States Gymnastics Federation, made it clear at the time to Traetta that he wanted to assert more control over the production of future gymnastics television events. Elite gymnasts were no longer just athletes to be lauded during international competitions. They were valuable commodities as famous as any Hollywood celebrities and professional athletes. In a 1993 poll of more than fourteen hundred Americans, nearly a decade removed from her Olympic moment, Retton was named the most popular athlete in the country, ahead of NBA star Michael Jordan, NFL quarterback Joe Montana, and NHL superstar Wayne Gretzky.

Fueled by Retton's success in the immediate aftermath of her 1984 Olympic performance, Bela Karolyi boasted at the time that membership at his Houston gym swelled to twelve hundred. The Romanian miracle worker was now doing the same in his new home. He and his wife made plans to expand.

Chapter 3

Pushing Boundaries

In just a few short years, the combination of grueling training tactics and a demanding coaching style cloaked in charisma helped the Karolyis turn the United States from an irrelevant nation in the gymnastics world to a force to be reckoned with. America's most ambitious coaches took note of the strict Karolyi philosophy, and a formidable list of imitators emerged.

As more clubs opened and eager students poured in, a small number of gyms and coveted coaches were developing reputations as champion factories that knew how to take the sport's best prospects and push them toward the type of fame and financial windfall enjoyed by winners like Retton. The competition for those few coveted spots on the national team was fierce and constant. Families of promising young gymnasts drove for hours each day to bring their daughters to leading clubs in hopes that their talent might be recognized by an influential coach with national connections. Some families moved to new states or split up so daughters as young as seven or eight years old could train at an elite club. For many gymnasts from Michigan and other nearby states, the path to potential stardom passed through an old abandoned school on the corner of Cedar Street and Mt. Hope Avenue in Lansing.

By the early 1990s, John Geddert had turned Great Lakes Gymnastics Club into a juggernaut. His gymnasts struck fear into their peers at competitions, and in turn, Geddert struck fear into his gymnasts. He intimidated fellow coaches, parents, and their pre-teen daughters with his demanding style. He hurled clipboards at gymnasts who didn't meet his standards. His voice boomed when he swore at gymnasts for making mistakes. One sharp yell could freeze everyone in the gym. And there was a lot of yelling.

His assistants warned the girls to keep a low profile on days when Geddert's ire was particularly high. They divided the gymnasts by age and skill level, and each coach worked with the rotating groups on a specific skill or apparatus. His wife, Kathryn, taught by the balance beam. Kim and Jill Hartwick—daughters of the couple who first opened Great Lakes—worked on the floor exercise and the vault. Kathie Klages, a fellow Central Michigan graduate, joined the Gedderts after working as a high school coach in her hometown of Spring Lake, Michigan. The future head coach of Michigan State's women's team, Klages won the United States Gymnastics Federation "Coach of the Year" award in Michigan in 1988 for her work with the Great Lakes girls. A host of male assistants cycled through the staff as well. They pushed the girls hard, but none of the other coaches was as ruthless as Geddert, according to the gymnasts who trained there. The assistants largely stayed quiet when he rampaged in practice or pulled a girl into a side room for a tongue-lashing.

Geddert's specialty was the uneven bars. Gymnasts say he would make his young athletes practice until their hands bled and their arms could no longer hold them in the air. When they lined up to stretch, Geddert leaned his weight on top of their small bodies and pulled their limbs to test the limits of their flexibility until they cried. He inspected their form during "crunchers," an exercise where they lay on their backs and hoisted their arms and legs in the air in a hollow body hold to strengthen their abs. If he saw one of the girls wasn't keeping her glutes tight in the position, he would step with his full body weight on the small bit of their backsides that wasn't taut, pinching it against the floor.

"Looks like we've got a flat tire," he was known to say.

The marks from his feet bruised their sides and stayed on their hips for days. Some gymnasts remember Geddert sitting beside them and slapping their legs hard enough to leave a handprint.

"I would literally have his handprints on the side of my leg, just because he could," says Heather Berry, a former elite gymnast who went on to compete in college. Berry remembers being kicked out of practice for a variety of reasons, some as trivial as Geddert not liking the way she did her hair on a particular day. She recalls Geddert snapping her bra the first time she wore one to the gym, drawing unwanted attention to her reaching puberty. When Geddert decided the girls would switch from a uniform of black leotards to white ones for their meets, Berry says he told her that she should start going to tanning salons to look better in the new uniform. At twelve or thirteen years old, the gymnasts worried about the switch in color because the white would make them look a few pounds heavier.

Weight was always an issue, as it was in many high-level gyms across the country. Geddert made frequent comments about girls gaining weight and placed them on strict diets. Later in his coaching career, other gymnasts say he punished the girls who were caught eating something they shouldn't eat by making them clean the gym bathrooms with a toothbrush.

Like Bela Karolyi, Geddert could turn on his charming side when he needed it. He was a strapping man who carried himself with a magnetic, cool confidence. His gymnasts craved his approval and would put themselves through torture to get it.

"The bad was really bad," says former Great Lakes gymnast Trinea Gonczar. "But the good was really good."

Geddert required each girl to give him a hug before they left the gym at the end of practice. He could crack a joke and flash a devil-may-care smile with the right parents to keep himself in their good graces. Rumors about his sexual conquests were as common around the gym as hearing him barking orders. The teenage gymnasts who traveled around the country with Great Lakes used to joke that Geddert's hotel room remained vacant most nights while he was out chasing women.

"You would have to be nuts not to know," Berry says. "It was well known about his extracurricular activities."

Shelby Root first met Geddert in 1985 when, at sixteen, she began training at Great Lakes. In an account revealed in the 2019 book *The Girls*, written by journalist Abigail Pesta, Root described how Geddert, her former coach, helped her advance in gymnastics to the point that she earned a college athletic scholarship. Root says Geddert also groomed her through a series of physical encounters that were increasingly more inappropriate and sexual in nature. When she was eighteen and no longer being coached by him, Root accompanied Geddert to an out-of-state gymnastics meet, where she wasn't competing. She described to Pesta an encounter she had while swimming with Geddert in the hotel pool.

> I remember he eventually had me with my back against the pool wall, and he was in front of me, one arm on each side, and he kissed me for the first time. I remember being surprised and not sure how to react, and I went along with it.... He moved my bathing suit bottom over to the side and proceeded to have sex with me. It was my first time, so I didn't have any experience and wasn't sure how to respond.

Geddert was married and eleven years her senior. Root had just gotten her braces off the previous year. She went on to describe to

36

Pesta how she fell in love with Geddert and continued to have sex with him after she went off to college, first to the University of Iowa and later to Central Michigan University, Geddert's alma mater.

Connie Root, Shelby's mother, told Pesta that after her daughter's eighteenth birthday she "suspected a sexual relationship," adding, "The sexual nature was not discussed, but, as a mom, I knew."

Geddert did not comment for Pesta for *The Girls* nor has he commented for this book about Root's revelations.

Years later, in a Facebook message sent to a former USAG staffer, Geddert acknowledged "past indescretions [*sic*]." He didn't mention Root specifically and described his "indescretions [*sic*]" as "my business," adding that they occurred at a time when he was separated from his wife for three years.

Geddert was also known to take time during trips to grab a beer with his loyal friend, Larry Nassar. Nassar, in the eyes of the gymnasts he treated, was the polar opposite of Geddert. He was "a puppy dog," awkward and androgynous compared to their machismo-filled jock of a coach. Geddert won their admiration by withholding. Nassar was overly eager to help or lend a kind word. He might tell an inappropriate joke from time to time, but he blushed when he did. He snorted when he laughed. He wore undersized track shorts and oversized glasses.

"He was a big dork, honestly," remembers former gymnast Laura Szczepanski-Scudder. "He was goofy, but he was somebody you learned to trust very quickly. A lot of things changed as he was in the gym more. He made it a little more tolerable. You went to him when you needed something."

In the gymnasts' eyes, Nassar was a hero. What Geddert broke, Nassar could fix. He was a ball of positive energy. The makeshift training room behind the heavy, brown doors inside Great Lakes could feel like a safe haven amid a world filled with threats. He greeted each girl with a smile and a soft voice asking how he could help. His trainer's bag was filled with solutions. He taped their ankles and wrists before practice. He usually had a few small candy bars to sneak someone who was having a bad day or in need of a treat that didn't comply with their restrictive diets. He had bottles of lotions to employ the osteopathic massage methods he was learning in school to help ease their pain. If that didn't help, he kept a steady supply of sample pills in his bag and handed those out as well.

The former gymnasts say Nassar found a way even before he had his medical license to write prescriptions for those who needed pain relief. If their parents couldn't afford the medication, he quietly asked other families if they'd fill the orders to help out. He created regimens that sometimes included up to nine Advil pills per day for girls who weighed barely one hundred pounds. Others took the small handful of pills he provided for them at the gym without knowing what they were. He had their trust.

When time to heal ran short, Nassar found more powerful drugs to help gymnasts get back on the floor. He administered cortisone shots. Berry says he provided her with a shot of Toradol—a potent painkiller, not intended for pediatric use, that is known to cause peptic ulcers and gastrointestinal bleeding—in 1994 when she was fourteen or fifteen years old and needed to compete in a regional meet on Michigan State's campus with an injured ankle. It wasn't until two years later, laid up in a hospital room to treat a stomach full of ulcers and still battling the chronic effects of masking an ankle injury rather than fixing it, that Berry realized Nassar might not have been qualified to perform all the treatments he offered.

Nassar also soothed the problems medicine couldn't help. He listened to their complaints and seemed to care about their well-being. When the girls needed surgery, he traveled to hospitals in Detroit or

Cleveland to be supportive and was among the first faces they saw after coming out of the operating room. When asked how he had time for those trips during his schooling, Nassar told the gymnasts and their families that it was a valuable part of his education.

Nassar didn't completely ignore the classroom as his time continued at Michigan State. He was happy to be around medical innovators at one of the few osteopathic schools attached to a public university at the time. In 1989, early in Nassar's second year of medical school, a senior associate dean at the school named Dr. Philip Greenman published a book titled *Principles of Manual Medicine*. The book and Greenman's long career teaching those principles were heralded by the osteopathic community and helped provide another layer of legitimacy to a field of medicine that still had many skeptics. Greenman earned international acclaim for a series of videos he created to explain the fundamentals and techniques of "manual medicine."

Greenman appears in the series of fourteen hour-long videos wearing his white lab coat inside a doctor's office. He starts by explaining that the roots of manual medicine stretch back even further than Hippocrates. Using a male model clad in a black Speedo, Greenman walks his viewers through a series of tests and treatments they should use to evaluate and help patients for different parts of the body. As a student at the same medical school at that time, there is little doubt Nassar would have watched the videos and noted the authority and legitimacy they lent to Greenman. Years later, Nassar would create his own set of videos—first on tape, then on YouTube—to stake a claim as an expert in his own specific field.

One of Greenman's videos was dedicated to treating the pelvic area, and it begins with a warning. Greenman tells the camera this is "one of the more complex and controversial areas of the field." He goes on to discuss in specific detail the proper hand placement and movement when working on the joints and muscles in that area. He uses both a skeleton and his Speedo-clad model to demonstrate the treatments Nassar would modify for his purposes in the years to come.

Nassar developed a fascination with working on that part of the body during his studies, and he did not keep that interest to himself. He spoke regularly with colleagues about the potential healing power that could be found by treating the pelvic floor.

"He emphasized it a lot," says Steven Karageanes, a former medical school classmate and longtime professional acquaintance. "I thought [the technique] was helpful, but there are a lot of other techniques that were helpful."

Nassar sought out Greenman on Michigan State's campus to ask about developing new treatments and manipulations in the pelvic region. Later, Nassar said in a letter to his superiors that it was Greenman himself who suggested the young doctor focus attention on the sacrotuberous ligament—a large, rough ligament that stretches from the pelvis to the lower back beneath the gluteal muscles. Nassar would eventually teach others that the ligament was the "grand junction" of the body, a place that could be manipulated using a technique called myofascial release to solve a multitude of problems occurring elsewhere in the body.

Working extensively in this "complex and controversial" area when so many of his patients were preteen or teenage girls did not seem to give Nassar significant pause. When he gave presentations or wrote about the pelvic area for textbook chapters, he referred to the perineum as the "no fly zone" and made it clear that a doctor should always get permission and put on gloves before treating the area. He told Karageanes that his patients kept their clothes on and that he never did internal work on the young gymnasts in his care, statements that turned out to be lies. When Karageanes asked Nassar if he was worried about a parent or patient getting mad or uncomfortable with where his hands were going even if he was doing everything correctly, Nassar laughed it off. He appeared to believe the health benefits outweighed the risk of backlash. Any other motives he had for his budding interest remained hidden.

At Great Lakes, when Nassar started to employ his new methods, few questioned the necessity or intent of what he was doing. He was the good guy. Nassar convinced Geddert to tone down a few of his conditioning drills and adopt healthier nutrition guidelines that were less focused on weight loss. At times, he held gymnasts out of practice when they were in danger of injuring themselves seriously. He asked the gymnasts about personal problems and offered advice. He conducted full physicals for them at the gym. He knew where many of the gymnasts were on their path through puberty and suggested remedies if their maturation had been slowed by small caloric intakes and the hard work of training.

As years passed, it was clear that Nassar's role was much more than just an athletic trainer. To his gymnasts, he was an advocate, a confidant, and a friend. Nassar was willing to help the Great Lakes girls wherever and whenever he was needed. He saw them at the gym and traveled to meets when they needed him. Other times, he told the girls to meet him at the medical facilities where he worked as a resident. He made house calls and invited the girls and their parents to his own modest apartment if he ran out of time to treat their aching bodies during practice at Great Lakes.

Behind the heavy, brown doors at the old Walter French school, he cautiously tested the boundaries of the trust he was building. One former gymnast remembers he started by unclipping her bra as she lay prone on his training table. After several massage sessions, it felt normal for him to remove layers of her clothing. Nassar started to slide his hands closer and closer to intimate areas as he worked on her hips and pelvis.

Another former gymnast, Sara Teristi, remembers Nassar rubbing ice cubes on her bare chest to treat an injury shortly after he arrived at Great Lakes, according to details she revealed in Pesta's book *The Girls*. Teristi said a rib cage injury when she was fourteen prompted Nassar to apply ice to her chest, first over her leotard and eventually on her nude upper body. At times, she said, Nassar would turn his back to her after his "treatments" and angrily demand that she dress quickly and get out of the training room. Teristi told Pesta she remembers a musty smell in the room, which she now believes was due to Nassar ejaculating. She recalls other times when Geddert would walk into the training room while Nassar was icing her chest and touching her bare nipples.

"They would stand there and have a conversation right in front of me," Teristi said. "John would joke about how small my 'tits' were. He said if I was lucky, they would get bigger."

Towels now hung over the skinny glass windows between Nassar and the gym full of coaches, athletes, and parents. Usually isolated and unmonitored, Nassar pushed further with many of the gymnasts who sought his help. His hands lingered by their genitals, and he touched them in ways that felt intrusive and uncomfortable. By then he had built up enough trust among the gymnasts that they assumed he wasn't doing anything devious. His most brazen acts, though, were reserved for the privacy of his modest apartment.

Sarah Klein, another Great Lakes gymnast, remembers visiting Nassar's one-bedroom apartment a few miles from Michigan State's campus by herself when she was only twelve or thirteen years old. Klein's mother thought of Nassar as a good friend. It was the early 1990s, and many parents at Great Lakes felt they owed Nassar a debt of gratitude for the amount of attention and care he showed their daughters. So when he called a select few of them to ask if their daughters would be willing to help him with some experiments he was conducting for his schoolwork, they didn't hesitate. The girls felt special to be picked for his study. Their parents had been just as effectively groomed.

The apartment was sparse, a second-story walk-up that was clearly the home of a student. Nassar's training table and a stack of gymnastics magazines were set up in the living room, which led to a small kitchenette and overlooked a local park. Nassar, single and approaching his thirties now, invited Klein inside and explained he wanted to compare the flexibility of cold muscles to the flexibility of warm ones. He pulled out the notebook where he had recorded the marks of other girls who had already participated in the same experiment.

He asked her to start by performing center splits in the family room. Klein lay with her torso and chin flat against the carpet and pushed her legs out at a 180-degree angle. Nassar crouched behind her with a ruler so he could measure how far her crotch hovered above the floor in the split. He jotted down notes, and then led Klein into his small bathroom where the tub was already filled with warm water. He told her he'd leave the room while she removed her clothes and hopped in.

For nearly a half hour, Klein soaked in the tub tucked into one corner of Nassar's small East Lansing apartment. An egg timer counted down the minutes. He popped in once, making a big, goofy show of casting his eyes skyward.

"I'm not peeking," he said with a giggle while he handed Klein a gymnastics magazine to keep her busy while she waited. Klein and the several other girls who sat in the tub—some in leotards, some completely nude—don't know for certain where Nassar spent the rest of those twenty minutes while they soaked or what he did to occupy the time.

43

Klein climbed out of the tub, toweled off, and dressed before returning to the living room. Nassar told her to drop into the center splits again and retrieved his ruler to see if Klein's midsection stretched any closer to the carpet after her time in the tub. Nassar thanked her and told her for a "reward" to climb on to the training table for a massage. There in his family room, with Klein naked and covered by a bedsheet, Nassar's hands worked their way across her body, and he put his fingers inside her vagina.

Teristi visited Nassar's apartment as well, according to *The Girls*. After several conversations with Pesta, Teristi unearthed a memory she said she repressed for decades. She recalled Nassar locking the door to his apartment and telling her to go into his bedroom and lie down on his bed. Teristi said Nassar then performed oral sex on her and anally raped her. She told Pesta she left Great Lakes after the rape and never saw Nassar again. It would take Teristi three decades to report the rape to police and the Michigan attorney general's office.

While it's not clear precisely when Nassar's sexual abuse of gymnasts began, it is clear that he spent the early years of his career in the sport growing gradually bolder and pushing boundaries.

"Looking back now," Klein says of that period, "I think that what Larry was trying to figure out was: Can I really get away with sexually abusing little girls?"

Chapter 4

What Price Glory?

Jamie Dantzscher doesn't remember the moment, but her parents do. The third of John and Joyce Dantzscher's seven children, Jamie was two years old when the television in the family's living room was tuned in to the 1984 summer games. As she watched Mary Lou Retton and her teammates soar to a silver medal in the women's gymnastics team competition, the toddler pointed to the screen declaring, "I want to do that." At least that's the way the story has been passed down.

It wasn't long before Jamie's uncle Kyle, who used to babysit Jamie and her siblings, was pulling cushions off the furniture inside the Dantzschers' living room and teaching Jamie how to do flips with a soft place to land. She was a natural, everyone agreed. At age seven, when Jamie finally joined a gymnastics club, A.V. Twisters near her home just outside of Palmdale, she moved quickly through the levels.

Gymnastics in the United States is divided into ten levels, based on a gymnast's ability to master more difficult skills. Once gymnasts reach level ten, a common plateau for collegiate-level gymnasts, the only thing left is to become elite, and few ever do. Roughly 120 young women compete at the elite level at any given time. The junior and senior national teams are selected each year from that pool of elite gymnasts, and every four years, under the current format, four women from the senior national team realize their ultimate dreams and are chosen to compete on the Olympic team.

By the time Jamie turned eleven, it was clear she had the raw talent to become an elite gymnast but lacked the appropriate coaching. Joyce and John Dantzscher made the decision to drive Jamie ninety minutes one way each day through the traffic and gridlock of greater Los Angeles, to "the Home of the Gliders," Charter Oak Gymnastics, the Covina gym run by the husband-wife duo of Steve and Beth Kline-Rybacki.

Beth Kline-Rybacki had been the first American woman to ever score a perfect ten on the floor exercise in a national competition. She made the 1980 Olympic team but was denied her Olympic moment when President Jimmy Carter made the controversial decision to boycott the 1980 Moscow summer games. Steve Rybacki worked construction and as a machinist to pay the bills in the 1970s while pursuing his real passion, coaching gymnastics. Largely self-taught, he immersed himself in the sport, attending clinics and reading whatever he could get his hands on. By the time Jamie came to Charter Oak, he had cemented a reputation as one of the best coaches in the country. Jamie would become one of his stars.

Working with the Rybackis complicated Jamie's relationship with her sport. She soon realized all that came with training as an elite-level gymnast. Steve Rybacki had a temper, and on many nights during practice, Jamie felt as if all he did was yell at her, his face red, the veins popping out of his forehead. On some days, Jamie felt as if Beth Kline-Rybacki wouldn't be satisfied until she'd reduced Jamie to tears. When Jamie wasn't performing to the Rybackis' satisfaction, she would often be told to go sit in the corner, the equivalent of a "time-out" given to a small child. It was humiliating.

The Rybackis demanded perfection. Skills had to be executed twenty times in a row. A single fall meant starting over. Some nights, Jamie didn't leave the gym until midnight, exhausted. The Rybackis, Jamie said, exercised total control—telling her how to stand, how to wear her hair, when to talk, when to pee, and what to eat. The Rybackis did not respond to multiple interview requests for this book as of press time.

John Dantzscher was a produce manager at Ralph's grocery store, a Southern California chain. Joyce Dantzscher was a bartender. With seven children, neither of them could afford the time to watch Jamie for the duration of her practices, which often exceeded thirty hours each week, and even if they had the time, parents were discouraged from observing what went on inside the gym. Jamie was mindful of how much her parents had sacrificed for her to try to reach her goal of becoming an elite gymnast and one day making the Olympic team. She felt stuck. Gymnastics became like work. Even the sight of the Grand Avenue exit off of California Highway 210, which led to the Rybackis' gym, eventually made her feel sick to her stomach.

The pressure to remain thin was ever present. Jamie says that she and other top gymnasts at the Rybackis' gym were subjected to daily "weigh-ins." Beth Kline-Rybacki, in particular, was constantly on Jamie about what not to eat and the importance of "looking good," which Jamie took to mean looking skinny in her leotard. At fifteen, she started making herself throw up and continued to battle bulimia and anorexia for more than the next decade. After one five-day stretch battling the flu and vomiting constantly, Jamie stepped on the scale at the gym and found that she was seven pounds lighter than her normal weight.

"We need to figure out how to keep this weight off," Beth Kline-Rybacki told her.

Jamie remembers meeting Nassar sometime in late 1994, shortly after she made the junior national team as a twelve-year-old. By then her life was consumed with gymnastics. She attended school full-time through sixth grade but by middle school had to take independent studies so she could maintain the demanding practice schedule set by the Rybackis. By high school, Jamie would frequently leave class early, doing her homework in the family van as her mother made the long drive to Charter Oak.

Much of that period is a blur, which is commonplace for victims of childhood trauma. Precise dates, times, and places get muddled in a mind filled with stinging memories. Jamie remembers being in what looked like a doctor's office as Nassar gave her a physical examination while she lay totally naked on his examination table. Not yet a practicing physician, Nassar finished medical school in 1993 and was still doing his residency when he first met Jamie a year later and treated her, alone, with no chaperone in the room.

Nassar groomed Jamie in a way that would become a routine he'd follow with dozens of national team gymnasts. Training sessions at the Karolyi ranch, where Nassar was a fixture, and national team competitions became his hunting ground. The ranch, roughly an hour north of Houston, was not yet the epicenter of America's effort to train future gold medalists, but even in the mid-1990s, an invitation for a gymnast to train at the periodic camps held by the Karolyis was coveted. Personal coaches of national team gymnasts, like the Rybackis, couldn't turn down an invitation to accompany their gymnasts to Texas and often found themselves deferring to the Karolyis and their grueling training methods. The morning warm-up lasted forty minutes and consisted of a leg workout followed by an upper-body circuit so demanding Jamie could barely feel her arms, let alone execute a full bar routine when it was over. The sessions left her exhausted, and the comments about her appearance only added to the pressure she felt to be perfect.

During her first visit to the ranch, Jamie says the Rybackis made it clear that the Karolyis wanted Jamie to lose weight, even though she weighed less than one hundred pounds at the time. Through her coaches, she says, they put it bluntly.

"They think you're fat," the Rybackis told her, relaying the Karolyis' devastating feedback. During meals, the young gymnasts were under the ever-watchful eye of their coaches and the Karolyis. As one former national team member put it, "every piece of food we put in our mouth, it equated to the commitment we had of making the Olympic team."

Just as he'd been inside of John Geddert's gym in Lansing, Nassar was a friendly counterbalance at the ranch, a relief from the physically and emotionally draining training sessions. He earned Jamie's trust at the ranch and during competitions by sneaking her food and candy, joking with her, and talking openly about how awful and demanding her coaches could be. Gradually over time, the nature of the conversations changed and became filled with sexually inappropriate language. Nassar described in detail the process of oral sex and told Jamie other gymnasts had mentioned to him that they'd given blowjobs. Not yet sexually active, Jamie didn't know what to make of Nassar's comments but dismissed them as harmless. It didn't even occur to her at the time that it was inappropriate for an adult male to talk about such things with a minor.

When Jamie was fifteen, she developed a urinary tract infection. Her doctor in California asked Jamie if she was sexually active, and when Jamie denied it, her mother remained unconvinced.

"Don't lie!" Joyce told her daughter.

"Who am I having sex with?" Jamie replied, defiant.

The thought never crossed Jamie's mind that it could have been Nassar's ungloved hands that caused her infection. He'd inserted his bare fingers into her vagina and rectum so frequently it became normalized. At the time, she never thought of it as sexual abuse, not consciously anyway. Jamie trusted Nassar, thought he was genuinely trying to help, so she didn't think twice about allowing him to touch her in places no doctor, or anybody else for that matter, ever had before.

Looking back, she wonders if her subconscious mind had a different level of awareness. When Jamie was thirteen, not long after she began training as a national team gymnast and only months after Nassar's "treatments," she developed suicidal thoughts. The long hours of training, the overwhelming pressure to be perfect and look thin had left her mentally broken. Her family had made huge sacrifices financially for her to remain in gymnastics. Whenever she wanted to quit, she felt a tremendous sense of guilt. Feeling trapped, she tried on separate occasions to suffocate herself with a pillow.

"I'd rather die than quit or do gymnastics," she said, reflecting on that time in her life.

Jamie never told anyone about what she was feeling inside. She suffered in silence.

Chapter 5

Absolute Fury

A year after Jamie Dantzscher made the US national team, a ground-breaking exposé of elite gymnastics and figure skating appeared in bookstores across the United States. Joan Ryan's *Little Girls in Pretty Boxes: The Making and Breaking of Elite Gymnasts and Figure Skaters* could very well have been based on Jamie's life story. Ryan was one of the first female sports columnists at a major daily newspaper, working at the *San Francisco Examiner* and later the *San Francisco Chronicle*. She originally took three months to research the world of elite gymnastics and figure skating for an article she was writing for the *Examiner* and wrote that she discovered "a story about legal, even celebrated, child abuse." Ryan then took a year's leave of absence to write her critically acclaimed book.

First released in 1995, *Little Girls in Pretty Boxes* exposed the abusive culture within elite-level gymnastics like no work of nonfiction before it. Ryan took aim at the tactics of some of the most high-profile coaches within the sport, including Bela Karolyi, writing that "Karolyi draws the most criticism of any gymnastics coach for mistreating his athletes. Perhaps it's because he's the most famous coach and thus the easiest target. Or perhaps it's because his track record of producing gymnasts with eating disorders is stunning."

In example after example, Ryan documented how Karolyi's mental and emotional abuse of gymnasts led to a diminished sense of self-worth for the young women he coached that frequently resulted in eating disorders. Erica Stokes, a former national team member, started making herself throw up at fourteen, around the time Bela Karolyi started calling her "a pregnant goat." Ryan described Stokes's experience in her book:

> [Karolyi] called everyone names: her teammate Betty Okino was a pregnant spider. Kim Zmeskal was a pumpkin or a butterball, Hilary Grivich was a tank. Erica tried not to take it personally, but the words burrowed into her brain like parasites. She began to see herself as if in a fun house mirror—squat, bloated, grotesque. She tried giving up food altogether, but she enjoyed eating. So she threw up.

An internal USA Gymnastics memo from December 1995, which dealt with recommendations on athlete wellness, noted "that self-esteem in all pre-adolescent and adolescent girls plummets as much as 30% from the self-esteem of girls in elementary school. The majority of competitive and elite athletes are in middle-school and high school." The girls and young women whom Bela Karolyi was routinely body shaming inside his gym were at one of the most vulnerable times in their formative years.

Little Girls in Pretty Boxes offered a counternarrative to the one commonly associated with the Karolyis. Many of the young women Ryan profiled never realized their Olympic dreams. The Karolyis, long held up as the creators of Olympic champions, are seldom judged by the collateral damage, those who never have their golden moments. Erica Stokes, weakened by bulimia and injuries, quit gymnastics in the run-up to the 1992 Olympics.

By far the most gut-wrenching story in Ryan's book is that of Christy Henrich. Henrich made the junior national team at age twelve. By thirteen, she was training more than nine hours a day. By comparison, the NCAA limits the time collegiate gymnasts can practice to twenty hours per week, but Henrich's coach at the time, Al Fong, held weekly practice sessions more than double that amount of time. When a judge told Henrich at a competition that she looked "fluffy" and needed to lose weight, she was crushed and subsequently developed an eating disorder.

In early 1991, Henrich retired from gymnastics, falling short of her goal of competing in the 1992 Olympics. By mid-1993, she weighed around sixty pounds. She'd tried valiantly to continue, fighting through injuries and competing at one point with a fractured vertebra in her neck, but weakened by years of forced starvation and bulimia, she was physically unable to go on. Suffering from anorexia, she continued to deteriorate after leaving the sport and died on July 26, 1994. Henrich had just turned twenty-two.

Little Girls in Pretty Boxes should have led to sweeping reforms within gymnastics, and for a time, it appeared as if it would. Ryan and the book were featured on *60 Minutes, Oprah, The Today Show*, and elsewhere. The media was suddenly paying attention to the high price so many young women paid while striving for Olympic glory. The book was even made into a Lifetime movie, but within the gymnastics community it had powerful critics.

Kathy Johnson Clarke, who won a silver team medal and an individual bronze medal on the balance beam at the 1984 Olympics, spoke candidly in the book about her battles with abusive coaches, overtraining, injuries, and bulimia. In the mid-1990s, when Johnson Clarke was working as an analyst for ABC and ESPN on gymnastics broadcasts, she served as a technical advisor on the Lifetime movie and remembers the reaction she received when she called USA Gymnastics, informing the governing body of the sport about her involvement with the film.

"What are you doing? It's bad for the sport," she was told. "I remember telling them specifically, that 'No, Joan Ryan loves this sport so stop making her out to be the bad guy. She's drawing attention to these things that you want to believe are rare.' I was never treated the same after. It was as if 'Oh, you spoke out against us.'"

In reality, little changed within the sport after the release of Ryan's book, and within elite-gymnastics circles, Ryan herself was treated as an ill-informed outsider. Jamie, who served as a stunt double for the Lifetime movie, remembers her coaches at the time dismissing Ryan and those she interviewed for her book as "losers and whiners." The tragic irony is that at the same time Jamie appeared in a movie highlighting abuses within her sport, she was being repeatedly sexually assaulted by Larry Nassar, the national team doctor.

When contacted after the Nassar scandal broke, Ryan could barely contain her anger.

"I literally felt fury. Just absolute fury that it happened at all and just the scale of it," Ryan said.

Rather than ushering in a new era of reforms, the abusive culture within the elite levels of the sport remained after the release of her book, abuses that were once again laid bare through media scrutiny that came with the exposure of Nassar's horrible crimes. One could argue the culture of elite-level gymnastics worsened in the immediate aftermath of the release of Ryan's book. By then, the physical and emotional abuse so pervasive in elite-level gymnastics clubs had become normalized. This is the type of setting that would serve as a safe harbor for Nassar for more than two decades.

"The book came out in 1995. They cannot claim they didn't know about the abusive culture. That's what makes me furious is that nothing changed," Ryan said.

To suggest that USA Gymnastics ignored the health and well-being of its elite gymnasts in the interests of pursuing money and medals would be an easy narrative to push. But it wouldn't be historically accurate. For a time at least, USA Gymnastics offered a well-intentioned Athlete Wellness Program, established even before Joan Ryan's exposé.

In the fall of 1994, USA Gymnastics was reeling after the death of Christy Henrich. The public perception was that elite-level gymnastics had a problem with eating disorders and that the sport's governing body had its collective head in the sand. The incoming president of USA Gymnastics at the time, Kathy Scanlan, took over her position soon after Henrich's death. A short time later, she tapped USAG Vice Chair for Women Nancy Thies Marshall to lead a task force to look at the way the sport responded to the health risks gymnasts faced.

Thies Marshall had been a four-time national team member and, at age fourteen, part of the 1972 Olympic team that included Cathy Rigby. In Scanlan she found a willing partner, someone who embraced the idea of addressing the sport's problems, such as abusive coaches, overtraining, and eating disorders. The two women would engage one another in many long brainstorming sessions, which led Thies Marshall to believe real changes within the sport were on the horizon.

By the mid-1990s, USA Gymnastics had grown to include more than seventy-three thousand athletes, coaches, and instructors. More than five hundred gyms across the country were registered under the USAG banner, and it fell on Thies Marshall and her team of experts to examine the governing body's response to what's known as the Female Athlete Triad. The "Triad" was first described in a 1993 meeting of the American College of Sports Medicine. Young female athletes who engaged in disordered patterns of eating, such as bingeing, purging, prolonged fasting, and the use of diet pills or laxatives, it was determined, were also at risk of suffering from menstrual dysfunction, or amenorrhea, and premature osteoporosis, or bone loss. That trio of health risks—disordered eating, amenorrhea, and premature osteoporosis—comprised the Triad and, at the time, it wasn't at all clear how many athletes were affected.

Task force member William Sands, then the director of research and development for USA Gymnastics, had conducted an unpublished study of elite gymnasts and found that 28 percent of them suffered from eating disorder problems. Around the same time, a survey of forty-two NCAA gymnastics programs revealed that 62 percent of collegiate gymnasts admitted to engaging in disordered eating.

Dan Benardot knew he had an uphill battle trying to change the mindset within elite-level gymnastics the first time he observed a national team practice in the early nineties in Colorado Springs. It was a five-and-a-half-hour-long practice, and there was no food or water in sight. Benardot, a nutritionist for the women's artistic program, would serve alongside Thies Marshall on the athlete wellness task force for USA Gymnastics from 1992 to 1996, and more than anything during that time period, he remembers struggling to get coaches to buy into the logic that gymnasts needed to eat more and eat more often in order to perform better.

Benardot explained to coaches that he understood their concerns about weight. It boiled down to simple physics—every pound a gymnast gained in body weight required an exponential amount of power to move it. But Benardot also understood the science of how food is broken down within the body—that blood sugar peaks within the body roughly an hour after food is consumed and in roughly three hours is used up entirely. And that's for a normal, inactive person. To deny food to a gymnast, somebody training upwards of six hours a day, literally means having a human being running on empty, eating into their muscle mass with each physically demanding routine. Under those conditions, which had become the norm, America's top gymnasts were wasting away.

"Our interest was: How can we intervene in what is a muscle-losing paradigm?" Benardot said.

Slowly and over time, Benardot got coaches to buy into his logic, to provide small snacks for national team gymnasts every three hours to maintain healthy blood sugar levels. Gymnasts rotated through his lab at Georgia State University in Atlanta for nutritional assessments. But there were limits to how far Benardot's message spread. He only made one trip, for example, to the Karolyis' Texas training facility. While he doesn't recall any direct resistance from the Karolyis, he similarly does not recall the couple embracing his message. Nor did Benardot know that at the same time he was preaching healthy nutrition for gymnasts, Larry Nassar was using food as a weapon, a lure to groom gymnasts at the Karolyi ranch, manipulating them and gaining their trust in an environment where they'd become so afraid to eat in front of their coaches that they had to sneak food into their dorm rooms.

Thanks in part to Benardot's efforts, the United States wound up with the heaviest women's gymnastics team to compete in the 1996 Atlanta Olympics. The gymnasts were by no means overweight. Their muscle-to-body-weight ratio was just far superior to their competitors in Atlanta, and it showed in their performance and appearance, as Benardot recalled.

"I still remember the coach from Romania coming up to me on the floor and saying, 'Dan, your gymnasts look like elephants.' And I said, 'Well, yours look like cadavers.'"

Benardot wound up with a gold medal for his contributions to Team USA during the Atlanta Olympics. He used to hold it up as one of his proudest accomplishments as a sports nutritionist. Ever since the Larry Nassar case, he's had trouble even mentioning it.

"I pound my head against the wall and say, 'What else could we have done?' "

Chapter 6

All That Glitters

In the summer of 1996, much of America was blissfully unaware of Joan Ryan's revealing book and the gymnastics community's struggle to create a healthy environment for its athletes. The country teemed with Olympic fever as it prepared to host the summer games in Atlanta just twelve years after Mary Lou Retton's gold medal performance in Los Angeles.

Atlanta was growing into a fitting host for the 100th anniversary of the first modern Olympics. The city buzzed and rebuilt itself in the years leading into its moment in the global spotlight. Newspapers breathlessly counted down the days before the opening ceremonies for what would be a star-studded two weeks of competition. NBA all-stars, tennis Grand Slam champion Andre Agassi, soccer star Mia Hamm, sprinter Michael Johnson with his golden shoes, and the ageless Carl Lewis were all among the athletes who would help the United States win forty-four gold medals on their home turf. None of those celebrities, though, shined as bright or burrowed their way deeper into the hearts of a nation than the seven teenagers who leapt, spun, and tumbled their way to America's first team gold medal in gymnastics.

Young girls from coast to coast crowded around their television screens in late July and practiced cartwheels on family room carpets for months afterward. At a time when American adults were starting to view female athletes with a new level of respect, their daughters were busy filling their heads with dreams of becoming the next Shannon Miller or Dominique Moceanu.

The oldest daughter of Paul and Camille Moxon was among those enamored with the sport. Camille had always loved gymnastics herself. She was several months pregnant in 1984 when she watched Mary Lou Retton and the Karolyis usher in a new era. In December of that year, she gave birth to her first child, a daughter, and named her Rachael.

Rachael was not an athlete as a child, but Camille noticed a graceful quality in the way she moved and in her posture. She naturally sat with her toes pointed in the way a ballerina is trained to position her feet. She enjoyed ballet, and after Camille introduced her to gymnastics, she fell captive to the sport's beauty. They snuggled on the couch together to watch the 1992 Barcelona games and recorded the television coverage on their VCR. They shook their heads in disbelief as judges awarded Shannon Miller with silver and bronze finishes instead of the gold they thought she deserved.

As new or updated athletic venues sprouted up all over Atlanta during the year before the 1996 Olympics, Camille and Rachael dusted off the videotapes from the shelves of their home in Kalamazoo, Michigan. They replayed the Barcelona games many times in anticipation of Miller's return to gymnastics' biggest stage. She would be joined by six other young women who captured the country's melting pot identity—the daughters of immigrants from Romania and China; the first black woman to win Olympic gold in gymnastics; a pair of self-motivated Midwesterners; and underdog Kerri Strug, an Arizona native who had battled through injuries and hardship to reach a second Olympic games.

Rachael, a precocious eleven-year-old, had studied all of their backgrounds. She scanned the television guide in the Sunday newspapers for upcoming events and read whatever articles she could find as the roster took shape.

She was a voracious reader, often spending hours beneath the shade of an elderly neighbor's apple trees with a book on summer days. The neighbor had problems with her vision, so Rachael eventually moved indoors to read to her and keep her company on a regular basis. The Moxons, devout Christians, encouraged their three children to find ways to help the less fortunate. They kept a tin on a hutch inside the family's modest dining room where the kids would drop spare change they found in parking lots or couch cushions. When the tin filled up, they sent what they had to an orphanage in Haiti. The dining room was also where the Moxons made a point to eat together as a family almost every night. Rare exceptions could be made if, say, a live gymnastics event was on the air during dinner time.

Rachael desperately wanted to try gymnastics for herself. She had little interest in other sports. She took swim lessons in the summer. She helped her mother clean another neighbor's house in exchange for piano lessons. She had a group of friends she met through a local co-op composed of families who homeschooled their children. But adding gymnastics to her weekly schedule occupied Rachael's thoughts for years while she petitioned her parents to sign her up at a local gym.

Camille held strong reservations about letting her daughter get involved in a sport with such demanding and dangerous training. She had read Joan Ryan's book and was aware of the eating disorders and injuries, the scarred underbelly of those spellbinding performances they saw on television. Rachael was tall for her age group and still working on taming her long limbs, which put her at greater risk for injuries in a sport that was notorious for causing them. Even at eleven years old, though, she held a preternatural ability to form a convincing argument.

As excitement for the Atlanta games grew, Rachael pressed her parents to let her give gymnastics a try. Paul and Camille were well aware by then that their oldest daughter "could argue water uphill." Whenever the family had a disagreement, Rachael made her case with logic and delivered it with zeal. It took time, though, to find the right words to talk her way into a gymnastics class. Camille researched nearby gymnastics clubs and found one in Kalamazoo run by Lubomir Geraskov, a Bulgarian ex-pat who won a gold medal on the pommel horse for his home country in 1988. Camille liked his focus on conditioning and making sure his gymnasts stayed safe while learning new skills. She had some good news to deliver to her daughter.

"Okay," she told Rachael. "You can do this. But if I even see a hint of you not eating, young lady, I will yank you out so fast your head will spin."

Camille continued to tell her that one of her parents would be at every practice and watching closely. Rachael had no objections. She was too giddy to care. She was a gymnast.

On the evening of July 23, 1996, the couch and both rocking chairs in the Moxons' small family room were filled by Paul, Camille, and their three young children. The occasion was special enough to warrant dinner in front of the television, which was flipped to Channel 9 when NBC's prime-time Olympic coverage came on the air.

The Atlanta games were only four days old and already infused with drama. The Soviet team that had claimed gymnastics gold in eight of the previous ten Olympics—a stretch dating back to the 1956 Melbourne Olympics, interrupted only by the country's decision not to send athletes to Los Angeles in 1984—was no longer competing under one flag. More than a dozen nations that claimed their independence after the USSR dissolved in 1991 were, for the first time, competing at the Olympics on their own. Russia remained the heavy favorite in the team competition, but the geopolitical changes of the last five years meant that the world's best gymnast—1995 World Champion Lilia Podkopayeva—was battling for her homeland of Ukraine rather than Russia.

The Russian men's team had claimed gold the previous night. Their female counterparts held a slight lead over Team USA and Romania heading into the second day of a two-day competition. The NBC cameras panned past tens of thousands of fans clad in stars and stripes ready to cheer their team to a comeback victory. The support was overwhelming. So was the pressure. One of the US gymnasts broke down in tears as the moment sunk in minutes before the competition began.

After a pep talk from captain Amanda Borden, the Magnificent Seven rose to the occasion. Propelled by a near-flawless opening routine on the uneven bars by Jaycie Phelps, the US team ignited the thirty-two-thousand-plus fans in the Georgia Dome with one awe-inspiring performance after another. As they approached their final rotation of the competition, the Americans had not only closed the gap with Russia but surged ahead of them for a commanding lead.

The Russian athletes made their way to the floor exercise mat with their characteristic, unshakable stoicism. But all eyes remained fixed on the vault and its long runway on the other side of the arena. As long as the US women avoided disaster and cleanly executed their vaults, they were all but guaranteed to stand atop the podium.

The first four vaulters had no issues. Moceanu—a fourteen-year-old wunderkind who often drew comparisons to Nadia Comăneci—and Strug were next. Both gymnasts trained under Karolyi. In

Olympic scoring, the worst score for each team in each event gets thrown out. They thought they needed one more good score to lock up the gold medal, and Strug and Moceanu each had two attempts to get it. None of the other gymnasts could remember Moceanu or Strug missing a single vault attempt in the month they spent together practicing in the lead-up to their trip to Atlanta. They tried their best to hold back smiles and celebrate.

Moceanu hit the vault smoothly and flipped high into the air on her first attempt. Her heels hit the mat first, but rather than striking a triumphant upright pose, her feet slipped from beneath her as if she'd landed on a banana peel. A roar caught in the throats of the crowd. The unexpected falter rattled Moceanu as she sat on the mat for a moment after her fall. Her next attempt was almost identical. To avoid a calamitous finish, America's hopes rested on the shoulders of four-foot-eight Kerri Strug.

The image of Moceanu's missteps stuck in Strug's mind as she sprinted toward the vault table for her first attempt. Her legs shot out in front of her body as she approached her landing, and she, too, fell. Her left ankle hit the mat like a javelin, absorbing the weight of her body before she landed on her backside. The landing aggravated a previous injury, and Strug hobbled to her feet.

"She is limping," announcer John Tesh reported to millions of American viewers hanging in suspense. "Kerri is hurt!"

The ankle felt loose as she limped back down the runway, kicking her leg down as she walked in hopes of popping the joint back into a comfortable place as she walked. Karolyi stood beside the raised platform and caught a glance from her worried eyes.

"Shake it off," he yelled in his thick Eastern European accent. "You can do it! You can do it!"

Strug looked less certain. Her teammates anxiously huddled nearby. The Americans were unaware at the time that the Russians had not done enough on the floor exercise to possibly close the gap. The gold medal was theirs, but Strug, her teammates, and the tens of thousands of chanting fans in attendance were under the impression that gymnastics history hung in the balance as Strug approached the runway for her final attempt.

The drama of uncertainty remained for television viewers too. The cameras zoomed in as she exhaled at the end of the runway. At home in Kalamazoo, Rachael could barely watch. The screen filled with Strug's face for a passing moment as she took her first strides. She built up speed as she ran, and then exploded off of the spring of the vault and shot herself high above the blue mats. The crowded Georgia Dome fell silent as she flipped through the air. Camille and Rachael held their collective breath in their home in Kalamazoo.

Strug's feet hit the mat in perfect unison. Her left foot shot up from the ground like it had landed on hot coals, but she held her balance. She threw her arms up into the air as the crowd roared in approval. Then she collapsed to her knees.

"Kerri Strug is hurt!" Tesh yelled above the cheers. "She is hurt badly!"

Marta Karolyi and a female athletic trainer rushed to the platform to help Strug to her feet and carry her off the platform while the judges submitted their scores. As they helped her down the short step, a man in his thirties stepped in front of the television camera and put his hand around Strug's back to help carry her. Marta Karolyi stepped aside, and the man picked Strug off her feet and carried her through a growing throng of coaches, trainers, and photographers as she grimaced in obvious pain. A team of coaches and trainers clad in red, white, and blue windbreakers crowded around her as her scores were posted in the arena. Tesh announced the results to the rest of the country.

"9.712! She has done it!" he said. "Kerri Strug has won a gold medal for the United States team."

Rachael and Camille celebrated back in Michigan. They had no idea that the man who held America's newest sporting hero in his arms at that moment lived only an hour down the road from them in Michigan. He was an athletic trainer named Larry Nassar, and at the conclusion of the Atlanta games, he was set to take over as the US gymnastics program's national medical coordinator—the top doctor for the top gymnastics program in the world.

Chapter 7

The Ranch

Many assumed the 1996 Olympics would be the career capstone of Bela Karolyi. Then fifty-three, he had served as the personal coach for both Dominique Moceanu and Kerri Strug at the Atlanta games, while his wife, Marta, was head coach. He retired from coaching after the Olympics and was inducted into the International Gymnastics Hall of Fame a year later. But disappointing finishes by the American women at the World Championships in 1997 and 1999 changed all of that.

The US women failed to win a single medal at either competition. In an effort to return to the top of the podium, USA Gymnastics president and CEO Bob Colarossi coaxed Karolyi out of retirement, hiring him after the 1999 World Championships to fill the newly created position of national team coordinator. Marta Karolyi would continue to work alongside her husband, but the new position meant Bela Karolyi would have ultimate authority over the training of national team gymnasts. The Sydney Olympics were nine months away and the last thing Colarossi wanted was another poor showing by Team USA. By hiring Karolyi to lead the women's artistic program, USA Gymnastics did more than just hand absolute power to arguably the most controversial coach in American gymnastics, it simultaneously elevated the profile of a place that in elite gymnastics circles was already known simply as "The Ranch."

If the Karolyis' goal was to take the best gymnasts America had to offer and put them in a place so free of distractions from the outside world that they could train in isolation, Bela Karolyi achieved that in 1984 when he started building his vision from the ground up. Everything about US gymnastics increased in scale during the 1980s and 1990s, and the Karolyi ranch was no different. It seemed destined to match the outsized personality of its owner. In 1983, Karolyi purchased fifty acres, miniscule by Texas standards, on land he'd discovered while on a hunting trip. He bought even more land in the years that followed, growing the parcel to two thousand acres in the heart of Sam Houston National Forest. The ranch would eventually include two gyms for the women's artistic program, totaling fifty thousand square feet; a training room; a dance studio; housing for three hundred gymnasts, coaches, and administrators; and a dining hall. Equal parts tireless worker and showman, Karolyi dug a man-made lake; grew his own vegetables; and raised exotic animals, peacocks, a camel, and miniature donkeys. He built a log-cabin home on the property for his own family.

The final leg of the drive to the Karolyis' legendary training facility begins roughly sixty miles north of Houston, southeast of Huntsville, Texas, more than five miles off of Texas Highway 2296. That's where Four Notch Road bends like an elbow at 90 degrees, giving way to a dusty and unnamed forest service dirt road. It's a rocky and bumpy ride, one the gymnasts who traveled it used to dread. To call it a two-lane road would be generous; a driver would have to come close to putting two wheels off the edge near the ditch to let an oncoming vehicle pass by.

Initially the road is bordered by dense forest to the north and open fields to the south, but about a half mile in, the red dirt shrinks, becomes rougher still, and is lined on both sides by the piney woods of east Texas. Two bridges, so narrow that only one car at a time can pass, eventually lead to a constricting single lane. Two and a half miles into the drive a sign appears at a fork in the road pointing the way to "Karolyi's Camp," and roughly a half mile beyond that, the ranch that launched so many gold medalists comes into full view.

After becoming national team coordinator in 1999, Karolyi insisted that gymnasts vying for a spot on the Olympic team make that trek to his ranch in New Waverly, Texas, for at least one week out of every month. The personal coaches of national team members, who were scattered across the country, resisted the idea. It was a direct threat to the control they exercised over their athletes. But USA Gymnastics had hired Karolyi to regain its competitive edge, and his role gave him unmatched oversight of the training process. They had no choice but to comply.

"They all freaked out when we weren't number one at Worlds," said Alyssa Beckerman, a national team member from 1997 to 2000. "When we went to the ranch you could feel it. It was palpable. There was anxiety in the air."

Through the years, media outlets have largely produced positive stories about the ranch, adding to its mystique. As recently as the spring of 2016, NBC Sports aired a fawning tribute to the Karolyis and their training facility titled *The Ranch: Home of an American Dynasty*. In the film, a seventy-three-year-old Bela Karolyi, by then retired from his days as a Team USA coach, projects a robust, warm, and grandfatherly image as he shows off his vegetable garden, his collection of exotic animals, and his skills at skeet shooting off the dock that juts out over the lake he built on his property. Marta Karolyi, by then in her final months as national team coordinator for the women's artistic program, is portrayed as the stern but caring taskmaster, who will, for the final time, select the then-five-member Olympic team from a roster of nine national team gymnasts. "These girls are like her daughters," the narrator says as the gymnasts gather around Marta in the final scene.

The reality was starkly different. National team gymnasts have gone on record expressing how much they hated going to the ranch, so much so that just the thought of it made some physically ill. Jamie Dantzscher remembers getting sick to her stomach on the drive there. Jordyn Wieber, a national team member from 2006 to 2012 and a part of the gold-medal-winning American team from the London Olympics, also dreaded the trips to the ranch from her home just outside of Lansing, Michigan.

"I would lay in bed at night, the night before I was supposed to leave for the ranch, crying and just saying, 'I'm not going to wake up. I'm not going to go in the morning. I'm going to get up and I'm going to tell my mom I'm not going,'" Wieber said.

Alyssa Beckerman recalled crying on the way to the airport, and Alyssa Baumann, a member of the national team from 2013 to 2017, said she had panic attacks the night before the drive from her home near Dallas to the Karolyis' ranch.

"I would be crying every single time. . . . It's not normal to react like that, just to go to a camp that's a drive away from home. I thought, 'What if I just roll my ankle before I go, so that I don't have to go?'" Baumann said.

A national team member from 2007 to 2011, Mattie Larson would hyperventilate and cramp up in her arms the night before each trip to the ranch, while struggling to get a few hours of restless sleep in her home in Los Angeles. Her mother would massage her shoulders and arms to loosen the tension, thinking all the while that Larson was simply anxious about sleeping so far away from home. It was always an early flight from Los Angeles to Houston, where the final leg of the journey to the ranch began, and typically Larson would have to wake up at 4:00 a.m. on the day she flew to Texas.

At fifteen or sixteen, she can't recall for certain, Larson was taking a warm bath the night before a scheduled trip to train at the ranch. As much as she tried to relax that evening, her mind raced with thoughts of what was to come.

"There's no chance I'm going to go tomorrow. What can I do right now, so I don't have to go?" she recalled thinking.

Larson stepped out of the bathtub, moved the bath mat aside, and splashed water on the floor to make it look slippery. She sat down on the wet bathroom floor and leaned back, slowly, lining the back of her head up with the rim of the bathtub. She lifted her head away from the tub, counted to herself "one, two, three," and then banged her head as hard as she could on the edge of the tub, yelling from the pain and pretending she'd slipped and fallen on the wet bathroom floor. The impact left a noticeable bump on her head. Her parents rushed into the bathroom to check on her. Larson's parents, both struggling actors, then witnessed what turned out to be a brilliant performance by their daughter. Larson pretended to have a concussion. When her father asked her what their phone number was, she acted like she couldn't remember.

"I had no other choice but to put on an Oscar-worthy performance," Larson recalled.

Larson was so convincing, her parents took her to the emergency room, where she was given tests to determine whether she had a serious head injury. Her plan worked. She got out of going to the ranch the following day. A month later, during her first day of training at the ranch, she was pulled aside by an icy Marta Karolyi.

"You know, Kim Zmeskal fell out of the top bunk when she was here at camp and she made it to practice the next day," Larson remembers Marta Karolyi saying to her. After that, she didn't talk to Larson for the rest of the camp.

From accounts of the culture at the ranch, many had ample reason to want to stay away. Jeanette Antolin, a national team member from 1995 to 2000, remembers one of her early encounters with

Bela Karolyi during a training session at the ranch. She was seventeen at the time. In the middle of the gym floor during practice, with other coaches and gymnasts within earshot, Karolyi grabbed her buttocks with one hand and told her, "You need to lose this."

"It's horrifying. I'm sure other people saw and not one person said anything. Not one person came up to me and asked me if I was okay," Antolin said of the incident. "The mentality at camp was no one felt like they could say anything. Everyone was so scared that their place was going to be taken, their spot was going to be gone if they stepped up and said anything. For coaches, I feel like they didn't want to say anything because they didn't want to jeopardize their own gymnast."

Body shaming was nothing new for Antolin. Her personal coach, Don Peters, would make her do morning weigh-ins in front of him while she wore nothing but a sports bra and briefs. In 2011, Peters, the head coach of the women's team at the 1984 Olympics, was placed on USA Gymnastics' list of permanently banned coaches following claims that he had sex with three teenage gymnasts, according to reports at that time. Antolin says Peters would routinely tell her she looked like she had gained weight. At seventeen, he put her on an eight-hundred-calorie-a-day diet while she trained roughly seven hours a day.

At the ranch, Antolin's bags were searched for food, and coaches closely monitored what she ate. While she never made herself throw up, she took a steady diet of laxatives during her final two years on the national team in order to get food out of her system as quickly as possible.

Alyssa Beckerman remembers becoming so obsessed with food in the run-up to the 2000 Olympics that she forced herself to eat nothing but carefully measured portions of oatmeal for breakfast, lunch, and dinner. She says she remembers her personal coach,

Mary Lee Tracy, poking her buttocks and telling her, "I can see the cellulite," and that the Karolyis, through Tracy, let it be known that they were monitoring what she ate.

Mattie Larson recalled that when she was seven, her personal coach, Galina Marinova, told her she looked like she "swallowed a watermelon." Marinova, Larson says, encouraged her to suck on a lemon wedge rather than eat before competitions. When Larson didn't make the 2008 Olympic team, she says that Marinova told her it was because she'd gained too much weight. Larson, who weighed less than one hundred pounds at the time, was never able to make herself throw up, but at sixteen she started taking laxatives, which was her way of purging food from her body. She became afraid of food and took laxatives daily until age twenty-two. Her biggest concern at the ranch during training sessions, she said, was that she would "shit my pants."

A tearful Marinova denies Larson's claims of body shaming. However, in November 2018, Marinova and Artur Akopyan, her codirector at her Hawthorne, California, gym, All Olympia Gymnastics Center, settled a lawsuit Larson filed against them more than two years earlier. The October 2016 lawsuit alleged Marinova and Akopyan, who also coached 2012 gold medalist McKayla Maroney, created an "abusive, harassing and degrading environment" that enabled Nassar's abusive behavior. Marinova and Akopyan agreed to settle the lawsuit with Larson for $1 million.

National team gymnasts training at the Karolyi ranch stayed either in cabins or a few hundred yards away from the main gym in a low-slung row of rooms that resembled a rustic roadside motel. The accommodations were hardly luxurious. The sheets and pillows were so uncomfortable that most gymnasts packed their own bedding. The water smelled like rotten eggs, in some rooms the showers had visible mold, and for years the ranch had no cellular phone service. Adding to the sense of isolation gymnasts felt, parents were forbidden.

However, the harshest critics of the ranch concede that the spartan surroundings fostered a sense of camaraderie. The Karolyis, for all their faults, were tireless workers and gracious hosts, at least to the other adults. On many evenings, Bela and Marta Karolyi would welcome the visiting personal coaches of gymnasts and USA Gymnastics staffers into their home. Over Bela Karolyi's homemade deer jerky, sausage, and apricot brandy, and with bottles of fine wine, the adults would carry on into the night, huddled in the modern kitchen inside the Karolyis' log-cabin home. Nassar, however, was rarely with the adults. More often than not, he was with the gymnasts, unsupervised, and frequently in their cabins, where they say he sexually assaulted them.

On the last evening of training camp, there was often a cookout, which helped the team bond. But the main purpose of the training camps wasn't to socialize. It was to push girls and young women, physically and mentally, like they'd never been pushed before, which often left gymnasts feeling pressured to train through painful injuries.

Beckerman trained for the 2000 Olympics with a wrist that had been broken for three years and hadn't fully healed. During a particularly hard practice at her local gym with her personal coach, Beckerman would typically be asked to perform three to five uneven bar routines, which would leave her completely exhausted. At the ranch, Bela Karolyi demanded she go further and perform seven bar routines. Beckerman recalls gymnasts "dropping off like flies" due to injuries. She got through the training sessions with a steady diet of painkillers and anti-inflammatory drugs.

Jamie had plantar fasciitis so painful that at times she had difficulty standing. She competed with a broken back, a sprained ankle, and broken toes, and required cortisone shots and a steady diet of Advil to numb the pain. Jeanette Antolin competed with stress fractures in her back and painful bone chips in her ankle but put off getting surgery on her ankle until after the Olympic Trials.

"We were all so broken down and injured. No one was taking care of their bodies. We were all malnutritioned. Most of us had eating disorders at the time. Most of us were being abused by Larry and not knowing it. That environment cannot create the best athlete," Antolin said of that period at the ranch. It was in this setting that Nassar became both a miracle worker and a willing accomplice. What the abusive training regime broke, Nassar was often left to fix, enabling gymnasts to train through painful injuries.

Tasha Schwikert wouldn't have had to see Larry Nassar at all had she not sustained an injury that, she says, was caused by Bela Karolyi. More than a month before the Olympic team was scheduled to depart for the Sydney Olympics, Schwikert and her teammates were at the ranch stretching, performing what's known as elevated splits. Designed to push the limits of flexibility, it's a challenging stretch even for top gymnasts. Rather than splitting their legs and forming a 180-degree line on the flat floor, gymnasts during an elevated stretch prop their front leg up on a stack of mats so they can extend beyond 180 degrees.

As the gymnasts performed their elevated splits, Bela Karolyi walked among them, pausing above Jamie with a disapproving look because her groin wasn't close enough to the floor. According to both Jamie and Schwikert, he forcibly pushed Jamie down by her shoulders beyond where she could naturally stretch on her own. The sharp pain Jamie felt in her groin brought her to tears and instantly provoked Karolyi's anger. He yelled at her, loud enough for the entire gym to hear, questioning her toughness. Schwikert witnessed the scene unfold as she stretched with her right leg extended and elevated on the stack of mats in front of her, her left leg stretched straight behind her. She told herself not to cry so she, too, wouldn't become the target of Karolyi's ire. When he ultimately did push her down by the shoulders, forcing her beyond the point she could stretch on her own, the pain was unbearable, but she fought back the tears.

The next day Schwikert could barely walk. She limped to Larry Nassar for treatment. Over the course of the following weeks, three to four times daily, Nassar inserted his ungloved fingers into Schwikert's vagina, telling her it was to massage the muscles around her injury. Like her teammates, she didn't question his intentions. After the 2000 Olympics, where Schwikert managed to compete, she was formally diagnosed with a partially torn tendon in her groin, which she attributes to Karolyi's overly aggressive stretching routine. When Schwikert was thirteen and on the junior national team, she remembers being awestruck by Bela Karolyi. It was almost surreal that she, too, would be trained by the legendary coach. Now she remembers Karolyi as the man who injured her at the most critical time of her gymnastics career.

"It just makes me angry," Schwikert said. "It was so unnecessary. We know our bodies. A coach shouldn't push you down to the point of tears. Everybody has their stopping point. That was the catalyst to me seeing Larry. Now my whole Olympic experience is clouded by the fact I saw Larry Nassar four times a day."

USA Gymnastics has never tracked injury data, but perhaps the most ambitious effort to understand the rate at which elite gymnasts become injured and require surgery was conducted by investigative reporter Scott Reid of the *Orange County Register*. In 2004, the newspaper published the results of a survey Reid conducted with nearly half of the roughly three hundred women who had competed on the US junior and senior national teams from 1982 to 2004. Among Reid's findings in his investigation was that more than 93 percent of the gymnasts interviewed suffered broken bones or injuries that required surgery and that nine out of ten gymnasts continued to train on injuries that resulted in broken bones or surgery.

Gymnasts, Reid found, were as likely to require surgery during their careers as NFL football players. One of the more interesting aspects of Reid's report is that there was a noticeable increase in injuries that required surgery for those gymnasts who competed after 1996. The rate of injuries requiring surgery shot up nearly 50 percent when compared to those gymnasts whose stints on the national team ended in 1994 or earlier.

Gymnastics officials at the time dismissed Reid's findings, saying their athletes were simply attempting more physically challenging routines and, therefore, increasingly more prone to injury. Bela Karolyi called the results of Reid's survey "a gross exaggeration."

"There are no problems with our sport," he told the *Register*. "We have an action-packed sport, and from time to time people get injured."

In an August 2016 interview with ESPN about the idea behind the ranch, Karolyi explained that the personal coaches of national team gymnasts were simply "creating queens of their own gyms." His intent was to hold training sessions at the ranch so intense that they'd match the pressure of international competitions and allow the nation's best gymnasts to measure themselves against one another. Using that yardstick alone, the formula was successful. But at what cost? That's the question that most troubles former Olympic medalist–turned–gymnastics commentator Kathy Johnson Clarke.

"Overtraining can work," Johnson Clarke says, adding that she never saw Karolyi-trained gymnasts unprepared for competitions.

But she also understood the inherent risks involved and that the Karolyis seemed incapable of recognizing when they were pushing their young gymnasts too hard.

"There was no ability on their part to realize they were breaking someone," Johnson Clarke says.

"The whole essence of their coaching and the whole essence of our system is compliance and if you want your dream to come true you comply.... There are people who can thrive on that and some do. But what about the people that don't? [Larry Nassar] only existed and only operated for as long as he did because we created a culture, we created a massive gray area, where nobody could see clearly."

In January 2011, the Karolyis entered into a long-term lease agreement with USA Gymnastics as the US Olympic Committee designated the ranch an official Olympic training site.

"This type of facility is an excellent model for the Olympic movement," USOC CEO Scott Blackmun said at the time. As much as the gymnasts dreaded the experience, the ranch would remain central to their training regimen for years to come.

National team gymnasts called it "the end room." It was the last room in the row of motel-like dorms at the Karolyi ranch, the one closest to the gym and the main road. There's a television on the wall in the corner of the room opposite the door and an overstuffed L-shaped sectional couch where gymnasts would unwind after long hours of two-a-day practices. Two training tables line the back of the couch, and opposite one of them there's a desk where gymnasts could do their homework. For years, Larry Nassar treated gymnasts on that table to the right of the door, and more often than not, this is where he sexually assaulted Mattie Larson.

When Larson was fourteen, her hips started hurting to the point where she had a piercing pain close to her pelvic region. As he did for so many other national team gymnasts, Nassar told Larson she was "butt dumb," and that her glutes were not firing properly, so, he needed to go internally to "adjust her."

Nassar would stick his fingers in her vagina for at least ten minutes. He'd start by having Larson lie on her back but eventually would have her flip over onto her stomach. By the end of the sessions, she remembers him being sweaty, breathing heavy, and leaning his body up against hers. "How do you feel? Better?" he'd ask. Larson would feel obligated to say "Yep." More than anything, she was incredibly uncomfortable and just wanted it all to be over. She and the other gymnasts at the ranch were told they had to see Nassar for "treatment," and so they did what they were told. It became routine. Even when Larson later had issues with her knees and ankles, Nassar came up with a similar rationale for penetrating her vagina with his fingers. As he'd done with multiple gymnasts, he'd tell her she was "favoring one side of her body," or "butt dumb," and repeat what he'd done before.

Alyssa Baumann was fifteen the first time Nassar penetrated her with his fingers in the end room. On several occasions, he did so while Debbie Van Horn, an athletic trainer for USA Gymnastics, who'd worked with Nassar at dozens of competitions since the late 1980s, was treating gymnasts on the other training table in the room. Nassar would drape a towel over Baumann's midsection while he inserted his fingers in her vagina for several minutes at a time. Baumann remains convinced that despite the covering, it would not have been difficult for Van Horn to determine what Nassar was doing to her. Van Horn has not commented publicly about what she did or did not know about Nassar's behavior, and neither she nor her attorney would respond to requests for comment for this book.

In 2014, Baumann almost went to her coaches to tell them what she was experiencing during her sessions with Nassar. She even rehearsed in her mind what she would say:

Hey, this makes me uncomfortable. I don't know what to do.

But the words were never spoken. The World Championships were approaching, and Baumann was mindful of her place on the team.

"I knew that if I had a problem, they wouldn't care. They would just see me as an issue and go on to the next girl. I didn't want to be a problem, so I just kept it to myself."

Nassar sexually assaulted national team gymnasts wherever he had access to them. He sexually assaulted Jamie in her own bed at the ranch. He would stretch her limbs there too, lying on top of her, crotch-to-crotch as he pulled her legs back behind her head. The first time he assaulted Jeanette Antolin was in 1997 in a hotel room in New York City, a week before the World Championships in Switzerland. It was her first big international competition, and although she would be an alternate, it was the furthest she'd come in her gymnastics career. Despite feeling uncomfortable and unsure about Nassar's invasive methods, the last thing Antolin was going to do was say anything that would jeopardize her place on the team. So, she remained silent.

The Karolyis, personal coaches of national team gymnasts, and athletic trainers other than Debbie Van Horn said years later they were not aware Nassar had access to gymnasts like Antolin inside their private rooms. This lack of awareness speaks to the lack of oversight of Nassar and of the medical staff in general. To hear former national team gymnasts tell it, Nassar went wherever he wanted to, and nobody within USA Gymnastics seemed concerned about his movements.

Nassar was so brazen, he sexually assaulted Kennedy Baker in the tunnel leading to the gymnastics floor at the HP Pavilion during the 2012 Olympic Trials in San Jose. Just minutes before the competition was scheduled to begin, Baker complained to Nassar that her Achilles was hurting badly.

"Can you do something?" she asked him, desperate for some relief from the pain.

"Yeah, I'll adjust it really quick," Nassar told her.

"You're gonna adjust it right now, in the hallway?" Baker asked, dumbfounded.

"Yep, we'll just do it right here," Nassar assured her.

"He told me to lay down, and he just basically fingered me, then I had to go compete," Baker said. Shaken by what had just happened to her, Baker fell during her second event, the balance beam. She finished in eighth place in the all-around competition, missing a chance to be part of the Olympic team, and remains convinced her performance suffered because of Nassar's sexual abuse. Like others, she remained silent out of concern she'd jeopardize her place on the team and because, like others, she also trusted Nassar and never processed at that time that he was sexually assaulting her.

Chapter 8

Money and Medals

What Marta and Bela wanted was automatons and
Jamie was never going to be that girl.

—ATTORNEY JOHN MANLY

For the US women's gymnastics team, the 2000 Olympics in Sydney, Australia, felt like living in a restrictive bubble. There was no "Olympic experience." The team wasn't allowed to take part in the opening ceremonies because of Bela Karolyi's concern that it was too close to the competition and would be too physically taxing. The American women didn't even stay in the athletes' village with the rest of Team USA. They were housed instead at Pymble Ladies' College, on Sydney's north shore, where their movements and diets were strictly monitored.

Alyssa Beckerman, an alternate for the six-member 2000 team, remembers frequently finding a welcome snack on her pillow—a chocolate, left there by Larry Nassar, who had access to the gymnasts' sleeping quarters, just as he did at the Karolyi ranch. Nassar never sexually assaulted Beckerman, but in Sydney, he continued to sexually assault Jamie in her bedroom, just as he had in Texas at the ranch.

Everything about these Olympics turned into a nightmare for Jamie. She was the US national champion on the uneven bars that year but was told by the Rybackis a short time after warm-ups that she wouldn't be competing on the bars or the balance beam. Jamie had sprained her ankle in practice the week before the Olympics, raising questions about her ability to perform. In her mind she knew she'd be able to compete through the pain. Her other ankle was already injured, and she still gutted out performances. She felt confident in her ability to manage the pain, but the decision was out of her hands. By not competing on the beam and bars, arguably her strongest event, Jamie would not be eligible to compete in the all-around competition, even though during the mock all-around competitions at the ranch she had placed first when pitted against her teammates. She was furious.

At the first chance, Jamie signed paperwork to be released from the team so she could get away from her coaches and the Karolyis to spend time with her family. Her parents had dug deep into their finances to bring all six of Jamie's siblings to Sydney to see her compete. She spent the first night away from her teammates at her family's hotel and, the next morning, was lounging with five of her siblings, watching the movie *Gladiator*, while her father and one of her sisters took a taxi to deliver tickets they'd no longer be using to former Team USA member Dominique Moceanu. Jamie dozed off during the movie and awoke to a knock on the door. It was her mother, and she was in tears.

"Your dad got hit by a bus," she said, sobbing. "We need to get to the hospital."

John Dantzscher and his twenty-one-year-old daughter, Jennifer, were riding in the back of a taxi through the streets of Sydney. While going through an intersection, the taxi was hit broadside by a bus. While Jennifer was able to escape the accident with relatively minor injuries and a few stitches, John suffered a massive head injury that, at the time, doctors feared might be fatal.

"They basically told me my dad wasn't going to make it, and that I could go in and say goodbye. I remember going in there and touching his hand and he was freezing. There was blood everywhere and they were drilling holes in his body everywhere," Jamie said.

Doctors told Jamie and her family that every five minutes John managed to hang on gave them hope he'd survive. During the lengthy wait for updates from the doctors, Jamie was visited by Kathy Kelly, the director of the Women's Artistic Program for USA Gymnastics. After expressing concern for Jamie's father, Kelly delivered another message, encouraging Jamie to keep any mention of the accident from the media. The reason was clear to Jamie: USA Gymnastics didn't want any bad press.

"I wanted to go off on her and I didn't," Jamie recalled.

Kelly did not respond to requests for comment for this book.

After weeks in the hospital in Australia, John Dantzscher was healthy enough to travel home, where he began his lengthy recovery. He had to teach himself how to speak again and do simple tasks. Jamie was fully aware that her Olympic career was over. She had already made plans to become a collegiate gymnast at University of California, Los Angeles.

The US women placed fourth in Sydney. Years later, in 2010, it was determined that the Chinese team had used an ineligible gymnast after falsifying her age, so the American women ultimately were awarded the bronze medal. At the time, though, the US performance felt like a failure. In a series of interviews, Bela Karolyi blamed the disappointing performance on the gymnasts, questioning their work ethic, and on the coaches, who, he said at the time, had too many competing agendas. In short, he blamed the poor performance on everybody but himself. Seeing these interviews, Jamie became furious. She told the assembled press in Sydney that Bela Karolyi "takes credit for what goes right but doesn't take the blame when things go wrong." She mentioned her two younger sisters, both talented gymnasts, and added, "I'll be damned before I'll let them go through what I went through here. As an athlete, to be in the Olympics, was great. But the way they treated me as a person, it was just wrong."

The response to Jamie's outspokenness was immediate and brutal. Sally Jenkins, a respected columnist with the *Washington Post*, excoriated Jamie in a column:

> Jamie Dantzscher's accusatory, finger-pointing trill was a far more graceless performance than our fourth-place finish. "Bela takes credit when we do good, and blames everyone else when we do bad—it's so not fair," she pouted. Actually, Bela Karolyi is everything the United States needs. You may not like this man with the bristling mustache, the eyes like burning glass, and the fierce booming voice; it may bother you to see him hulking over tiny bodies and urging them to deadly feats, but he is the maker of modern gymnastics, transforming it from a sport of delicacy to power. Without him, the United States doesn't turn out Mary Lou Rettons, it turns out, well, Jamie Dantzscher....The problem is not that Karolyi has too much control of U.S. gymnastics, but that he hasn't had enough.

The message was clear: dare to question Bela Karolyi and you will be dismissed as a whiner. What Jenkins didn't know while writing those blistering words was that Jamie had shown uncommon grit, time and again, competing for her country through painful injuries, including two injured ankles in Sydney. She didn't know Jamie's father was battling for his life in a Sydney hospital, and she most certainly didn't know that Jamie was being victimized, repeatedly, by the doctor assigned to the Olympic team. Nobody other than Jamie knew all of this at the time.

When contacted about her column from 2000, a gracious Jenkins was more than willing to atone. In a December 2018 column, Jenkins acknowledged she, like many other journalists at the time, was blinded by the pursuit of Olympic gold and didn't see or fully understand the human cost.

"Many people are tangentially responsible for this ecosystem that harbored Nassar and other abusers for so long. Including yours truly....I was not nearly interested enough in how, or at what cost, the Karolyis collected their haul of 97 Olympic and World Championship medals. I was too busy admiring the gold and making a living off the beauty of the performances that those young women turned in, despite the unimaginable circumstances."

"Every gymnast is impossibly brave, but obviously what Jamie Dantzscher was dealing with was tougher than most. I hate that I added to her pain," Jenkins added in a separate comment for this book.

Shortly after the 2000 Olympics, Nancy Thies Marshall, the former 1972 Olympian and USA Gymnastics vice chair for women, watched her vision of a comprehensive athlete wellness program die a slow death. One of the ideas Thies Marshall was most excited about was a mentoring program, aimed at helping the current national team members find their voices. The idea was to pair a current national team gymnast with a former Team USA member, somebody who could act in a "big sister" role, someone who would have a firsthand understanding of the demands of overtraining, injuries, and maintaining a healthy body image. Somebody who'd survived practice sessions with an emotionally abusive coach or, in the worst case, a coach who was sexually abusive. During the run-up to the 2000 Olympics, however, the personal coaches of national team gymnasts resisted the idea. To them, the mentoring program was just opening the door to having one more voice in the ear of their athletes.

In spring 1999, Thies Marshall had met in Tempe, Arizona, with roughly forty former national team gymnasts. The purpose of the meeting was to provide training to the group of women so they could better serve in their role as mentors to the young gymnasts competing for Team USA, with whom they'd eventually be paired. It was a diverse group. There were women in the room that day who'd competed on the US national team in the 1960s, 1970s, and 1980s, women who, Thies Marshall thought at the time, undoubtedly had emotional and physical abuse, and in extreme cases, sexual abuse, as part of their personal narratives.

"The idea was we were going to train the mentors in several of these topics that they were going to run into in interacting with their athletes. 'Here's what you do if....' I mean, we'd all experienced the weight of being at that level. The goal was to help our current national team members not feel alone. That they could talk to somebody that had experienced the same high-level pressure," Thies Marshall said.

Thies Marshall will never know the answer, but she is tortured by the question: What if? What if the mentoring program would have taken root and flourished? Would a young gymnast who'd been sexually assaulted by Larry Nassar have confided in an older mentor? Would the abuse have stopped, sparing hundreds of women the same fate?

"If a national team member had said, 'I don't feel comfortable. This is weird. He makes me feel weird,' I'm confident there were former national team members that were involved in the mentoring program who, if they would have heard that, they would have acted," Thies Marshall said.

In June 1999, USA Gymnastics published its Athlete Wellness Book. Edited and coauthored by Thies Marshall, the one-hundred-page handbook was to be the definitive resource to produce healthier athletes, a handbook of information for gymnastics coaches and administrators. The foreword to the book was written by Larry Nassar, who by then was well established as the national medical coordinator.

"Those of us on the health care and administrative staff at USA Gymnastics are proud to be working with the young men and women drawn to this sport," he wrote. "The publication is a valuable text, meant to enhance our effectiveness as teachers, coaches, parents, administrators and health care providers."

It makes Thies Marshall nauseous when she considers that Nassar was preying on young women and girls at the same time he wrote those words and presented the public face of a physician concerned about athlete safety.

In the fall of 2000, shortly after the Sydney Olympics, Thies Marshall met with Bob Colarossi, then president and CEO of USA Gymnastics, to update him on the progress of the Athlete Wellness Program. Unlike previous conversations she'd had with his predecessor, Kathy Scanlan, Colarossi seemed indifferent, offering no ideas of his own and simply nodding as he listened to Thies Marshall speak about her team's initiatives.

"There was this sort of blank stare," Thies Marshall said. "There just wasn't engagement in the effort." Colarossi declined to answer questions about the meeting or his time at USA Gymnastics.

A short time after returning home, Thies Marshall received a phone call from USA Gymnastics headquarters in Indianapolis. It was Kathy Kelly, the director of the women's program. Kelly informed her that the budget for the Athlete Wellness Program was being cut in half. Thies Marshall was crushed. The mentoring program, barely off the ground, would be one of the casualties of the slashed budget. She didn't feel comfortable being a "token spokesperson" if she couldn't make any substantive changes, so she quit

USA Gymnastics, agreeing with Kelly that it would be best if she simply resigned her position.

While it's not clear whether Bela and Marta Karolyi played any role in the demise of the Athlete Wellness Program, they certainly made their opinion of it known in a 2004 *Orange County Register* article written by reporter Scott Reid, telling him the program was unnecessary.

"These girls are all healthy," Marta Karolyi said. "We don't really need special help or anything like that."

From 1999 through 2004, the same time period in which the Athlete Wellness Program was scuttled for financial reasons, president and CEO Bob Colarossi was lauded for bringing in more than $20 million in sponsorship revenue to USA Gymnastics.

"What's so sad for me is I feel like we were really at the threshold of building the scaffolding to put guardrails in place and then the whole conversation changed to, 'How are we going to become the most dominant country in the world in this sport?'" Thies Marshall said.

Part II

UNHEEDED WARNINGS

Chapter 9

The Pitbull

The red brick façade of Holden Hall towered over Rachael on a warm June afternoon as she and her father, Paul Moxon, unloaded a week's worth of luggage on the south side of Michigan State's campus. She hobbled toward the front doors of the seven-story building, dragging her healing left foot in a walking boot, to check in for the first day of summer camp. It had been more than two months since she broke her foot during a tumbling pass over Easter weekend.

Rachael stood quietly by her dad's side while they greeted James Muffett, one of the camp's founders. Muffett helped start the Student Statesmanship Institute in the mid-1990s with the goal of introducing high school students to the legislative process through the lens of a Christian worldview. The campers spent their days studying real bills and playing the role of legislators arguing for or against them. Each night, they held a worship service and heard from a motivational speaker. They met with actual lobbyists and, at the end of the week, argued their positions on the floor of the state capitol building in Lansing. The six-day program was packed with long hours of intensive work.

Rachael was fifteen years old when she learned about the camp in the spring of 2000. Less than a year from finishing her high school–level courses, she was already fascinated with the law. Rachael was homeschooled, and the Moxons were part of a co-op in the Kalamazoo area that offered a set of elective, higher-level courses for the students based on different areas of expertise among the parents in the group. One parent taught physics, another calculus. Rachael's favorite class, though, was debate. The idea of going to a camp where she could spend a rigorous week in the shoes of a politician thrilled her.

She kept her excitement hidden behind a timid veneer as she collected her room assignment and registration details from Muffett. Rachael was painfully shy in her early teenage years. Muffett recalls she barely shook his hand and stood ramrod straight while he tried to break the ice. She had trouble making eye contact. Muffett met plenty of shy teenagers at his camp each summer, but Rachael stood out.

Oh my Lord, he thought to himself. *This might not work for her.*

Rachael found her dorm room down one of the long corridors in Holden Hall. She settled onto the bed and loosened her walking boot for a few minutes of rest. Gymnastics had remained a regular part of Rachael's life since she convinced her parents to let her give it a shot in the wake of the 1996 Olympics. She was not an elite gymnast and harbored no dreams of Olympic glory, but she was drawn to the practiced discipline of the sport. She spent enough time in the gym for inevitable injuries to arise. She suffered from wrist and back issues. This time around, she was overcompensating for stress fractures in her shins when a bone in her foot gave way.

An added benefit of the mock legislation camp being at Michigan State that week was the convenience of getting to see the doctor who had been helping her cope with some of her injuries, Larry Nassar. An appointment with Nassar normally required a round trip of more than two hours to reach the office and then another hour in the exam room. Rachael had started to see him for back issues a few months before she broke her foot, and he offered to help her with the broken bone as well. Her parents scheduled an appointment with him for that Thursday to save an extra journey from Kalamazoo to East Lansing.

Rachael initially shied away from the idea of seeing Nassar the week of camp. Her mother, Camille, normally accompanied her on visits to Nassar's office, but since Paul was spending the week at Michigan State as a camp chaperone, he would be the one in the room with her this time. She didn't like the idea of her dad witnessing some of the ways Nassar treated her back, which included her lying on his exam table wearing only underwear from her waist down. Camille suggested Rachael should tell Nassar to focus only on her foot and to skip the back treatments this time around. She agreed to the compromise. An abbreviated version of her regular appointments was better anyway, given the busy week.

At camp, Rachael settled into her daily schedule, growing steadily more comfortable with the small group of peers on her legislation team. They ate meals together in Holden Hall's dining area. They attended study sessions inside one of the large building's classrooms, and most of the group played volleyball in the recreation area just outside its doors. Muffett, Rachael's dad, and the other chaperones helped corral the students to their wing of the dorm and made sure lights were out by 10:00 p.m.

Thursday morning came quickly. Rachael and her group were finalizing their arguments for the capstone debate at the state house the following day when Paul came to collect her for the doctor's appointment. She regretted having to duck out of preparations and used the short trip to the sports clinic to tell her dad what she was learning.

Rachael and her father checked in at the reception desk in a large, welcoming lobby on the fourth floor of the reflective, glass-paneled building at 4660 South Hagadorn Road. They walked to the end of the hallway and stepped into Nassar's corner room. A small bench for parents sat just inside the door. His exam table was in front of a large window opposite the room's entrance, and a short countertop with a sink and bottles of lotion lined the wall in the far corner.

Nassar decorated his office with photographs of the famous gymnasts he had helped. His arm was wrapped around them in some of the pictures. Others were autographed or accompanied by thankyou notes adorned with little hand-drawn hearts and messages of love. Prominently featured among the small collage was an image of him in a red, white, and blue windbreaker on the floor of the Georgia Dome helping Kerri Strug after her gold-medal-clinching vault. Rachael, like so many other girls who came through the office, looked at that picture and felt lucky to be in Nassar's office. This was the man who fixed the world's best gymnasts, and not only was he her doctor but he also treated her like a friend.

Rachael, because she was spending the rest of her day at camp, wore makeup and dressed up more than she normally would for a doctor's appointment. Nassar noticed almost immediately. "You look beautiful, and so grown up," he told her when she and her father arrived at the office.

Paul found the comments a little odd but assumed it was just the doctor's awkward attempt at small talk with his teenage patient. Rachael thought nothing of it at the time. Nassar often found ways to compliment her when she visited, a kind word about the shoes she was wearing or her long, brown hair.

The appointment that June was shorter than most. Nassar examined Rachael's foot and told her the fracture looked fully healed and that she could stop wearing her walking boot. Nassar told her he would see her again soon for another follow-up appointment and hugged her goodbye. Pleased, Rachael returned to her group at camp.

The following day, Rachael and her fellow campers were bussed to the capitol building, craning their necks to admire the 130-year-old edifice and its stately, domed ceiling. They found their seats in the ornate, large room where state representatives propose and vote on new laws. Rachael reviewed her notes and ran through the details of her group's mock legislation presentation that served as a climax of the weeklong camp.

When it came time for her to speak, Rachael's voice boomed off the old walls. The rest of the hall, filled with dozens of her peers and many of their parents, fell silent. Rachael's parents smiled knowingly. Their daughter might be reserved, but she was not one to shy away from a cause she thought was just.

She held the room's attention for several minutes and gracefully parried away a rebuttal from students arguing the other side of her bill. Muffett sat in the back of the room with his mouth agape. He could not believe he was watching the same timid, meek girl who struggled to shake his hand a week earlier. He felt like he was watching a lion learn to roar.

Rachael's experience at camp solidified her interest in public policy. She returned to the camp year after year and eventually worked as a counselor, creating her own moot court track for students who wanted a slightly different experience. Muffett looked forward to greeting her each summer. His earlier doubts about the once-shy camper were long gone. From that first Friday when she took center stage at the State Capitol, Muffett had a new nickname for her: "the Pitbull."

Rachael's Christian roots and curious mind combined to push her to search for a clear vision of right and wrong at an unusually young age. She was struck by the power that laws and the ideas behind them had in shaping the world around her. She decided to step away from gymnastics to focus on a new passion. When most kids her age were studying for their driver's licenses, Rachael—having already completed high school–level requirements—signed up for a yearlong paralegal program.

Before she turned eighteen, she worked as a legislative aide for state politicians in Michigan. Within a few months of her eye-opening moment on the floor of the Capitol at summer camp in 2000, Rachael started making regular trips to Lansing to volunteer on the campaigns of candidates who professed values similar to her own.

Her trips to the MSU Sports Medicine Clinic continued too. Medical records show she visited Nassar's office a total of five times, but Rachael remembers making several other trips he did not document during the nearly two-year stretch that she was under his care. The appointments that followed her camp-time checkup were all ostensibly to monitor the healing in her foot, but Nassar rarely missed the opportunity to "check her alignment" and work on her back.

That process involved Rachael lying facedown on the training table as Nassar, without putting on gloves, massaged her back with one hand and penetrated her vagina with the other. He pulled Rachael's shorts down her legs and draped her with a towel. He positioned his own body directly between Rachael and her mother, who was always in the room for these treatments. His back blocked Camille's view of exactly what his hands were doing and where they were going.

Nassar explained at Rachael's first appointment that he could help her with hip and back issues by manipulating ligaments near her pelvic region with a technique called myofascial release. The common physical therapy treatment uses sustained pressure on the sheath of connective tissue around a muscle to help improve the range of motion or relieve pain in that area of the body. It does not include the therapist putting any part of his or her hand inside a patient's vagina.

Camille and Rachael had previously learned through a family friend that some physical therapists use a different technique that requires them to put their fingers inside the patient. When Nassar's fingers went inside her, Rachael assumed he was trying this other technique. She didn't think to tell her mother exactly how Nassar was touching her because she assumed her mother could see what he was doing. How, she figured, would a respected doctor feel comfortable making small talk with her mom as he did these things unless they were legitimate?

Nassar took advantage on many occasions of the vagueness of language that people frequently use when talking about the private areas of their body. When patients told their parents that Nassar touched them "down there" or "in their privates," the specifics were ambiguous enough for him to explain away his hand placement with legitimate medical reasons for working near their genitalia. Nassar never noted doing any type of internal work in Rachael's medical records, and years later he initially denied putting his fingers inside her.

Rachael stopped seeing Nassar in the fall of 2001 when she was sixteen years old. He told her the broken foot was fully healed, and while she still had some problems with her wrist that needed medical attention, he had done all he could do for her.

Toward the end of Rachael's time seeing Nassar and in the months that followed, Camille noticed bit by bit that she was seeing less of the roaring lion that emerged at summer camp. Rachael was increasingly more timid and uncomfortable around new people.

She grew tense whenever they were in public and in particular when a man she didn't know entered the room. If they were in line at the grocery store or a sandwich shop, Rachael asked her mom to stand behind her as a buffer between her and the next person in line. Eventually, Camille started reflexively positioning herself between her daughter and any man whom they didn't know.

Late one night in the winter of 2002, not long after Rachael's seventeenth birthday, Camille decided she needed to ask her daughter about the behavior she had been noticing for several months. As they stood side by side in front of the kitchen sink, washing dishes—Camille's favorite setting for heart-to-heart conversations with her children—she brought up Rachael's growing anxiety around others.

"You know, honey, this has been happening for a little while now," Camille said. "What's going on?"

Rachael, always direct, did not mince words. "I think Dr. Nassar abused me," she said.

Camille's stomach dropped. Rachael told her mother she wasn't sure how much of what Nassar did to her was sexual abuse and how much was a medical treatment. She didn't know when her appointments crossed the line, but she was certain they did.

Rachael recalled one of her final visits when Nassar rolled her onto her side, covertly unclipped her bra, and massaged her breast. He told Rachael and Camille he was working on the muscles around her rib cage to help relieve shoulder pain. She remembered looking at him and noticing his eyes were closed. His face was flushed. She looked down to see a clear erection bulging in Nassar's dress pants.

Camille could see the same scene replaying in her own mind. She knew immediately which appointment her daughter was referencing. Camille had seen the bulge too. At the time she couldn't be sure if her eyes were lying to her. She knew Nassar's wife was pregnant with their first child and dismissed what she thought she was seeing as involuntary. Her brain wouldn't allow her to connect Nassar's arousal with her teenage daughter lying on the table.

Camille stood by the stack of half-clean dishes in her kitchen and asked questions. Rachael, next to her, answered them as best she could. She stuck to facts, stoic as she worked her way through the details she could recall.

In the weeks and months that followed, Rachael and her parents waded through discussions about what to do next. They bought her a journal to record her unfolding thoughts as she processed the trauma of sexual abuse. They collected her medical records. Who could help them stop Nassar? Who would listen? Most of all, Rachael and her parents were stuck on the concern that if they did report what happened to her, no one would believe her.

Life marched forward while they weighed their options. Rachael worked as a legislative aide while she continued online paralegal school. Camille continued teaching her two younger children. At night, they would watch the news. The story captivating the country during the first few months of 2002 didn't provide any escape from the trauma Rachael was trying to process.

At the same time Rachael was seeing Nassar, a small team of reporters from the *Boston Globe*'s "Spotlight" team were uncovering a coordinated effort by the Catholic Church to hide sexual assault allegations made against priests in Massachusetts. The *Globe* published its lengthy investigation in its first Sunday paper of the new year. The story soon became a daily topic in national news.

For much of America, the *Globe* story was a revealing, alarming tale that dragged a typically taboo subject into unavoidable public view. It shed urgent light on the uncomfortable topic of child sex abuse, the long-lasting trauma it can cause, and the way that powerful institutions can enable predators. For Rachael, watching Catholic leaders fight the accusations and conduct damage control was a regular reminder of the incredibly long odds sexual abuse victims face when speaking out against someone in a position of respect and power.

The prospects for those seeking justice are not encouraging. Even offenders who don't have that power are overwhelmingly unlikely to be punished. According to data compiled by the FBI in 2017, fewer than five out of every one hundred people who commit sexual assault are arrested for their crimes. And among the small group who get arrested, only about 10 percent are ever incarcerated.

As Rachael watched the Catholic Church scandal unfold in 2002, she saw the amount of public pressure required to effect change. She told her parents that if she was going to report Nassar and find any success, she would have to do more than just tell the police. The general public would need someone to be the face of the story to remain interested and engaged. She would need to sit for interviews. Anonymous reports wouldn't be enough. She was going to have to stand alone and point her finger at a man who was beloved by two different monolithic institutions—a powerful Big Ten university with a popular athletic department and a national sports organization that produced the Olympic team's biggest stars.

Rachael had seen the way the gymnastics world reacted to complaints about poor treatment and physical abuse made by famous gymnasts like Jamie Dantzscher and Dominique Moceanu. She had read Joan Ryan's damning book about the culture in gymnastics. She knew that the sport and its many fans were willing to live with open secrets about the bad actors that surrounded the girls they loved as long as they kept winning.

She knew there was a chance—a pretty good chance—she could share the worst moments of her life with the world, and the world would shrug and move along. She believed the law in Michigan gave her until her twenty-fifth birthday to decide if she wanted to report Nassar to the police. The Moxons decided Rachael needed to be the one to make the final decision on how to proceed. She didn't yet see a fight she could win.

Her pragmatic mind constantly chewed through her options. She felt certain that her interactions with Nassar weren't an isolated incident. How many others like her were out there? Had any of them tried to report him? Rachael followed her hypothesis to its logical conclusion. If others had spoken up, Nassar had been convincing enough to silence them. She was right.

Chapter 10

Spartan Silence

The first known complaints about Larry Nassar came just months after he officially became an employee at Michigan State University. In the five years before Rachael wrestled with her own decision about how she would address what happened to her, at least five young women told coaches or athletic trainers working for the Spartans' athletic department that Nassar was doing things that didn't seem right. All of them received a similar response: they didn't understand what they were talking about.

Larissa Michell was the first. In the fall of 1997, she sat cross-legged on the floor of Michigan State coach Kathie Klages's cramped office inside Jenison Field House, the three-story, brick, art deco building that has served as a home for a variety of Spartans sports teams since 1940. Michell was sixteen years old and among the most advanced gymnasts in the Spartan Youth Gymnastics program. She remembers the skin on the backs of her thighs prickling against the dirty, green carpet as she tried to sort through her emotions. She was horrified at the realization that her new doctor might be sexually assaulting her and mortified that her teammates and coaches were going to know about it. She was intimidated looking up at Klages, who was sitting at her desk and mentioning the far-reaching implications of the piece of paper that she was at that moment waving in front of Larissa's face.

The modest office adjacent to the gym where Michigan State's gymnastics team practiced belied how far Klages's coaching career had risen. The former Great Lakes assistant and old friend of John Geddert left that gym in the summer of 1990 when the university hired her to be the new head coach of its women's program. Klages had a softer touch than her old boss and was using it to produce impressive results with the Spartans.

As Michell sat in the office, Klages was fresh off winning her first of several Big Ten Coach of the Year awards. Her teams had been ranked among the top fifteen collegiate squads in the country for most of the two previous seasons. As part of her duties as coach, she also oversaw the budding youth program that practiced on Michigan State's campus in the evenings after her college girls had finished for the day.

Klages had been thrilled when Nassar, her friend from their days together at Great Lakes, accepted a position as an assistant professor and a team physician at Michigan State that summer. She felt he would become an asset to the program, so much so that his presence would be part of the recruiting pitch that Klages and the other Spartan coaches gave to prospects. Nassar was reaching celebrity-like status in the sport a year after USA Gymnastics made him its national medical coordinator. His new job at Michigan State would not get in the way of that role. His contract required him to spend a large portion of his time doing volunteer outreach work at other organizations such as USA Gymnastics and a local high school in nearby Holt, Michigan.

Michell knew of Nassar and his stellar reputation when she injured her back in September, just weeks after he moved into the MSU Sports Medicine Clinic on the edge of campus. When she visited him there, he also suggested that he could see Michell during her practices at Jenison Field House right after he was done helping the college gymnasts with their post-practice treatments. Once or twice a week she stepped away from her training and walked down the three flights of broad, cement steps to the bottom floor of

Jenison to see Nassar in the small room where he treated Spartan athletes and other gymnasts who trained in the building. Those sessions lasted up to an hour, long enough for one of the assistants who worked closely with Michell to wonder what was happening.

Michell told the assistant, without going into detail, that she didn't feel comfortable with her treatments. Shortly thereafter, the assistant elevated Michell's concerns to Klages.

In her subsequent meeting on the old, green carpet in Klages's office, Michell nervously described what Nassar did to her, making it clear Nassar had penetrated her vagina with his fingers. Klages told Michell she had known Nassar for a long time, and she believed he wouldn't do anything that would harm a patient. Klages called other gymnasts into the office and asked if the doctor ever did anything inappropriate to them. After several said no, Michell suggested Klages speak with one of Michell's friends, who was a couple years younger. The two of them had spoken previously about Nassar, and her friend had expressed similar concerns about the way Nassar touched her. The other girl confirmed to Klages that Nassar touched her in places that made her uncomfortable.

The pair of gymnasts sat together on the office floor, feeling as if they were in trouble. Klages was an upbeat, maternal figure for the girls in the youth program, and they had a sense they were disappointing her. She brought in the older collegiate gymnasts to tell Michell and her friend that there was nothing wrong with what Nassar was doing. If Nassar was trying to help, the younger girls thought, they must be the ones with the dirty minds.

Klages told Michell she could file a formal report if she wanted to go forward. But even just the accusation, she said, could have a very big impact on her life and on Nassar's life. She assured her again that Nassar was a good doctor and an even better man. She held the form up in front of Michell and asked her to make a decision. Michell told her not to file the report and then rushed out the door, sprinted to the nearest bathroom, and burst into tears. Klages didn't tell the parents of the young gymnasts about what had been discussed inside her office that day. There's no indication she told anyone, except Nassar.

Michell visited Nassar a few days later for her next appointment in his office. "So, I talked to Kathie," Nassar said as he sat next to her on his stool and once again assured her that what he did to her was strictly medical treatment. Michell was flush with embarrassment again.

"I'm so sorry," she told him. "This is all my fault and was just a big misunderstanding." Then she hopped onto his training table, where Nassar penetrated her again. She recalled that day years later as more painful than others. "It felt like he was angry with me," she said.

Christie Achenbach was a sophomore member of the Spartans' cross-country and track teams when Michell's complaints were shooed away. Achenbach earned a scholarship at Michigan State after winning all-state honors for four straight years for the high school in her tiny hometown a couple hours to the north. She didn't know the name Larry Nassar until later in her college career when a host of other doctors couldn't figure out how to fix a problem she was having with her hamstring.

After a string of stumped specialists and an unhelpful round of acupuncture, the school's athletic trainer suggested Nassar might be able to help. He was an unconventional doctor, Achenbach was told, but he was achieving great acclaim and results with some of the country's top gymnasts. In his office, Nassar explained to Achenbach that his treatment was unique and on the cutting edge of osteopathic medicine.

She called her coach, Kelli Bert, a day or two after the appointment. Bert said years later she doesn't remember the phone call.

Achenbach says she told her coach that Nassar didn't use a glove or lubricant like a gynecologist would use before inserting his finger into her vagina. Instead, she told the coach, Nassar rubbed his hand on the outside of the region until it became naturally lubricated. Achenbach was immediately certain this was inappropriate but was too shocked and nervous to say anything at the time.

Achenbach remembers Bert telling her Nassar was an Olympic doctor and knew what he was doing. She called a fellow teammate who had seen him in the past, but the teammate didn't have a similar experience. She told her parents, and they, too, assumed Achenbach was misinterpreting the actions of the doctor. The twenty-one-year-old small-town student had kissed only one boy at that point in her life. She wasn't confident enough about what happened to her to push back harder. She never saw Nassar again, but her attempt to sound an alarm about his actions was swiftly muted.

Tiffany Thomas shot a wide-eyed stare at the graduate student athletic trainer in the room with her the first time Nassar sexually assaulted her. Thomas was a freshman outfielder for the Michigan State softball team, a star recruit from California who came to East Lansing in 1998. She developed a back injury during her first semester on campus that caused bouts of debilitating pain. The team's trainers referred her to Nassar.

She lay unclothed from the waist down on Nassar's training table when she shared her look of panic with the trainer in the room. She got an insouciant shrug in return. Thomas spoke to the supervising trainer, a woman named Destiny Teachnor-Hauk, who dismissed her concerns and said the treatment was normal. It wasn't until a year and a half later, in March of 2000, that anyone told her differently.

Thomas and the Spartans were in Boca Raton for the Florida Atlantic Invitational tournament during Michigan State's spring break when her back pain flared. Athletic trainer Lianna Hadden was traveling with the team and trying to get Thomas healthy enough to play. Nothing seemed to be working. Thomas says she hobbled to Hadden's room and asked if Hadden would consider trying the things that Nassar normally did for her when she saw him back on campus. When she described the intravaginal treatments, Hadden gasped.

"I'm not doing that to you," Thomas remembers her saying as tears welled in Hadden's eyes. Thomas cried too. Her initial misgivings seemed to be confirmed. They talked a bit further, and Hadden suggested that when the team returned to East Lansing, the two of them should discuss Nassar's treatments with Hadden's supervisor. Hadden didn't know that Thomas had already tried that route once. The following week, Thomas took a seat in the bleachers inside Jenison Field House with Hadden and Teachnor-Hauk. She walked the two of them through her experience with Nassar.

"He does this to everyone," Teachnor-Hauk told her again, just as she had more than a year earlier.

Teachnor-Hauk, according to Thomas, said Nassar worked with some of the country's best athletes, that Michigan State and its athletic department were lucky to have him at their disposal. She told Thomas that the treatments were necessary to keep her healthy enough to play, so if she felt uncomfortable seeing him, she had two options: suck it up or stop playing.

Thomas had grown to think of campus as a second home despite her experience in Nassar's office. But her chronic back pain continued to increase in intensity to the point where it was hard to walk some days, let alone swing a bat or dive for a fly ball. In 2001, she returned home to California, abandoning the sport she loved and her college studies, feeling certain that nothing Nassar did to her on his training table ever helped her back, nor was it designed to do so.

Within a year of Tiffany Thomas's departure, Lianna Hadden found herself in the midst of another emotional conversation with another star athlete shaken by an encounter with Nassar. Jenny Rood came to Michigan State with a volleyball scholarship and her father's permission to "punch any boy in the nose who tried to put his hands where he shouldn't." Shoulder, back, and leg injuries were keeping Rood from matching the high expectations she had set for her first few seasons as a Spartan. Her coaches and team trainer suggested she should visit a man that her teammates had jokingly dubbed "the crotch doc" because of his unusual technique. The athletes put up with some discomfort because Nassar was also known as "something of a wizard," a highly demanded physician with a "miracle treatment."

Nassar told her at the appointment that he would apply pressure to the pelvic area. He said nothing about exactly where he'd put his hands or the way her body might react to his stimulation. Rood, inexperienced, believed her body would only react to an intimate touch if she wanted it to react. As Nassar continued his procedure, she lay on the table frozen in a storm of confusion, fear, and embarrassment. Nassar chatted as he worked, like a dentist making small talk during a routine appointment.

She recalls "trying to desperately understand why I couldn't control what was happening to my body. . . . I felt like my body had just betrayed me, and I had built up such a wall of protection in my mind around Nassar that my first reaction was to question myself, to blame myself."

Rood's mind raced with possibilities as she tried to weigh her options for what to do next. She worried that she would be deemed a liar or looked down on if she told anyone what happened to her. She was afraid her peers would look at her differently or that she might be accusing an innocent man. After giving it some consideration, she decided she needed to say something.

Rood asked Hadden, the trainer whom she and her teammates called Lili, if there was a way to file a general complaint. She was still shy and confused about the specifics of what happened to her during her appointment. Hadden took her claim seriously and asked follow-up questions. She wanted to know if Rood thought what happened to her was a crime. Had Nassar physically hurt her?

Rood wasn't ready to discuss details. She wasn't physically hurt, and she wasn't sure that what happened was a crime. She wanted her experience noted, though, in case others had the same misgivings and could perhaps validate the way she felt. She learned that no such reporting mechanism existed. She resolved to stop Nassar if he tried to touch her pelvic area again. It was the best she could think to do.

Nassar's reputation and his personality unmoored both patients and colleagues. It was hard to square their vision of the man with the stereotypical image of a sexual predator.

Even police failed to see through Nassar's smoke screens. Detectives from Meridian Township, the chartered community made up of two towns on the eastern border of Lansing, took only two weeks in the fall of 2004 to dismiss a seventeen-year-old's claims that she was sexually assaulted by Nassar.

Brianne Randall was not an elite athlete. She had no reason to revere Nassar, and she wasn't referred to him by someone who understood his place in the sporting world. She made no mention of his Olympic credentials when she visited the Meridian Township police station one day after her second appointment with Nassar to treat scoliosis.

Randall's first appointment with Nassar was uneventful. He evaluated her back while her mother and a medical student remained in the room and suggested a physical therapist might help. A month later, on September 16, 2004, Randall returned on her own for a follow-up appointment at the MSU Sports Medicine Clinic, where Nassar aggressively rubbed his ungloved hand on her vaginal area and her breast. The following day, she and her mother reported her experience to the police before visiting the local hospital to complete a rape kit as part of a standard procedure for collecting evidence.

Nassar arrived at the police station two weeks later to speak with Detective Andrew McCready. He came armed with some written material and a PowerPoint slideshow he used at medical conferences to explain pelvic floor adjustments. Nassar took the detective step by step through his presentation, explaining the way muscle fibers in that area of the body connected to the lower back and the hamstrings. Nassar told him the treatment was medically appropriate and mentioned other medical journals and training videos that verified its legitimacy.

McCready summarized his discussion with Nassar in a total of six sentences. He told investigators who reviewed the case years later that he didn't record the interview or retain more extensive notes. He reviewed the slideshow Nassar created but did not seek out any medical journal. He did not interview any medical expert to ask about the treatments, explaining that his department didn't have the money or time to consult expert witnesses. He did not record any questions or responses about the differences between what Randall described and the way Nassar described his technique. He did not mention Randall's claim that Nassar also massaged her breast.

He did not contact anyone at Michigan State to see if Nassar had received any other complaints. He did not forward the case on to prosecutors.

McCready completed fourteen sexual misconduct investigations during his time as a detective. He sent thirteen of them to the prosecutor's office for review. When asked by investigators years later, he said he would handle Randall's case differently if he could do it over again and included it was "not [my] best work."

Two days after McCready spoke to Nassar, he spoke with Randall's mother to explain that what happened to her daughter was medical treatment. Ellen Speckman-Randall pushed back about specifics such as Nassar not wearing gloves and being alone in a room with a seventeen-year-old girl while he touched her in private areas. McCready wrote in his report that he informed Randall's mother there was no way to prove if Nassar wore gloves or was alone in the room. It's not clear if he ever asked the doctor those questions and, if so, how Nassar answered them.

Speckman-Randall recalls a meeting with Nassar after police informed her they considered the matter closed. The doctor told her that it was clear her daughter wasn't as comfortable with her body as some of the high-level athletes he treats on a regular basis but that her complaint "had merit." Speckman-Randall left the conversation with Nassar under the impression that he knew he had been "put on the radar screen."

Years later, the police department and township manager would issue a formal apology to Randall, who then went by Brianne Randall-Gay, and invite her to work with them to improve their sexual assault investigations. McCready has not discussed his role in the case publicly, but told investigators that he was fooled by Nassar's lies. He reportedly apologized to Randall-Gay privately. His supervisor, who signed off on the closed investigation, declined to be interviewed by investigators and told a reporter from Deadspin.com that he had no memory of the complaint.

Kathie Klages told police she has no recollection of the conversations in 1997 described by Larissa Michell (now Larissa Boyce). Track coach Kelli Bert told reporters she had no recollection of the conversation Christie Achenbach described. Lianna Hadden said the same thing when asked about her conversations with Tiffany Thomas (now Tiffany Thomas Lopez). Destiny Teachnor-Hauk, likewise, told investigators multiple times that she had no memory of a conversation with Thomas in the bleachers of Jenison Field House. Six young women say they told remarkably similar stories to five different adults in the early years of Nassar's career at Michigan State, and not one of the adults can remember.

Nassar portrayed himself publicly as an innovative expert on a rare medical treatment. He used medical jargon and his self-proclaimed expertise as effective weapons against a steady stream of complaints during his first seven years as a Michigan State employee. But medical knowledge, while it may have been enough to easily swat away questions from the young women and Meridian Township police in 2004, was not the only tool he used for deception. To those who knew him personally, Larry Nassar was a selfless pillar of good virtue in their community. He was willing to help anyone at any time. It was hard for friends and close colleagues to conceive of his doing anything that wasn't intended to serve others. His shield of a sterling reputation, though, was about to face its stiffest test yet.

Chapter 11

Hide-and-Seek

Kyle Stephens had long, brown hair and a mouth full of braces in the spring of 2004 as her time in the sixth grade drew to an end. While traveling on a field trip in the final weeks of the school year, she huddled toward the back of the bus with a close friend to share secrets. Kyle's friend told her a story about being touched inappropriately by her cousin. As she listened, Kyle realized something similar had happened to her.

She mustered the courage after a week or two to say something to her mother. She was nervous about her parents' reaction because she knew how much they liked the man who molested her. Her mother's shadow filled the doorframe of her dark bedroom as Kyle lay down on the top bunk of her bed tucked beneath a set of rainbow-patterned sheets. She wasn't quite sure how to start.

"Mom," she said. "When Larry rubs my feet, he rubs them on his penis."

Kyle could feel the shock in her mother's response from across the dark room. She was scared and ashamed, worried in her twelve-year-old mind that she was the one who had done something wrong. Her mom asked her to climb down from the bed so they could go to the living room and talk to her dad.

Kyle already feared her father. He had high expectations for his daughter, and they butted heads frequently while she was growing up. He could be volatile. He struggled with an injury that kept him out of work and took a cocktail of prescription drugs designed to combat his constant, debilitating pain. She was wary around him and would tell fibs from time to time to avoid a harsh reaction. She repeated what she had said in the bedroom minutes before, and Kyle's father started asking questions. He was skeptical. She was scared. Kyle clammed up, unable to unload the long list of details about her experience in the basement of Larry Nassar's home.

Katie Stephens, Kyle's mom, had helped the Nassars pick out their new home years earlier. While Nassar stayed busy at Michigan State and traveling around the country for USA Gymnastics events, Katie helped his wife, Stefanie, go house hunting. In the summer of 1998, the Nassars settled on a fifteen-hundred-square-foot split-level ranch inside a suburban subdivision in Holt, a Lansing suburb. Surrounded by a pleasant hodgepodge of public parks, shopping centers, and winding residential streets, the Nassars' home was built into a hill that sloped away from the street. It looked deceivingly small from the front with the walkout basement and the big backyard hidden from view.

Kyle, her parents, and her big brother, Erik, were regular visitors. Katie had met the Nassars through her work as a physical therapist at Michigan State, and they became fast friends. The families got together most Sunday afternoons and holidays to cook dinner together and relax. While the adults chatted upstairs, Kyle and Erik usually scampered down to the basement, where they spent hours watching Disney movies and cartoons.

At some point each Sunday, Nassar would volunteer to check on the kids. He would settle in next to Kyle on the couch to watch television with them or suggest a game of hide-and-seek. There was no shortage of good hiding places in the basement.

Blue carpet covered the main room downstairs. A pair of couches pointed toward an electric fireplace and the television. A piano sat against one wall. Doors to two other bedrooms and a guest bathroom lined the left wall. Nassar also had a "clinical room" where he kept a training table, shelves full of tape and lotions, and a hoarder's load of medical records. Nassar frequently invited gymnasts whom he couldn't fit into his work schedule to come to his basement, where he'd have them lie on the training table and he would administer one of his back treatments.

During games of hide-and-seek, Kyle liked to hide in the unfinished part of the basement. She would wedge herself under a sink next to the washing machine or in a little nook next to the furnace. Nassar would wander into the area and pretend not to see her. There, Kyle remembers watching him unzip his pants and expose his penis. He kept a white bottle of lotion with blue lettering in the room and masturbated in view of where she was hiding. The first time it happened she was next to the furnace.

"If you ever want to see it or touch it," Nassar told her, "just ask." She was six years old.

Nassar grew bolder during these visits as the years passed. He sat next to her under a blanket while she and Erik watched movies. He pulled her feet into his lap to massage them while his penis was exposed and rubbed it against her. He slipped his hand into her shorts and eventually put his fingers inside her.

At twelve, when her bus ride conversation with her friend led her to speak up, Kyle was too young to fully understand what was happening to her. She wasn't ready to talk about the entirety of what Nassar was doing on the night she first told her parents about their friend's behavior.

Kyle told her parents only that Nassar used his penis at times when he massaged her feet. Their reaction scared her from sharing any more. They found her story far-fetched, hard to believe. They decided to consult a psychologist and chose a Michigan State professor named Gary Stollak.

Dr. Stollak invited Kyle's parents and Nassar to his home office for a meeting to confront him with the accusations. Nassar denied doing anything wrong. Unlike his previous denials, Nassar gave no medical explanation for what Kyle claimed he was doing. He could not explain away his touches with jargon and slideshows. It was his word versus the word of a twelve-year-old girl. The other adults in the room knew Nassar frequently spent time in the basement with Kyle and her brother. They had seen him in the past offer to massage her feet. Nonetheless, as their meeting drew to a close, Kyle's parents and the professional psychologist chose to believe Nassar.

Kyle was waiting at home when her parents returned from the meeting along with Nassar. They called her into the living room and explained that it wasn't right to lie about such a serious thing. They asked her to apologize to Nassar as he sat across from her and played the role of a concerned friend. She refused.

"No one should ever do that to you," Nassar told her. "If anyone ever does that to you, you should tell someone."

Her parents continued to send her to appointments with Stollak in the months that followed. She tried to say as little as possible during the half dozen or so sessions in his drab home office. Being alone with an older man scared her. Kyle doesn't recall Stollak asking her any questions about what happened in Nassar's basement during their time together. He worked from the premise that what she had told her parents had been untrue, and their discussions were more akin to sexual education lessons than a search for truth.

Stollak's role as a licensed psychologist obligated him under Michigan law to report any suspicion of child abuse. There is no record of him reporting Stephens's story to police or child protective services. Years later, when Kyle's story was made public, Stollak told a judge in Michigan that he had no memory of seeing her as a client. He said he suffered a stroke that impacted his memory and explained that he disposed of his former patient files when he retired in 2010.

Kyle's relationship with her father went from bad to worse during the time she was seeing Stollak. When she argued with her dad on any subject, he told her she was a liar and constantly reminded her that she had falsely accused their good friend. He snapped at her frequently and told her she needed to apologize to Nassar. For nearly another year, she held her ground, but her dad would not relent.

She was in the living room once again when her father's patience completely expired. "You need to tell the truth," he said to her.

She resisted at first. She watched the skin around her father's jaw stretch tight. She saw his eyes narrow in determination and felt the intensity as he held his face within inches of hers.

"You need to tell the truth or I'm going to make your life a living hell," he said.

Kyle blinked tears away from her eyes. She had run the sexual abuse through her head like a horror movie on loop during the last year as others tried to convince her it hadn't happened. She would continue to do the same throughout her teenage years, forcing herself to relive the trauma so as not to forget that it was real. It was not just a bad dream.

Nassar had stopped abusing her, but she would continue to fantasize about catching him somehow. She would think about hiding recorders when her family visited his house and coaxing him into a conversation about what he did to trap him. She watched as Nassar's image of unimpeachable good character—already strong enough to convince her parents that she was a liar—continued to grow stronger.

As a thirteen-year-old, she was not ready to give up completely, but she also knew she couldn't keep battling her father. If the life she had lived over the past year was not already a living hell, she knew she wasn't prepared to endure one. Her father must have seen the resolve slipping from her face.

"So are you ready to tell the truth, then?" he asked.

"Yup," she said.

"So you were lying, then?"

Kyle gritted her teeth and huffed out her nose.

"Yup."

Chapter 12

Statute of Limitations

Rachael never returned to gymnastics as an athlete after her string of injuries as a teenager. The long hours she once spent in the gym were instead occupied by her new love for the law.

After completing enough college-level courses to meet the school's requirements, Rachael enrolled in the Oak Brook College of Law a few months after her nineteenth birthday. She was one of roughly fifty new students in the small, Christian-based correspondence course program headquartered in Fresno, California. She found the format more practical than a brick-and-mortar law school because it would allow her to earn a degree for roughly the same price as buying a new car. The low cost gave her a chance to choose future jobs based on their value to the world rather than their likelihood to help her pay down student debt.

The remote classes—she studied at home in Michigan save for one week a year when the group met in Fresno—appealed to a young woman who was still grappling with how to trust the world around her. The aftershock trauma of sexual abuse can be far-reaching, unpredictable, and impossible to compartmentalize. For Rachael and many others who suffered Nassar's abuse, those tremors showed up in unexpected places and could be paralyzing.

Nassar groomed her and others with his goofball personality and by convincing Rachael and her parents that he genuinely cared about her. He used good to mask evil. It wasn't dark corners and long shadows that reminded Rachael of danger in the wake of abuse. Instead, friendly gestures and small acts of kindness set off the alarm bells in her head. Each time someone else's hand grazed hers, Rachael was left to wonder whether it was a sympathetic touch or someone testing her boundaries. She viewed compliments through a skeptical lens, wondering constantly about the person's true intentions. Was she trusting someone she shouldn't trust?

"It basically takes every normal interaction and not only turns it on its head, but uses it against you," Rachael said. "So, you just don't engage with people. You shut them off. You put up walls."

Flipping the poles of good and bad shook Rachael's faith. She worked through her questions by writing in a private journal. Publicly, she started a blogging account on Xanga.com, where she wrote about justice, forgiveness, and a biblical worldview. She found solace and hope in the words of others like C. S. Lewis. The British author wrote about his own faith coming temporarily unmoored during World War II.

Her blog attracted the attention of a young Canadian man interested in theology. Jacob Denhollander first found Rachael's Xanga page on the recommendation of a mutual friend. They traded comments with each other about what she was writing and their similar views of the world. Longer messages followed about their personal lives and the ways in which both arrived at their strongly held beliefs. After a couple years, they decided they should meet. Jacob traveled to Michigan to meet Rachael and her family in person. Before the visit, he brushed up on his gymnastics knowledge to help break the ice.

It was the summer of 2008, and the US team was preparing to battle China for a gold medal on the latter's home turf in the Beijing games. Rachael had stopped training in the sport but had not lost her love for it. She coached preschoolers for a few years and contin-ued to follow the rise of America's up-and-coming gymnasts with her mom. Rachael kept tabs on Nassar too. She periodically searched his name on the internet, hoping to find another complaint or someone casting a faint bit of doubt about his intentions. What she found instead was that his fame and beloved status had only grown stronger.

Nassar's picture appeared on the front page of the *Lansing State Journal* in a profile about his work in the weeks leading up to the 2008 Olympics. The article outlined Nassar's career in gymnastics and the way he helped famous Olympians such as Kerri Strug and Shannon Miller. The headline dubbed him Team USA's "Dream Builder"—a moniker he provided to the reporter himself.

"I always think of myself as a dream builder," he told the reporter that summer. "It's great to see people live out their dreams and achieve their goals."

Nassar's most valuable quality to the coaches and gymnasts was how fast he could get the girls back to work. The most common areas of injury in gymnastics are wrists, ankles, and backs. Routine hyper-extension makes some types of back injury nearly inevitable for gymnasts who train for long periods of time, especially those who followed the intense practice ethos widely accepted by the world's top coaches. Discs slip, vertebrae fall out of line, and pain follows.

Most physicians tell younger patients the best way to fix these problems is through rest. Elite-level gymnasts, though, have small windows of time to reap the rewards of their years of hard work. The coaches who invest countless hours in training them know that developing one superstar can change the trajectory of their own careers. Missing weeks or months of training represents a major blow for both gymnast and coach. Nassar told them he had a shortcut.

He told his gymnastics patients he had treatments that could alleviate their pain and allow them to keep practicing. He used his pelvic floor adjustments when other doctors might have explored options for surgery or other forms of treatment. One gymnast said she saw Nassar for months before someone recommended she get a bone scan when her pain continued to persist. The results showed she had eight fractures in her back. Whether the treatments worked was nearly irrelevant. They were enough to convince gymnasts and coaches they were safe to keep going at a time when stopping was not an option.

Physicians who knew Nassar professionally say he was not a genius. He was a specialist who became an expert in a specific procedure geared toward helping lower back and pelvic injuries, both common among gymnasts. Medical experts say the treatments, when administered under the right circumstances, are a useful type of therapy. When done properly, the therapy is always completed with gloves, a third-party chaperone, a thorough explanation, and usually after all less-intrusive options have been exhausted.

Coaches who worked with him appreciated how much he knew about the sport. In the same 2008 article where Nassar talked about making dreams come true, his old friend John Geddert said he valued Nassar's ability to shape a rehab program around his gymnasts' injuries.

"Most doctors that don't know the sport will simply tell you to get off of it, rest, get out of the gym," Geddert told the *Lansing State Journal*. "That wastes very valuable time, especially when you're dealing with national-caliber athletes who can't afford to take time off."

Kathie Klages told the same reporter Nassar was the "most amazing doctor I've met in my entire lifetime." USA Gymnastics president Steve Penny called Nassar an important member of the team who "can be trusted and has [the athletes'] best interest in mind."

Such heaping praise helped Nassar accrue more than a dozen "Contributor of the Year" awards at the state, regional, and national level for his work with gymnasts. By 2008, with the Beijing games approaching, Nassar was traveling to fewer events. He had three children under the age of ten at home, the oldest of which had been diagnosed with autism. He continued volunteering as a doctor, but also dedicated time to teaching Sunday School at his local church. He was still eager to attend the biggest meets, though, and was on his way that summer to his third Olympic games as the head physician of the US women's team.

Toward the end of Jacob's first visit to Michigan, Rachael decided she wanted to tell him about Nassar and how he had sexually abused her. They slipped away from a family gathering to a small elementary school playground across the street from her home on the night before he was scheduled to return to Canada. Jacob had been just as thoughtful and engaging as his online messages thus far, and Rachael thought he deserved to know about an event that in many ways shaped her teenage years. She also wanted to see how he would react.

Jacob listened quietly while they sat on swings and Rachael revealed what very few others in her life knew at that point. He didn't recoil. He nodded along and told her he was sorry to hear what Nassar had done. He didn't question her story or how she had handled the aftermath. He offered her support and told her that his feelings for her weren't any different from what they had been before.

Jacob passed the test. A year later, in August 2009, they were married in Kalamazoo. The newlywed Denhollanders moved into a small apartment with plans to eventually relocate closer to Jacob's home in Canada. They borrowed a bed from friends and found a cheap dining room table, holding off on most furniture until they had a more permanent place to live. They did splurge for some bookshelves. They both agreed that a home is not a home without a set of well-stocked bookshelves.

Rachael also passed the bar exam in 2009, completing her long-term goal of becoming an attorney, but she watched the last months of that year slip by with dread. Her twenty-fifth birthday would arrive in December. When she looked it up years earlier, the statute of limitations to hold Nassar criminally responsible for what she knew was sexual assault appeared to expire when the victim turned twenty-five years old. Time was almost up.

She continued to comb the internet in hopes of finding some reason to believe she stood a chance. She knew she would have to overcome both the loyalty that many felt to the institutions where he worked and the personal love so many of his patients had for him, even those who didn't yet realize he was taking advantage of them when he said he was helping them.

Rachael grew despondent. She struggled when she thought about the hundreds of other young women whom Nassar treated, certain that she wasn't the only one who had been abused. Jacob did his best to console his new wife. They talked through all her potential options, but each led back down a path that reminded her she would be one small voice standing up against a famous man and the humongous, lucrative institutions that supported his work. She felt powerless.

On the eve of her twenty-fifth birthday, Rachael lay awake in a borrowed bed in her sparsely appointed apartment and stared up into the darkness. She had already accepted the reality that there was nothing she could do, but the finality of the date filled their room with a sense of loss. Jacob felt like they were mourning the death of a loved one. He wasn't sure if he had seen his wife cry before, but there were tears that night as her hope faded.

Rachael resolved not to give up. She would share her story to corroborate Nassar's actions if another victim ever came forward. She knew now, though, she couldn't stop him on her own. She would need help, and she had no idea where she would find it.

Chapter 13

"Souls Fall . . . Like Snowflakes"

Souls fall into hell for sins of the flesh like snowflakes.
—OUR LADY OF FATIMA

In 2009, John Manly was adrift. Some days just getting out of bed was a struggle for the attorney. He was full of rage, drinking alcohol to take the edge off and popping off at work—at one point he was sanctioned $20,000 by a Los Angeles judge for accusing the diocese of withholding information about an abusive Catholic priest he was suing.

"You're trying to withhold this until he dies!" Manly accused the attorneys from the diocese.

Manly's father, from whom he'd once been estranged for roughly a dozen years, died of lung cancer in 2006. Years of representing victims in priest abuse cases had shaken his Catholic faith. He questioned everything, even whether life itself was worth living. One night, not long after the death of his father, Manly, himself a married father of four, took a lonely drive from his home in Costa Mesa down Pacific Coast Highway with a loaded Glock .45 handgun in the passenger seat. He was thinking about ending it all.

Manly's life had reached a turning point years earlier in 1997. That's when he met Ryan DiMaria and started a five-year court case that would change not only his personal fortunes but also the trajectory of his career. In the 1990s, Manly worked primarily as a real estate and construction defects attorney, defending large commercial developers. He excelled at thorny cases other lawyers avoided, so much so that colleagues took to saying, "When things get fucked up, call Manly."

The work required Manly to deal with people and the press, and both came easily to him. But Ryan DiMaria's legal case was something new for Manly. DiMaria had been sexually abused as a seventeen-year-old by a priest. And not just any priest. DiMaria had been abused by Monsignor Michael Harris, the longtime principal at Mater Dei High School in Santa Ana, Manly's own alma mater.

Nicknamed "Father Hollywood" because of his matinee-idol looks and charismatic personality, Harris was perhaps the best public speaker Manly had ever seen outside of Bill Clinton and self-help guru Tony Robbins. When he gave communion to Manly during his time at Mater Dei, Harris would lock eyes with him and, in a dramatic low voice, say, "John, the body of Christ." It was mesmerizing. But it was all a façade, an act designed to mask an abusive past.

DiMaria was abused when Harris was principal of Santa Margarita Catholic High School from 1987 to 1994, a school in Rancho Santa Margarita that Harris helped found after he left Mater Dei. It was no small thing for Manly, with his strict Catholic upbringing, to represent someone who was suing not only his church and a Catholic school but also Manly's former high school principal.

In 2001, DiMaria's case turned on a critical California Supreme Court ruling. The state's highest court ordered the diocese to produce a 1994 psychiatric evaluation of Harris from St. Luke Institute, a church-owned psychiatric facility. The report revealed that Harris was sexually attracted to postpubescent adolescents and that there were multiple cases of young men who had come forward saying Harris sexually molested them. The church had proof Harris preyed on teenage boys for years and had buried it.

DiMaria had originally asked for $150,000 in his lawsuit, enough to cover his counseling fees. With the revelation that the church hid Harris's abusive past, DiMaria was ultimately awarded $5.2 million, an historically large settlement for a priest abuse case. With this stunning outcome, John Manly's career as an attorney advocating for victims of child sex abuse was on its way. For more than a decade, he would travel the country representing hundreds of priest abuse victims, winning hundreds of millions of dollars in settlements for his clients. The work was rewarding professionally, and it made him wealthy, but it also brought with it memories of a past Manly had long since buried.

Manly's father, World War II army veteran John C. Manly III, had been on the way to conduct a land invasion of Japan when two atomic bombs ended the war. His mother, Mary, was a talented opera singer who studied under legendary soprano Rosa Ponselle and later performed on national television. From his father, Manly had a sense of service to a cause bigger than himself. He joined the Navy Reserve after completing law school, serving as an intelligence officer before his discharge in 2004. From his mother, Manly inherited a flair for the dramatic, but it was his personal experience that led him to develop an intense hatred for bullies.

Born in San Mateo, California, in 1964, Manly and his parents relocated to Santa Ana when he was eight. His father, the son of a small-town attorney from Grinnell, Iowa, went on to become a paralegal for the army after World War II, helping to prosecute Japanese war criminals at military tribunals in the Philippines. The nameplate Technical Sergeant John C. Manly had on his desk in Manila now sits on his son's desk inside a law firm in Irvine, California. Eventually Manly's father took a job selling industrial batteries and phone systems.

Manly's mother insisted on raising him in parochial schools. She had a quote from Our Lady of Fatima she was fond of saying: "Souls fall into hell for sins of the flesh like snowflakes."

A staunch Catholic, Mary Manly made certain her son didn't eat meat on Fridays, went to confession on many Saturdays, and attended St. Catherine's military school in Anaheim during the week. Founded by Dominican nuns, roughly half of St. Catherine's students boarded at the school. Not Manly. With his brush cut, pressed khaki uniform, his belt buckle and shoes shined daily, he'd board the public bus to school each day, mindful of the looks that often came his way during what was a period of mounting public sentiment against the Vietnam War and those in uniform. The atmosphere at the school wasn't any more welcoming.

Manly remembers the physical violence—teachers who routinely struck him with wooden paddles and eighth graders who'd shove the younger students, like Manly, in the urinal and then pull the handle to flush, soaking his uniform.

"I just remember getting the shit kicked out of me. A lot," he said of his time at St. Catherine's. When he'd complain to his father about the bullying, the message he received in return was simple: "Fight back."

When Manly was ten, his parents' circle of friends and acquaintances included several members of the John Birch Society, a conservative political group that became a haven for far-right conspiracy theorists. One night, during a dinner party at his house attended by several couples, one of the male guests became drunk and started denying the Holocaust had ever happened. Manly wasn't old enough at the time to fully appreciate his parents' political beliefs, but he never knew either of them to hold any anti-Semitic views.

"Get the fuck out of my house!" Manly's father hollered at his guest. "I had friends that liberated those camps. Get the fuck out!"

Manly watched, stunned, as his father, who rarely cursed, physically removed the man from their home. Manly's father had hardly been raised in a progressive household, but he had a base-level understanding of right and wrong and would pass that quality on to his son.

Manly vividly remembers another encounter at one of his parents' dinner parties that occurred during that same time period. His mother, the former opera singer, wanted him to join the All-American Boys Chorus, a choir group founded in Orange County in the early 1970s by Father Richard Coughlin, a gregarious priest from Boston with a thick Irish brogue. She invited Coughlin over for dinner and to meet her son. At one point during the evening, Coughlin took Manly into a bedroom, away from his parents, and had him sing a few notes. It was then that Coughlin explained to him that part of the choral practices involved doing military-style formations.

"We do inspections and they'll inspect you in your underwear," the priest said. Manly remembers staring at him, confused. Then he remembers freezing as Coughlin twice groped his genitals through his clothes.

Coughlin, Manly later discovered, had left a trail of sexual abuse, dating back to his days as a parish priest in Boston in the late 1950s. Of those who would later file civil suits against Coughlin before his death in 2004, five had been members of the All-American Boys Chorus, which Manly never wound up joining.

When Manly was fifteen, his parents went through a contentious divorce, and it was around that same time that another priest, a Jesuit who'd become part of Mary Manly's social and religious network, began to play a far more influential role in her son's life. Father Donald McGuire had been a parish priest in Chicago in the early sixties before traveling the world to lead retreats. He was perhaps best known as Mother Teresa's spiritual advisor.

What Manly didn't know as a fifteen-year-old was that in the early sixties McGuire molested a boy in Europe and continued to sexually abuse boys in Chicago while teaching at Loyola Academy. He was forced to move from the Archdiocese because he couldn't get another assignment there. He went on to molest dozens of children in Illinois, Wisconsin, and elsewhere. Convicted in 2008 on federal charges of taking a teenaged boy across state lines and out of the country for sex, McGuire was sentenced to twenty-five years in federal prison and died as an inmate in 2017. A series of criminal and civil proceedings against McGuire revealed the Chicago Jesuits concealed his crimes for more than forty years, enabling him to abuse dozens of boys.

When Manly's parents were going through their divorce, it was McGuire who took Manly aside and told him he would be his foster father and that he shouldn't have contact with his biological father. He frequently brought Manly to a retreat in Big Bear Lake, California, and, on multiple occasions, molested him.

"He didn't rape me but he certainly raped my psyche," is how Manly describes the encounters with McGuire at Big Bear Lake.

For decades Manly buried the incidents from his childhood with Coughlin and McGuire. He never spoke about them, not even with his closest friends or loved ones. They remained locked in a part of his memory he wouldn't allow himself to explore. Through the years, if a conversation ever turned to his childhood experiences with priests or his Catholic upbringing, he'd simply say, "We all have our stories," or something equally dismissive.

Manly's early legal career hardly reminded him of the sexual abuse he'd endured as a child. Most days he was just trying to figure out a way to pay the bills. He graduated from Pepperdine Law School in 1990 flat broke and remembers pulling quarters from the ashtray of his 1983 Volkswagen GTI to pay for a movie. He was twenty-five, had $80,000 in student loans, and another $25,000 in credit card debt. The bank refused to give him a car loan. In the mid-1990s, Manly's law practice consisted of one office cubicle he rented at the Irvine Spectrum for $300 per month. He had a secretary but couldn't afford to pay her a salary, so she worked hourly from 5:00 p.m. until midnight.

All of that changed in 1997 when he took on the Ryan DiMaria case, a new turn that would ultimately lead to representing hundreds of priest abuse victims. To Manly, the seemingly endless stream of shattered lives—mostly men struggling with anxiety, depression, and suicidal thoughts because of the sexual abuse they'd suffered as children—was "like drinking out of a fire hose." The pressure, the stress, and the memories that the priest abuse cases conjured up within him almost destroyed him.

He was years removed from being the high-powered attorney with a national reputation, the fierce advocate for child sex abuse victims, who would meet Olympic gymnast Jamie Dantzscher in an airport conference room. Jamie was struggling as well. Neither of them was in a place mentally to put the sport of gymnastics on trial yet.

Valorie Kondos Field still calls Jamie Dantzscher the "GOAT"— Greatest of All Time. And for "Miss Val," as she's known to her athletes, to hang that label on any gymnast is saying something. Kondos Field led the UCLA Bruins to seven NCAA National Championships. Jamie played a pivotal role in three of those titles. Kondos Field still recalls Jamie's first collegiate performance in 2001. She knew what Jamie had been through, the emotionally abusive climate Jamie experienced on the national team, and the toll it had taken on her. Not wanting to push her new gymnast too hard in her first competition, Kondos Field limited Jamie to two events, the floor and uneven bars. Jamie scored perfect tens in both. She would go on to register twenty-eight perfect ten scores as a Bruin, at the time a school record, and be inducted into the UCLA Athletics Hall of Fame.

More than anything, her experience at UCLA made gymnastics fun again. She fell back in love with the sport. But she was far from healed, far from whole as a person. Jamie continued to struggle with an eating disorder that started when she was fifteen. As a UCLA sophomore, she barely ate enough to sustain herself. While training and competing that year, her daily diet frequently consisted of a cup of coffee in the morning, perhaps half of an energy bar or half of an orange, and then some chicken salad she would pick at later in the day. She once lost eleven pounds in a month, becoming so thin her coaches grew concerned and insisted she see a counselor on campus to discuss what was an obvious eating disorder.

For as much as she excelled at UCLA, life after college was a different story. After graduating with a bachelor's degree in psychology in 2005, as her friends started getting married and launching careers, Jamie was lost. It was the first time since her early childhood that gymnastics didn't dominate every aspect of her daily life. Throughout her early to mid-twenties, she bounced from one gymnastics coaching job to another to pay the bills, went through a string of bad relationships, and self-medicated with alcohol. During one physically abusive relationship, she ended up getting chronic active Epstein-Barr virus, an illness with symptoms similar to mononucleosis. Jamie sank even further into a deep depression and started having suicidal thoughts. In 2010, she overdosed on sleeping pills and had to be hospitalized.

"I remember at that point just asking myself, 'Do I want to live or do I want to die?' I was even a little surprised at that point, 'cause I was like, 'I want to live.'"

That same year, Jamie quit drinking. She found a psychiatrist she trusted, who cut back the antidepressants she was taking, and for about three years she stopped dating. At no time did Jamie consider that her ongoing cycle of self-destructive behavior might be attributed to the sexual abuse she suffered as a teenager. That realization wouldn't come until years later.

Chapter 14

The Perfect Storm

While Rachael, Jamie, and others struggled through life after gymnastics, John Geddert was thriving. By 2011, he was already the most decorated gymnastics coach in Michigan history. He'd coached more than twenty US national team members at his Twistars USA Gymnastics Club, which he opened in 1996 after leaving Great Lakes Gymnastics. None of his students was more promising than a powerfully built five-foot-two gymnast from nearby DeWitt named Jordyn Wieber. She was Geddert's biggest star, and in 2011, her first year on the senior national team, she won the all-around competition at her first senior-elite event, the American Cup. Barring an injury, Wieber seemed destined to become Geddert's first Olympian.

Mandatory training sessions at the Karolyi ranch continued, but they were less frequent since Bela Karolyi stepped aside in 2001, handing the role of national team coordinator to his wife, Marta. With fewer trips to Texas, the role of gymnasts' personal coaches took on added importance. In 2011, few coaches within the sport had higher profiles than Geddert, who was then fifty-three.

The demanding coaching style that continued to push Geddert forward was also wearing thin on some at his gym. At the time that his star gymnast was hitting her peak, Geddert was also navigating police investigations that threatened to send his elevated status in the sport crashing down to earth. Geddert's hair-trigger temper led to allegations of assault and battery in multiple incidents at Twistars.

In the first incident, reported in November 2011, the parent of a Twistars gymnast who also worked at the club as a coach told state police that during a heated argument after an evening practice, Geddert followed her into the parking lot, screamed obscenities at her—among other things calling her "white trailer trash"—and physically assaulted her by stepping on her foot and chest bumping her to prevent her from leaving.

In the second incident, in October 2013, eleven-year-old gymnast Makayla Johnson (she later changed her name to Makayla Hampton) told state police that Geddert pulled her off the floor during a Twistars practice to discipline her. Hampton and her grandmother, Jacqueline Hampton, both described that night. Hampton says she had a mental block and had been unable to perform a round-off, back-handspring layout. Geddert's frustrations with the young gymnast's limitations boiled over for everyone on the gym floor to see. Fuming, he pulled Hampton into the locker room, alone.

"I felt scared. I thought if I went in that room, he would choke me or something," Hampton told police.

Once inside the locker room, Hampton says, Geddert screamed at her and stepped on her foot so she couldn't back away. He then grabbed and twisted her arm, she says, pushing her into the wall and down onto a bench. Hampton says she can't recall specifics of what Geddert said. She only remembers being in tears and afraid. She then returned to practice to do conditioning drills as a form of punishment. Jacqueline recalls picking her granddaughter up from practice and seeing Geddert pacing the gym with a threatening look on his face. During the car ride home, Hampton broke down in tears as she described the incident. The next night, Jacqueline had her granddaughter file a report with the Michigan State Police.

On the same evening that police interviewed Hampton, they showed up on Geddert's doorstep in Grand Ledge, Michigan, to question him about the incident. It was after 10:00 p.m., and Geddert had a glass of wine in his hand when he answered the door to find two state troopers on his front porch. His wife and son were at home at the time. He led the troopers to his basement for the interview.

Geddert told them Hampton "got her ass chewed" but denied stomping on her foot and said he only grabbed her arm to guide her to a chair, even demonstrating on one of the troopers how he'd touched the young gymnast. When asked if it was normal to touch a gymnast in this way or whether he had her permission to touch her at all, Geddert responded with a question of his own: "Is this something I need to call a lawyer on?"

Geddert, with his career potentially on the line, instead turned to a close and loyal friend who he knew could help. Shortly after reporting the incident, Jacqueline received a series of text messages from an unexpected source. It was Larry Nassar, pleading with her not to pursue criminal charges against Geddert.

"Just ask to drop it, if you are not 100% sure you want to close John's gym and have him banned from USAG for the rest of his life," Nassar said in his text message, adding, "Having the police come to his house was a huge lesson for [John] already....If you are able to tell the PA [prosecuting attorney] that you want to drop the case it would go a long way for sure. Remember this is not just about John but also effects [sic] every family at the gym. If John makes changes everyone wins. If John is banned from gymnastics, solo, many many people are affected....I have nothing to gain by being deceitful and everything to lose. My life is about honesty and trust or there is not a single person that would see me."

Nassar went on to explain that "John just sent a policy out that from now on all staff members are not to be allowed to be with a gymnast alone and not allowed to be in any room without the door being open."

Whether such a policy ever existed at Twistars is unclear, but if it did exist, it was either ignored or it simply didn't apply to Nassar. He saw hundreds of girls on his training table in a room at Twistars, with the door closed and without another adult present. Parents would routinely sign their children up on Monday evenings and wait hours for a chance to have their daughters treated by the man who worked on Olympians. The Twistars gymnasts would gather near the start of the vault runway waiting for their turn to enter the double steel doors to Nassar's training room. Once inside, while on his training table and surrounded by shelves of cleaning equipment, dozens of those girls and young women say Nassar sexually assaulted them.

Geddert was never criminally charged in either the 2011 or 2013 investigations. After the 2013 incident involving Hampton, he was ordered by the Eaton County Prosecuting Attorney to complete counseling.

It turned out that these incidents were part of a pattern that stretched back decades earlier, to Geddert's days at Great Lakes Gymnastics. In a December 1986 report, filed with Lansing police, Geddert was accused of pushing a teenaged male (a police report of the incident has the person's age redacted because he was a minor at the time) down a staircase and kicking him in the middle of the back. Geddert denied pushing or kicking anyone and told the investigating officer he merely escorted the teen and his friend out of the gym after they'd disrupted his class.

In a 1990 incident, also reported to Lansing police, a male gymnast, who'd been going to Great Lakes gymnastics for two and a half years, accused Geddert of pushing him down from behind during a confrontation at a practice. Geddert told police the gymnast was being disruptive, that he grabbed the gymnast by the shirt, saying, "When I talk to you, you listen," and that the young gymnast then jerked away from Geddert's grasp and fell to the floor without being pushed. Neither of those cases resulted in criminal charges either.

While it's not clear what prompted it, in the spring and summer of 2014, USA Gymnastics paid Don Brooks, a Lansing private detective, to investigate the history of complaints against Geddert. Brooks interviewed Hampton, among others, about her reported assault inside the locker room. Brooks said it would be professionally inappropriate to discuss his findings, which he turned over to USA Gymnastics in September 2014. It's unclear if the organization did anything with the information he provided.

In late February 2019, the Michigan attorney general's office announced that it was taking over a criminal investigation of Geddert. Makayla and Jacqueline Hampton both spoke once again with state investigators. Multiple complaints about Geddert's coaching tactics had previously been investigated by the sheriff's department in Eaton County, Michigan, but none had resulted in criminal charges by the county's prosecuting attorney by the time the state took over the case.

Larry Nassar was well aware of John Geddert's aggressive personality. He'd seen Geddert's fiery temper on display at Twistars and dating back to their days working together at Great Lakes Gymnastics. What's not clear is how much Geddert knew about Nassar's serial sexual abuse. On at least one occasion, however, Geddert walked into the trainer's room at Twistars while Nassar was penetrating a young gymnast with his fingers, according to the woman's court testimony.

"All I remember is him [Nassar] doing the treatment on me with his fingers in my vagina, massaging my back with a towel over my butt, and John walking in and making a joke that I guess my back really did hurt," the woman testified.

Just how much Geddert saw, whether he knew the young gymnast was being penetrated, remains unclear. Geddert allegedly was in a position to hear complaints about Nassar's treatments on two other occasions, according to a report commissioned by the United States Olympic Committee in 2018.

Boston-based law firm Ropes & Gray conducted more than one hundred interviews and reviewed more than a million pages of documents in a probe into Nassar's misconduct led by two former federal prosecutors. Many of the survivors of Nassar's sexual abuse didn't speak with investigators from Ropes & Gray out of concern about the independence of the investigation. But the final report was surprisingly critical of both USA Gymnastics and the USOC. Much of it centered around who knew what and when about Nassar's sexual assaults, including Geddert.

A former Twistars gymnast told the investigators that in 1998, her mother reported an inappropriate treatment by Nassar to Geddert, who then "arranged for the gymnast not to see Nassar again for one-on-one treatments, but took no further action." A second former gymnast, who trained with Geddert in the 2000s, said her mother "reported Nassar's conduct to the tight-knit Twistars community, but that no action was taken." The Ropes & Gray report cites survivor interviews in each case and does not provide answers to key questions. What did the mother of the gymnast tell Geddert in 1998? To whom in the Twistars community did the report get delivered in the 2000s, and how much of that concern made its way to Geddert?

Perhaps the better question is, given the culture inside Geddert's gyms—Great Lakes and later Twistars—what did gymnasts and their parents feel comfortable sharing with Geddert about Nassar? Many of Geddert's former gymnasts remained silent and afraid of him years after they ended their careers and shied away from sharing their experiences with anyone asking questions. Former Great Lakes and Twistars gymnasts, their parents, and former office employees and coaches, who'd worked shoulder-to-shoulder with Geddert, were reluctant to say anything critical about him. Many of them cited his intimidating and vindictive personality. All of them were mindful of the power he wielded within the local gymnastics community.

Priscilla Kintigh was there the day Geddert started as head coach at Great Lakes Gymnastics. She was coached by him, worked later as his office manager at Twistars, and had a son who was also coached by Geddert. All told, she's known Geddert for more than thirty-five years.

"John and Larry were like this perfect storm," Kintigh said. "You become so unapproachable that your own gymnasts don't feel comfortable telling you what's going on. There's no way any of the girls would have felt comfortable saying anything to John [about Nassar]. Kids were terrified of him."

By 2011, the lack of any meaningful oversight of Larry Nassar within John Geddert's Twistars USA Gymnastics Club had become routine. As the decades-old partners who started in an abandoned school building in Lansing reached the pinnacle of their sport together, a similar dynamic was about to play out on the world's biggest stage.

Chapter 15

Fierce Five

By fall 2011, the American women had once again established themselves as a dominant force in international gymnastics. The London
Olympics were less than a year away. At the World Championships
in Tokyo that October, Jordyn Wieber continued her breakout year,
winning the individual all-around competition and leading Team
USA to an all-around team gold medal. Wieber's success marked
yet another career high point for John Geddert. He was by Wieber's
side the entire time as her personal coach, but by then, Geddert was
also head coach for the national team's women's artistic program,
a prestigious position within elite gymnastics circles that he'd keep
through the London Olympics.

Geddert was present in Tokyo in 2011 when a teammate of Wieber's, McKayla Maroney, spoke openly about Larry Nassar's sexually
abusive behavior during treatment sessions. Just how much Geddert
heard or understood about that conversation remains to this day a
matter of conjecture, but it raises questions about how much Geddert knew about Nassar's predatory behavior.

Nassar was obsessed with Maroney. She says he started sexually assaulting her when she was thirteen and a new member of
the national team. On hundreds of occasions at the Karolyi ranch in
the so-called end room and at international competitions, Maroney
says, Nassar vaginally penetrated her with his ungloved fingers. In

an October 2017 Twitter post, she first described a horrific incident with Nassar that happened inside the team hotel in Tokyo.

Maroney traveled all day and night with her teammates and says Nassar provided her with a sleeping pill for the lengthy flight. Still groggy by the time she finally reached the team hotel, Maroney recalls being alone with Nassar inside his hotel room for what she's since described as "the scariest night of my life." She told NBC News she remembers bawling and being naked on the bed with Nassar on top of her. Nassar penetrated her with his fingers while rubbing his erect penis against her. She was fifteen.

"I thought I was going to die that night," Maroney wrote about the incident.

In a victim impact statement submitted to the court at Nassar's federal sentencing hearing, Maroney's mother, Erin Maroney, wrote of the emotional toll Nassar's abuse took on her daughter.

"This experience has shattered McKayla," Erin Maroney wrote. "She has transformed from a bubbly, positive, loving, world-class athlete into a young adult who was deeply depressed, at times suicidal. At times, I was unsure whether I would open her bedroom door and find her dead."

The competition in Tokyo was a turning-point moment for Maroney. For the first time, she realized that she wasn't being "treated" by Larry Nassar at all. She knew she was being sexually assaulted. She woke up the day after the incident in the hotel room determined to tell somebody. Later that day after a training session, she was riding back to the team hotel along with teammates Jordyn Wieber, Aly Raisman, and Alicia Sacramone. John Geddert sat in the front passenger seat of the van full of gymnasts, who themselves were seated in multiple rows in the back as the driver wound his way through Tokyo traffic.

"Last night Larry was fingering me," Maroney blurted out, loud enough for others in the van to hear. There was a noticeable gasp.

When interviewed in 2018 by CNN and NBC about what was said during the van ride, Raisman said she recalled Maroney describing in graphic detail what Nassar had done to her the night before inside the hotel room. Wieber remembers Maroney saying, "he basically fingered me last night," and she also remembers Sacramone then rebuking Maroney for speaking those words out loud. Sacramone says she doesn't remember reacting that way at all to Maroney and declined to comment further about the conversation in the van, as did Geddert, who referred questions about the van conversation and anything else to his attorney, who also declined to comment.

When details of Maroney's comments were made public in 2018 during a series of media interviews with CNN and NBC News, Geddert texted Wieber in an apparent attempt to set the record straight, telling his former star gymnast he *didn't* hear what Maroney had said about Nassar during the October 2011 van ride in Tokyo. Wieber said she "think[s]" she believes her former coach, but she also struggles to this day to reconcile her feelings about both Geddert and Nassar.

Nassar, after all, was the doctor Wieber had been going to see since age seven or eight for various injuries, and there's no doubt in her mind that, at times, he helped her, especially when she suffered from severe back pain. But Nassar was also the man who, when she tore her right hamstring at age fourteen, sexually assaulted her. He was the man who'd abused her trust.

Wieber says she was fully aware of Geddert's abusive treatment of young gymnasts at Twistars, the demeaning language, the throwing of clipboards. Her own experience was different. There was the time she recalls early on in her training at Twistars that Geddert called her an "idiot," but after a meeting with Wieber's parents, Geddert never used that type of language with her again. She recognizes Geddert's contribution in helping her reach great heights in competition, but when asked if she had a daughter if she'd want her to be coached by Geddert, Wieber doesn't hesitate to answer.

"No. Just because I don't think he's a good person. I think part of why I was able to have success with him as my coach was because I was able to separate him as a person and him as a coach. I thought he was a good coach for me, specifically, but I know that he's not a good person," Wieber says.

When asked if she believes Geddert knew of Nassar's sexual abuse, she says she'll never know that answer for certain.

As the 2012 London Olympics approached, there was great anticipation that the American women would once again capture team gold. The women's team had not stood atop the Olympic podium since Kerri Strug's heroics in Atlanta. *Sports Illustrated* featured the team on the cover of its Olympic preview, the first time the magazine had placed American gymnasts on its cover since 1996. Led by team captain Aly Raisman and reigning world champion Jordyn Wieber, the team that traveled to London also featured Gabby Douglas, who would become the first African American gymnast to win the individual all-around gold medal; McKayla Maroney, who would turn in a near flawless performance on vault, her strongest event; and Kyla Ross, at fifteen the youngest member of the team and a rising star. Initially dubbed the "Fab Five" by the media, the quintet ultimately chose their own nickname while in London—the Fierce Five. The second name stuck.

Shortly before the London Olympics, Dr. Bill Moreau was appointed the USOC's managing director of sports medicine. At some point either prior to or during the first few days of the Olympics, Moreau became aware of the practice Larry Nassar had of treating gymnasts outside of the central USOC medical clinic. Moreau was concerned enough about Nassar's treatment methods, in particular his practice of treating young gymnasts alone, that he confronted Nassar about it. Moreau declined to answer questions from the authors, but he told the former federal prosecutors who conducted the USOC's internal investigation of the Nassar case that he spoke directly to Nassar about his treatment protocols.

It "would be safer for you" to treat the gymnasts next to other athletes, Moreau told Nassar. A chiropractor by training, Moreau understood firsthand how the hands-on approach Nassar took with his young athletes could potentially lead to uncomfortable moments. He went on to explain to Nassar that he "shouldn't take care of athletes alone" because in the absence of any chaperone or witness, Nassar would have a hard time defending himself if a dispute ever arose with an athlete. Moreau said he told Nassar he personally would never treat patients alone and stressed that Nassar shouldn't either. Nassar, Moreau said, responded that Marta Karolyi "won't let me" treat gymnasts next to other athletes (both Bela and Marta Karolyi declined to comment regarding questions posed by the authors).

Moreau told investigators he followed up his conversation with Nassar and visited him while he was treating gymnasts. It was an open setting, Moreau said, and Nassar treated gymnasts next to athletic trainer Debbie Van Horn, as he had for years, while multiple gymnasts were present. Moreau concluded, "There was no reason to believe the treatment setting was unsafe or inappropriate."

What Moreau didn't know when he signed off on Nassar's treatment methods is that he had sexually assaulted every member of the Fierce Five. Aly Raisman, McKayla Maroney, Jordyn Wieber, Gabby Douglas, and Kyla Ross would all eventually come forward publicly to identify as survivors of Nassar's sexual abuse.

Wieber remembers the time during the Olympics that she and Raisman were in their private room on the third floor of the townhouse where the women's team stayed in London. They were one of the very few Olympic teams in any sport that stayed outside of the athletes' village. Marta Karolyi's room was on the first floor. On the second floor, opposite a room shared by Kathy Kelly, the director of the women's artistic gymnastics program, and Jenny Zhang, the personal coach for Kyla Ross, there was a common room with a couch and a television where Nassar and the athletic trainers had set up treatment tables. Maroney was alone in that room with Nassar, lying on a treatment table, when she texted Raisman and Wieber.

"Larry has his fingers all the way inside me. Come down and rescue me," Maroney texted her teammates.

Wieber and Raisman immediately went down to the second floor and discovered Maroney on the treatment table as they walked in. They flopped on the couch for the duration of Maroney's session with Nassar so she wouldn't feel so alone and in the hopes their presence would make Nassar stop.

After the 2012 Olympics, Nassar, like other members of the medical staff, was subject to an evaluation filled out by a USOC staff member. He received high scores for "clinical acumen" and for being "very dedicated to his female athletes." But Nassar received an "unsatisfactory score" on "functions as a team player," and the evaluation noted he "does not appear to trust other medical providers to work with his athletes." The evaluation concluded that the USOC shouldn't consider Nassar for another Olympic appointment. The London games would be Larry Nassar's final Olympics, but his work with the US national team continued for another three years, and so, too, did his sexual abuse of America's best gymnasts.

Despite the trauma they were enduring at the team's nearby townhouse, the Fierce Five lived up to their pre-Olympic hype, winning team gold and four other individual medals, securing their place as one of the most decorated teams in US history. They were wildly popular after their performance in London. Feted at the White House, McKayla Maroney's unimpressed-face photo with President Barack Obama immediately went viral. They rang the bell at the New York Stock Exchange and attended the MTV Awards, and a smaller group of them threw out the first pitch at a Los Angeles Dodgers game. Everybody, it seemed, wanted to celebrate their golden moment. Behind their smiles at public appearances there was a dark truth the gymnasts carried with them, one they only allowed themselves to share in private moments with one another.

Lonny Biegel is the sort of man who doesn't like surprises. As the security director for special events for USA Gymnastics from 2003 to 2012, Biegel was responsible for the security of the national team gymnasts as they traveled after their performance in London on the forty-city Kellogg's Tour of Gymnastic Champions. At five foot nine, 260 pounds, Biegel was hard to miss as he escorted the Fierce Five on public appearances or stood watch inside packed arenas on the Kellogg's tour.

Biegel doesn't mince words, which is something you might expect from a man whose nickname is "Pitbull," and, when those words come, his thick Queens accent is unmistakable. He's worked for thirty-nine years in private security. His first big client was Sammy Davis Jr., and there have been dozens of high-watt celebrities since, from Barbra Streisand to Britney Spears.

The Kellogg's tour began in San Jose, less than a month after the closing ceremonies in London. During the second stop on the tour, in Ontario, California, McKayla Maroney and Aly Raisman both were injured after falling during their dismounts on the uneven bars. Raisman suffered bruises on her knees but wasn't seriously hurt. Maroney fractured her tibia, and while she missed several stops on tour, she made appearances to sign autographs.

During each performance, Biegel had a list of USAG staffers and event staff who were authorized to have access to the arena and be around the team. He can't recall precisely when it happened or in which city, but at different points during the tour, Biegel remembers asking the question: "What's Dr. Larry doing here?" Nassar would show up unannounced.

It wasn't unusual for male doctors to work with gymnasts on tour. But Biegel says he developed an understanding with the head athletic trainer for the women's program, Debbie Van Horn, and her colleague, Jamie Broz, that whenever a male doctor was on-site to treat a female gymnast, Broz or Van Horn were to be present at all times as female chaperones. It was a message he says he also expressed directly to doctors who joined the tour stops in different cities to work with the gymnasts.

Biegel says he always told the doctors he wouldn't allow cameras or cell phones in the training room or any pictures to be taken of the gymnasts while they were receiving treatment, and, he says, he explained to the male doctors in particular that he would always want at least another female inside the treatment area to act as a chaperone. "I took full responsibility for that," Biegel says.

When Nassar started appearing unexpectedly at the arenas on tour, though, Biegel couldn't help but notice that he followed a protocol all his own. He routinely treated gymnasts behind closed doors, alone. Biegel says he expressed his concerns about this at the time, initially to two USA Gymnastics staffers: Jill Coy, the managing director of the Kellogg's tour, and Jordan Dillon, the marketing manager. He says he had no reason to suspect anything nefarious about Nassar. He just didn't feel comfortable with a middle-aged man treating young female gymnasts without a female adult present.

At the time he raised his concerns, Aly Raisman was eighteen; Jordyn Wieber, seventeen; Gabby Douglas and McKayla Maroney, sixteen; and Kyla Ross, fifteen. Biegel went so far as to suggest the alternative of using a curtain over a doorway, hung with tape on PVC piping, and stationing a female security officer outside the curtain, the idea being to still provide the gymnasts some privacy but also the reassurance of an adult female within earshot while they were on Nassar's treatment table. He says he suggested this possible approach to both Coy and Dillon.

"Jordan Dillon was the most vocal of it, to say, 'Mind your own business, it doesn't concern you,'" Biegel said. When asked if those were her exact words, Biegel responded, "Absolutely. I would swear on a stack of Bibles."

When contacted about Biegel's account, Dillon, who left USA Gymnastics in January 2019, said, "I have never been Mr. Biegel's supervisor, so I'm not sure why he would say that he came to me to express concerns, especially about a realm of which I had no involvement nor oversight. If he means that he came to me to chat as a colleague, I can also state that I do not recall that ever happening."

Coy, who left USA Gymnastics in 2013, wouldn't comment.

Biegel says he discussed the issue of Nassar treating female gymnasts alone on five or six occasions and did so at least a few of those times with Ron Galimore, the longtime chief operating officer of USAG, who resigned in November 2018.

"Don't worry about it. The girls have it under control," Biegel says Galimore told him, meaning the female athletic trainers who worked with Nassar.

In written responses to questions from the authors that Galimore says were reviewed by his attorney, Galimore called Biegel's account "slanderous" and stressed he would never refer to female members of the USAG professional staff as "girls."

" 'The girls have it under control' would never come out of my mouth," Galimore wrote. He denied ever speaking with Biegel about Nassar's treatment practices on the post-Olympic tour. He said he only visited the tour "a handful of times" and that Biegel may have mistaken him with someone else.

"I was not aware that Nassar was conducting treatment sessions with athletes alone, nor that Nassar went to gymnasts' hotel rooms during competitions at Karolyi Ranch," Galimore added.

Chapter 16

What's Wrong with This Picture?

One of the false narratives oft repeated in the retelling of the Larry Nassar story is the notion that "everybody loved Larry." While it's true Nassar built up a reputation as the go-to doctor for gymnastics injuries and established a powerful trust with parents, some of whom consented to having their minor daughters treated by him alone in his office or in his own home, it's equally true that Nassar clashed with medical professionals and his superiors at USA Gymnastics. Many disliked Nassar.

Former USAG president and CEO Steve Penny says Nassar "had a strong sense of entitlement which I did not like." It was well known in USAG circles that Penny had a dislike for Nassar and the feeling was mutual. Nassar spoke openly about Penny's tense relationship with gymnasts, coaches, and members of the athletic training staff, and Penny referenced the friction between him and Nassar in a June 2017 court deposition.

At six foot four, 250 pounds, Penny was an intimidating figure inside the organization's Indianapolis offices. He could be warm and engaging. But, like other volatile leaders within elite gymnastics, Penny was also quick to lose his temper. He screamed at people. He threw papers. Women in particular became targets of his bullying, according to multiple accounts of USAG staffers. It was not uncommon for him to reduce them to tears. At one point, Penny had to make a formal apology before the USAG board of directors for his verbally abusive behavior toward staffers. Leslie King, the longtime vice president of communications, was the one most often in Penny's firing line.

"He knew it got to her," one former USAG staffer said. "He knew she'd go into her office, close the door and cry." King declined to discuss Penny's professional demeanor.

Penny did have a softer side. He'd often go through periods of great remorse about losing his temper with subordinates and apologize profusely to them, according to former staffers. Occasionally he'd buy them gift cards as a way to make amends.

At his core, Penny was a marketer and a skilled one at that, a "big idea" guy who understood the value of public relations and personal relationships. He'd worked in the marketing and promotions department of the Seattle Mariners, had a stint at Turner Broadcasting System as an Olympic researcher, and served as the media and public relations director for USA Cycling in the early 1990s. *New York Times* sports columnist Juliet Macur wrote of that period in Penny's career, noting that he was skilled in selling the sport of cycling and its rising star, Lance Armstrong.

"Penny was so good at selling cycling back then that Armstrong started calling him Dime," Macur wrote.

Penny joined USA Gymnastics in March 1999 and was touted as someone who could help grow the sport through partnerships with corporate sponsors. When he became president in April 2005, he quickly developed a reputation as a micromanager. But there was no question that under his watch the sport of gymnastics grew into an even greater financial success story. In January 2018, the *Sports Business Journal* noted that "the organization had been a commercial rocket ship."

From 2005 to 2015, revenue from membership shot up 75 percent. By 2015, fees from the nearly two hundred thousand members—a group that includes club-level gymnasts, coaches, and club owners—topped $12.4 million. Sponsorship dollars were pouring in to the tune of $3 million to $5 million a year, and Penny reaped the rewards. His annual salary more than tripled from $205,000 in 2005 to $628,445 in 2015. As Penny's salary grew, so, too, did his considerable ego.

"He developed a God complex," one former staffer said.

"His ego got larger and more dangerous," said another.

Staffers began to sense that Penny felt *he* was as responsible for the gymnasts' success as the gymnasts themselves. And when they did succeed, he loved basking in their limelight. He insisted on being the person to announce the Olympic team on NBC. At the 2016 Rio Olympics, he sat between Bela and Marta Karolyi where the cameras would capture him while panning the crowd. After the American women won gold in London in 2012, Penny accompanied them on many of their appearances on late-night talk shows and to the MTV Video Music Awards.

Much of the tension between Nassar and Penny stemmed from Penny's efforts, not long after he became president and CEO of USAG, to rely more heavily on medical professionals other than Nassar to direct athlete care. When Penny replaced his predecessor Bob Colarossi as the head of the national governing body, he reached out to the Indianapolis-based St. Vincent Sports Performance and its longtime executive director Ralph Reiff to explore ways in which St. Vincent could assist in the care of national team gymnasts. Reiff is a well-respected certified athletic trainer who has been a fixture at amateur sports competitions dating back to the early 1980s. He served alongside Nassar on a USAG medical task force. Penny's executive assistant, Renee Jamison, in a November 2018 deposition, described one particularly contentious meeting of that task force where Nassar's insecurity about protecting his turf boiled over.

"Dr. Nassar was very rude to Ralph Reiff during the meeting," Jamison testified, adding, "each time Mr. Reiff tried to bring up suggestions on more ways that St. Vincent's could help our athletes, Nassar was rude and would speak of ways in which that wouldn't work and wouldn't be practical."

"I left the meeting feeling like I had been in some testosterone turf war," says a former USAG staffer who attended the meeting.

Nassar grew increasingly territorial when it came to his treatment of national team gymnasts. He built personal relationships with them. When he wasn't treating athletes, he could be found at multiple competitions on the gymnastics floor, or "field of play," as it's referred to, with an expensive Canon camera strapped around his neck. He snapped photos of gymnasts going through their routines just as he had decades earlier when he was working at Great Lakes during his time in medical school. He made photo books, which he presented to gymnasts as gifts; gave them flash drives with photos; and sent them pictures in text messages and through social media. He became "friends" with many of them on Facebook and commented on their posts and pictures.

"We hated the fact that he was always, like, kind of creeping on us and taking photos all the time," Jordyn Wieber says. Nassar's incessant practice of taking photos on the field of play, on the team bus, and elsewhere wore on the gymnasts and raised eyebrows among his colleagues on the medical staff.

"He was going around with this camera, and I'm thinking, 'What's an athletic trainer taking frickin' pictures of gymnasts for?'" says Don Rackey, the men's head athletic trainer for USA Gymnastics from 1996 to 2016.

Rackey worked gymnastics competitions with Nassar dating back to the mid-1980s. He was Nassar's roommate for well over one hundred nights at three different Olympic games and during dozens of other international competitions.

"I don't know what kind of pictures he was taking, when they're straddling the bar or their legs are way apart, I don't know. But I always thought it was weird," Rackey says. "Why is an athletic trainer, whose job is to sit here and make sure you're taking care of injuries, now the team photographer for the women's team?"

It wasn't the only thing that struck Rackey as odd about his roommate. He remembers Nassar being overly protective of his computer. "He had that thing on him 24-7," Rackey says, and while other medical professionals would care for athletes in open treatment areas, within full view of their colleagues, Nassar would often take gymnasts alone into more private X-ray rooms, behind a closed door. Rackey had seen some of the videos Nassar posted on his website, videos in which Nassar demonstrated massage techniques near the pelvic bone. He thought perhaps that's what Nassar was doing while he was alone with the gymnasts. Still, he wondered to himself, "Why can't you treat them out here like we all do?"

On at least one occasion, around the time of the 2008 Beijing Olympics, Rackey remembers Nassar openly discussing a technique Rackey had never heard of before.

"I can manipulate the spine by going through the vaginal canal," Nassar told him.

Rackey didn't find the comment surprising at the time. After all, Nassar was an osteopathic physician, trained in manipulating the body through pressure points and massage. He'd used creative techniques before, such as acupuncture and taping to treat injured gymnasts. Perhaps this was one more of his outside-the-box ideas.

"He must've learned that in school," Rackey remembers thinking.

What's Wrong with This Picture?

USAG athletic trainer Tim McLane remembers a similar conversation with Nassar from the late 1990s or early 2000s. The two were speaking about manipulation techniques, and Nassar pointed out to McLane something he'd discovered in the book *Myofascial Pain and Dysfunction: The Trigger Point Manual*. The book was written by Janet Travell, who is perhaps best known as the personal physician of President John F. Kennedy, and it's seen as an authoritative source on manipulative techniques. McLane remembers Nassar mentioning that within Travell's book there's a description of an unconventional way to treat the obturator internus, the hip muscle that originates in the pelvic region, by going into the vaginal canal.

"I said, 'Really? That's probably not a good way to go after that,'" McLane recalls telling Nassar.

"Oh yeah, I wouldn't do that," Nassar replied. "No, we wouldn't do something like that."

"For me the most embarrassing part is I didn't pick up on something. That's what I beat myself up about," McLane says in hindsight.

Likewise, Rackey never allowed himself to consider that Nassar actually performed the invasive technique on young gymnasts, and certainly not while he was alone with them behind closed doors. Rackey says he didn't put the pieces together at the time: the pictures Nassar was constantly taking of young gymnasts, the overly protective attitude Nassar had about his computer, the closed-door sessions with gymnasts, the open discussions about intravaginal treatments.

"You're not putting two and two together, because Larry's this family man, teaching in church, looked up to in the community. Just because he says 'You can do it,' do you think he's doing it? I would never have thought," Rackey says.

The athletic trainer who had by far the closest working relationship with Nassar while he was with the national team was Debbie

Van Horn. The two met at the 1988 Olympic Trials and would go on to work together at gymnastics competitions worldwide for the next twenty years. Nassar would later describe Van Horn as one of the most influential women in his life.

Van Horn and her attorney did not respond to multiple interview requests. She's described by fellow trainers as "painfully shy" but remarkably dedicated to her sport. Like Nassar, she served as a volunteer for USA Gymnastics and only received modest travel stipends. She once slept in her car at a competition in order to be there to treat athletes. It was Van Horn who was often a few feet away from Nassar at the Karolyi ranch, working on gymnasts on her training table while Nassar, on multiple occasions, penetrated gymnasts on his table.

While Nassar describes Van Horn as one of the "necks" that controlled his "head," fellow trainers say Van Horn's passive personality made it highly unlikely she'd ever challenge or question Nassar's medical methods or his behavior inside the treatment room.

"I have a pretty big mouth. If I didn't agree with Larry, I'd tell him and [Van Horn] wouldn't. She would do whatever he said," says Melanie Seaman, an athletic trainer who worked on and off with the USA Gymnastics medical staff from 1995 to 2006. "I find it very hard to believe that [Van Horn] had no idea this was going on because she was with him all those times. She was with him more than anyone else," Seaman says.

In 2010, it was the head of USA Gymnastics, Steve Penny, who finally questioned why Nassar, then a forty-seven-year-old man, would be taking so many photos of young gymnasts. In his June 2017 deposition in the Mattie Larson lawsuit, Penny acknowledged he first raised the issue with Kathy Kelly, who, at the time, was director of the women's artistic program.

What's Wrong with This Picture?

"I didn't understand why he would be taking so many pictures," Penny said in the deposition. "I could understand why he might be taking pictures outside of the field of play but I didn't understand why he might be taking pictures on the field of play."

In the deposition, Penny said he didn't know if Kathy Kelly ever directed Nassar to stop taking photos, but that's not quite what he told investigators from Ropes & Gray, the law firm commissioned by the USOC to investigate the Nassar case:

"Mr. Penny stated to the Independent Investigators that he did not suspect that Nassar had any nefarious intentions in taking these photographs, but he asked Ms. Kelly to tell Nassar to stop. Ms. Kelly thereafter spoke with Nassar, who agreed to end his practice of taking photographs at meets and other competitive events."

Chapter 17

A Formal Complaint

The walls in Larry Nassar's exam room at Michigan State were a mosaic of pictures and posters of gymnasts in leotards and personal thank-you notes written on bright stationery in bubbly, swirling script. In spring 2014, Amanda Thomashow entered the exam room and, like most of Nassar's new patients, darted her eyes across the busy walls trying to digest the taped-up monument to his famous patients. The iconic image of Kerri Strug limping from the vault platform in Atlanta still loomed large. Strug's photo was joined now by dozens of other girls, including some from the 2008 squad that won silver medals in Beijing and the famous group that won gold in London.

Thomashow, twenty-four, was not a gymnast. The oldest of three sisters, Thomashow grew up blocks from Michigan State's campus, close enough to hear the cheers coming from the football stadium on Saturday afternoons from their backyard. Her parents enrolled their daughters in the youth program at Jenison Field House in the late 1990s, but Amanda abandoned gymnastics shortly after breaking her wrist as a grade schooler. She decided very early the injuries and intensity weren't worth it for her.

She spent her high school years as a cheerleader at Lansing Catholic High School before enrolling at Michigan State, the university where her father served as the director of the university's plant research laboratory and her mother had obtained a medical degree.

She graduated in 2012 and was planning to head back to campus and enroll in graduate courses to work toward her own medical degree that summer. She decided she wanted to become a neurologist. She still loved Michigan State, but after two dozen years of steeping in the school's tradition, her green-and-white blood was jaded. Thomashow's jaw didn't drop at the sight of Nassar's celebrity connection flushed out on full display on his walls. If anything, she found the photographs and notes a bit off-putting.

Hip and back pain from old cheerleading injuries nagged her after college, which is why she found herself in Nassar's office on March 24 for her first errand on what was scheduled to be a busy day off from work. She mentioned her appointment to a coworker a day earlier at the retail shop where they took inventory, folded clothes, and helped customers. The coworker, another East Lansing native, by chance had visited Nassar for an injury of her own in the past.

"Oh really?" she said when Thomashow mentioned his name. "He's kind of a creep."

Thomashow laughed. "What do you mean?"

Little warnings and bits of advice weren't rare among the girls and young women Nassar treated. Along with the string of pointed cries for help that had been ignored in the past, there was a steady undercurrent of uneasiness about Nassar's methods and his friendly demeanor. Gymnasts prepped their peers for a feeling that was going to be "weird" or "icky" when they lay out on Nassar's training table. Athletes from the Michigan State teams he treated did the same.

Skeptical parents harbored reservations about the way Nassar interacted with their children. Some members of the church where he volunteered as a Sunday school teacher had raised concerns in the past. Even Facebook, where Nassar interacted and scheduled appointments with many of his young patients, found his pattern of behavior odd enough to disable his account a few years after he joined, according to police reports.

Nassar's reputation still smothered all doubts. At this point, he had been working at Michigan State for seventeen years. Inspired by his oldest daughter, he started a charity to get autistic children involved in gymnastics and was approaching the end of his second decade with the US national team. His coworkers laughed off the Facebook ban as a misguided algorithm. Parents who whispered concerns to other gymnasts' parents as they watched practice were waved off as being paranoid. For most, the hunches and misgivings never amounted to enough to speak up against the dedicated doctor—a man who they were told was a key, rare asset to helping their daughters achieve their dreams.

Thomashow knew that her younger sister, who was still in gymnastics and training at Twistars, had seen Nassar for treatment in the past. Her mother, a pediatrician, recommended Nassar to some of her patients. She had gone out of her way to help Thomashow schedule an appointment and assured her that there was no need to worry, Nassar was the best. So, she brushed off her coworker's concerns about Nassar's personality and showed up at the MSU Sports Medicine Clinic the following morning.

She took a seat on Nassar's training table as Nassar wheeled his chair up next to her and a young female resident took her place a few feet away from them. They chatted about her family and about her injuries. Nassar nodded along and occasionally reached out to touch her thigh. He had her stand and examined her gait. He touched her hip and then left his hand for several seconds on her butt. Thomashow shot a confused, concerned look at the resident in the room and thought she saw the woman return a similar expression. Neither said anything at the time.

Nassar sent her down the hall to get X-rays for her hip injury. He showed her the images and pointed out that one of her hips was out of place. He recommended some exercises she could try to fix her issues and asked her to try a couple of them. She mentioned one of the twists he had her attempt actually caused some pain in her shoulder. Turning back to the X-rays, he suggested to the resident who was still there with them that she should check in on a patient in a different room.

When the door closed and the resident was gone, Nassar turned to Thomashow and told her he thought he could do a few things to help alleviate her pain right away. The appointment had already been long, almost an hour, and uncomfortable. She figured the sooner she agreed, the sooner she could leave.

Nassar asked her to lie on her side on the training table and massaged the shoulder she said was hurting with one hand. With the other hand, he reached over her and into her shirt. He cupped her breast in his hand in what he later described to investigators as an attempt to release tension in tissues that ran between her shoulder and the ribs beneath her breast. Thomashow believed the doctor had other intentions. She asked him to stop.

He told her to flip over onto her stomach as he walked to a counter in the far corner of the room where he kept a large bottle of hand lotion. He massaged her lower back and worked his way toward her pelvic floor. He placed three fingers over her vaginal opening and massaged the area, coming "extremely close" to inserting a finger inside of her vagina. Thomashow says it took her a couple minutes to process what was happening and muster the courage to tell him to stop.

"I'm almost done," she remembers him saying, before he walked back to the far corner of the room and stood for a conspicuous length of time with his back toward her. She noticed he appeared to have a large bulge in his pants.

Nassar insisted she schedule another appointment as soon as possible. Thomashow sat in shock as he tried to open a calendar on his computer. She remembers scanning the room as she tried to come up with excuses not to return and seeing the dozens of smiling faces on the pictures hanging from Nassar's walls.

"Oh my god," she thought. "He does this all the time!"

Thomashow knew immediately that what happened to her in Nassar's exam room was sexual assault. She said so out loud as she settled into a chair at her therapist's office less than an hour later. The visit was previously scheduled, the next item on her list of appointments and errands for the day.

"Okay, Amanda," the therapist told her. "Do you want to leave now to report this to police or should we finish your session first?"

She needed to tell her mother first. She needed to process exactly what had happened and come up with a plan for how to proceed. Two weeks later, she returned to the MSU Sports Medicine Clinic building at 7:00 a.m. on a Monday morning, arriving early in hopes of avoiding a chance run-in with Nassar. She had called Dr. Jeff Kovan, a fellow physician and the head of the small group at the clinic, over the weekend and explained her concerns. Dr. Kovan agreed to meet with her as soon as possible and for privacy ushered her up a back staircase—the same one Nassar frequently used for his after-hours appointments.

Thomashow apologetically explained to Kovan why she felt violated. She told him Nassar massaged her vaginal area with three of his fingers in a circular motion for more than a minute. She told him about the touchy-feely exam before then and the resident leaving the room. She told him she'd heard from other friends that he made them uncomfortable as well. She mentioned she had checked Nassar's Instagram page and could not understand why a fifty-year-old man was liking so many photos of young girls.

According to Thomashow, Kovan chuckled at the last comment. He said Nassar had told his colleagues years earlier that he had been flagged for suspicious behavior on Facebook but that it was a misunderstanding because he used the site to keep in contact with his young patients. Facebook doesn't publicly share information about any action it takes against individual accounts, but a spokeswoman said the company removes accounts that exploit children. They monitor potentially exploitative behavior with technology that can recognize child nudity in images and also rely on other users to raise concerns about problematic messages or activity. When an account is removed, it can't be reinstated. Someone would have to create a new account to rejoin the site. Nassar's coworkers knew his access to Facebook was restricted at one point, but he later returned to the site and continued to use it and other social media to communicate and schedule appointments with his young patients.

Kovan assured her Nassar was an expert of pelvic floor manipulations but said he would send her concerns through the proper channels.

Three weeks passed before Thomashow heard from anyone else at the university. In mid-May, she received a phone call from a woman named Kristine Moore, who told Thomashow she was an assistant director at the university's Office of Inclusion. Part of her job was to investigate complaints of sexual assault to see if they violated Title IX policy.

Thomashow recalls Moore sounding surprised as she laid out the same details she had described to Kovan weeks earlier. Kovan, Thomashow says, had clearly not relayed all the information from her complaint. In notes about her conversation with Kovan, Moore wrote that he did not seem to take the complaint seriously and was defending Nassar. After hearing more details from Thomashow, Moore told her she believed they should meet in person and open a Title IX investigation.

Congress passed Title IX of the Education Amendments in 1972, making it illegal for any university to allow discrimination on the basis of sex. The law created more opportunities for women in research, on athletic fields, and in many other areas of campus life. Through a series of Supreme Court rulings and legislative changes through the 1980s into the early 2000s, Title IX also became a tool used to hold universities responsible for keeping their students and employees safe from sexual violence. If schools didn't meet the US Department of Education's standards, they could be punished by losing federal funding.

Universities appoint Title IX coordinators to oversee the process of investigating and adjudicating claims of assault and harassment. In 2011, the US Department of Education crafted what has become known in the higher education industry as the "Dear Colleague Letter," which reshaped the Title IX process with detailed guidelines that each university should follow to be compliant with the law. The list of changes included lowering the burden of proof to show that sexual violence occurred to a "preponderance of the evidence," which is a lower bar to clear than the standard of "beyond a reasonable doubt" that exists in criminal courts. It also required schools to respond to claims of sexual violence in a timely manner; make greater efforts to inform those who report incidents about their options for pursuing justice; and offer them support services for counseling, academic assistance, and personal safety.

Two months after the new guidelines went into effect, the Department of Education's Office for Civil Rights received a complaint from a Michigan State student alleging, among other concerns, that the school was too slow to respond to her report of being sexually assaulted by a pair of athletes on campus. Another complaint about the university's response to a different case three years later prompted

166

the federal agency to launch its own investigation, which would eventually expand into a review of Michigan State's overall handling of sexual violence complaints against students and employees.

The investigation, one of dozens that the department conducted at universities across the country during that time, reviewed three years of grievances against Michigan State and eventually found the school fostered a "sexually hostile environment" on campus. The investigators reviewed 150 different claims sent to the office that handled Title IX complaints and found "significant concerns" with about 20 percent of them. Specifically, the federal investigators found that in multiple cases involving university employees, the Title IX office had evidence of inappropriate conduct but failed to respond adequately, and the behavior continued. They also discovered Michigan State failed to maintain complete grievance files, which "could potentially prevent the Title IX Coordinator from recognizing related incidents or patterns of incidents that need to be addressed."

Those missteps were related to cases other than complaints about Nassar. As part of its resolution with the Department of Education, Michigan State agreed to make several changes and provide documentation for all prior complaints of sexual abuse or harassment by the end of 2015. Michigan State didn't send those documents until nearly a year after their due date, and when they arrived, Thomashow's complaint about Nassar was notably missing. The university later said it omitted Thomashow's report by mistake.

Federal investigators were in the process of scrutinizing Michigan State's Title IX operation as Thomashow's claim started to make its way through the system. Her call with Moore prompted the school to begin its first official investigation of Nassar on May 15, 2014. Four days later, Michigan State president Lou Anna Simon had a discussion with one of her senior advisors, Paulette Granberry

Russell, a woman who had directed the university's diversity and inclusion efforts since before Simon took over leadership in East Lansing.

Granberry Russell met routinely with the president to make sure Simon was briefed on any diversity or Title IX issues that might become "hot-button topics." If a high-profile employee were involved in a complaint, members of Michigan State's Title IX office say they knew Simon would want to be aware. Granberry Russell learned about the complaint against Nassar on a Friday morning. She reviewed the file and sent an email to Simon: "We have an incident involving a sports medicine doc."

Their discussion took place the following Monday morning. Granberry Russell would say years later in court that she couldn't recall whether she and Simon met in person or spoke over the phone. She also couldn't remember if she specifically shared Nassar's name with Simon, who claims she didn't know the identity of the "sports medicine doc" until several years later.

Physical evidence from that time shows that Granberry Russell scratched a couple notes on the outside of her file folder that held the agenda for her meeting with Simon. "Sports Med," she wrote, "Dr. Nassar, SA." SA served as shorthand for sexual assault. Simon's printed notes for the same meeting included a bullet point for "Sexual Assault Cases." In the margin next to it, she jotted down three letters in pen and underlined them: COM—College of Osteopathic Medicine. For the first time, whether Simon knew his name or not, a complaint about the school's resident gymnastics celebrity had reached the highest office of the university.

Almost any noteworthy event that occurred on the Michigan State campus eventually found its way to the desk of the university's long-serving president. A decade into her stay in office, Simon was known as an omnipresent manager who had constructed a culture that prized loyalty and longevity.

Many of her closest advisors were fixtures on campus. Granberry Russell was in her sixteenth year in the same job. Simon's general counsel, Robert Noto, had served for nineteen. One of her most ardent and powerful supporters on the board of trustees, Joel Ferguson, had first been elected to his spot in 1986. Simon herself was a rarity in higher education, a woman who rose through the ranks to the top of a major university without ever changing her zip code.

Simon moved to East Lansing in 1970 after spending the first twenty-three years of her life in central Indiana. She was born to blue-collar parents and worked in her grandfather's lumberyard before earning a scholarship to Indiana State University, where she studied mathematics. She came to Michigan State for a doctorate in higher education and transitioned into teaching on campus when she finished her own classes.

She charted a course toward a role in the university's administration but never abandoned her background in math. Statistics and data served as her compass as she rose through the ranks. She first landed on the board of trustees' radar as a presidential candidate in the early 1990s. She didn't get the position that time around, but was elevated to provost—the highest academic officer of the university.

She got her shot as interim president in 2003 and took over the position on a full-time basis two years later, more than thirty years after she first came to East Lansing. She made it her business to know the minute details of running every facet of the university.

"You would never handle a sensitive topic without making sure Lou Anna was aware of it because you'd get your head back on a plate," a former longtime MSU administrator said.

During Simon's leadership, Michigan State thrived under the metrics often used to measure success in higher education. The school's endowment tripled to more than $3 billion under her watch. The land-grant school with a strong agricultural foundation grew the scope and amount of research it produced in a number of scientific fields.

Many employees were in awe of Simon's seemingly tireless involvement in and knowledge of the way an institution with thousands of employees and tens of thousands of students operated. She was a "data wonk" who processed information like a robot and held the dispassionate disposition to match.

Michigan State's profile grew on a global stage with Simon steering the ship. She understood the importance of fundraising and embraced the role athletics and branding could play in helping those efforts. She threw her support behind athletic director Mark Hollis, football coach Mark Dantonio, and basketball coach Tom Izzo— three more high-profile employees who had deep roots and long tenures in East Lansing.

Simon involved herself more directly in the world of college sports in 2012 when she took over as the chair of the NCAA's executive committee. A week before she was installed in that position, the organization levied unprecedented sanctions against fellow Big Ten school Penn State. The penalties stemmed from the university's administrators ignoring warnings about assistant football coach Jerry Sandusky's misconduct with young boys. Sandusky was later convicted of forty-five counts of child sex abuse.

Simon told reporters at the time that she used the scandal playing out in Pennsylvania as a chance to remind all of her employees how they should react to concerns or allegations of sexual abuse.

"The right thing is saying something when you see something, and doing something after you said something," she said. "It's really that simple."

Chapter 18

"A Great Bullshitter"

Sexual assault investigations on Michigan State's campus, like at some other universities, often travel down a pair of parallel tracks. On one track are the Title IX investigators. On the other are campus police officers. At a university that has its own police force, a complaint made about an on-campus incident to either of those groups will trigger reviews by both of them. The police send their findings through the legal system, where claims are required to meet a higher burden of proof than in the Title IX process. Title IX cases are decided by the university's investigator or, in some instances, a panel of trained university employees. During those investigations, the two groups will occasionally share information for the sake of efficiency.

Sergeant Valerie O'Brien of the Michigan State University police interviewed Nassar on the afternoon of May 29, 2014, two weeks after Amanda Thomashow's complaint was made official, in a small, windowless room inside the university's police station.

O'Brien and the Title IX office's Kristine Moore had talked to Thomashow together the same morning. Thomashow told them about the doctor's lingering touches early in the appointment. She recalled how he sent the resident out of the room, and about the odd comments he made and about how she had to tell him he was hurting her as his finger crept close to penetrating her vagina.

Thomashow told them that when she asked him to stop, he replied "almost done," and continued for several more seconds. She

171

mentioned how she found it odd that he walked to a counter on the other side of the room and stood for a notably long time with his back to her. Thomashow says she told the two women that she believed Nassar lingered in the corner because he was aroused.

Moore and O'Brien took notes and asked questions. Moore jotted down in her notes that Nassar's standing in the corner was "weird" and that he was "maybe erect." Moore later said Thomashow didn't specifically mention Nassar being aroused, and her notes were a reflection of her own suspicion at the time. It's not clear if O'Brien felt that was a red flag as well, but if she did, she did not raise it as a question when hours later she sat down to speak with the doctor. Moore and O'Brien both declined interview requests for this book.

Nassar arrived at the station wearing slip-on Nike sandals, jean shorts, and a T-shirt. He carried a black backpack slung over one shoulder. On a video recording of the interview, Nassar begins by asking O'Brien if he can pull out a laptop to explain his methods. He had the computer out of the bag and partially opened before he looked at her for an answer.

O'Brien explained he was under investigation but let him know he wasn't being forced to speak with anyone from the police department.

"Any time you feel you want to get the heck out of here, get up and walk out," O'Brien told him. "My feelings won't be hurt, okay?"

Nassar leaned forward on the small table between them, an embodiment of relaxed confidence as he started to explain to O'Brien the root of what he portrayed as a big, unfortunate misunderstanding. Nassar was eager to defend himself, but mostly he acted as if he was at the police station that day to help the officers solve a problem with his expertise.

"I'm taken by surprise, but at the same time I feel like crap that someone would feel that I was doing something inappropriate to them. This is how I make my living," Nassar said. He punctuated his words by jabbing his pointer finger into the table. "This is what I do. I've helped scores of people with these personal issues."

"Which is good to hear," O'Brien interjected, leaning back from the table, hands in her lap. "It's good to hear you feel bad that she feels that way."

"Well yeah," he cut back in. "Because I feel like this little deviant, and that's not who I am. That's not right. Of all the freaking people, I'm the only guy even allowed in with the national team. It's all other females. And it's because of the essence of who I am, it's the trust."

His hands continued to add emphasis to each point like a politician standing before a stump speech podium. "If I did something wrong, do you know how quickly that would spread like wildfire?"

"Right, right," O'Brien said.

Nassar grew more animated, his voice rising in indignant, authoritative disbelief.

"It's my twenty-seventh year with the team, or whatever, since 1986!" he spit out, exasperated. "I'm telling you with those kids, it would go Boom-chuck-a-woom-chuck-a-boom-chuck-chuck, you know what I mean?"

The interview lasted more than two hours. Nassar did the majority of the talking. He settled into the rhythm of a lecturer speaking to students. He told O'Brien he likes to talk to his patients about their social life and their families to build trust. He told her how he checks in with them constantly as he treats them to make sure what he is doing is working. O'Brien told him that she believed both he and Thomashow were describing pretty much the same interaction and this might be a matter of perception.

He suggested that perhaps Thomashow had been sexually abused in the past, and that's why she had a negative reaction to a doctor manipulating those parts of her body. It was his job to pick up on those things, he told O'Brien. He shook his head. That's what usually set him apart, he said, and he was kicking himself for missing the fact that he made a patient feel uncomfortable.

As their discussion wound to a close, O'Brien mentioned that he might have the option of taking a polygraph test if he was interested.

"It appears to me that you're telling me the truth," O'Brien said. "Unless you're a great bullshitter and, you know, you've pulled the curtains over *my* eyes this whole time."

Nassar's head snapped back as he laughed along with her.

"But in combination with what I'm seeing here today," O'Brien continued, "you know, I feel like you're telling me the truth. You're coming in here voluntarily. You're wanting to clear your name. That's what a polygraph can be used for, just to clear your name."

She thanked him for responding so promptly and thoroughly to her request to talk to him. He threw up his hands and thanked her back.

"I got a chance to purge, so thank *you* for that," he said. "It was nice to be able to purge, to let it out. That helps. I appreciate that." They chatted for a few more minutes. Nassar offered an explanation: maybe it was as simple as his being too distracted and not having explained himself enough to make Thomashow comfortable, just an unfortunate misunderstanding. O'Brien told him that sounded perfectly plausible to her.

"Thank you for being you," he said as he started to gather his laptop and pack his things. "You were good. It was comfortable talking to you."

On the other side of campus, Moore was assembling a panel of four experts who she hoped could explain pelvic floor treatments and provide professional opinions on whether what Nassar was doing was a legitimate medical procedure or sexual assault.

The first two women she tapped were Destiny Teachnor-Hauk and Dr. Brooke Lemmen. Teachnor-Hauk, the certified athletic trainer who dismissed Michigan State softball player Tiffany Thomas's concerns about Nassar in the early 2000s, had worked side by side with Nassar for nearly two decades. Lemmen is a fellow osteopathic physician who studied under Nassar, worked with him in 2014, and considered him a "very good friend." Moore also turned to William Strampel, the dean of the osteopathic college and Nassar's boss, for a couple more suggestions. Strampel recommended two other female osteopathic doctors who were then employees at Michigan State—Lisa DeStefano, who first met Nassar in 1988 when they enrolled in medical school together, and Jennifer Gilmore, who worked under Nassar while she was a medical fellow in the 1990s.

The assembled experts—all Michigan State employees with ties to the doctor—touted Nassar's reputation during their interviews with Moore. DeStefano told Moore pelvic floor treatment "is what he does and he is famous for it." Teachnor-Hauk, the same athletic trainer who sat next to Thomas in the bleachers at Jenison Field House and listened to her tearful account of being sexually assaulted by Nassar, told the Title IX investigators she had never received a complaint about Nassar in seventeen years working beside him.

The three doctors said they typically would perform those types of procedures over a patient's clothing, but explained skin-to-skin contact would make it easier to effectively treat a problem. They explained that the appropriate treatment would come "very close" to the vaginal opening, but a patient might not understand the technical difference. Moore's report doesn't mention asking any of them about Nassar's apparent arousal. All four experts stated with certainty that what happened to Thomashow was medical, not sexual, in nature.

On July 10, Moore met Thomashow in her office on campus to deliver the results of their investigation. Moore used a printed diagram of the female anatomy to attempt to explain to the twenty-four-year-old woman across from her why she had confused the doctor's treatment with sexual touching. She also had literature to give to Thomashow about services for victims of sexual abuse available to her on campus, which to Thomashow appeared to be sending mixed messages after she was just told she was not assaulted. Thomashow was irate. She stormed out of Moore's office and slammed the door behind her. Thomashow was scheduled to sit for her MCAT exams two days later but now could not stand the thought of spending her professional life inside a doctor's office. She took the test, but knew her desire to follow her mother's footsteps and become a doctor was already dead.

Moore finalized her investigation weeks later with a written report that, as a matter of Title IX policy, is shared with both the complainant and the accused person. In the conclusion of her twenty-three-page report sent to Nassar and others at the university, she wrote that while Nassar's treatments didn't rise to the level of sexual assault, it "brought to light some significant problems that the practice will want to address." Moore, an attorney by trade, wrote that the treatments and the lack of explanation Nassar provided before performing them could open the practice and the university to potential legal liability and are "exposing patients to unnecessary trauma."

The version of Moore's report that Thomashow received, however, didn't include any mention of "significant problems." The conclusion section in Thomashow's version of the report was significantly shorter and said her complaint was "helpful in that it allows us to examine certain practices at the MSU Sports Medicine Clinic." The university later defended its decision to create two different reports, calling it "standard practice," but a review conducted later by the *Lansing State Journal* found that Thomashow's was the only Title IX report at Michigan State during a three-year time span from 2013 to 2015 that included two different versions of a conclusion.

Nassar met with Strampel, the medical school dean, the day after Moore submitted her final report. He had told the dean months earlier when the investigation began that he "definitely [has] to completely change my treatment for sure." Strampel sent him an email on July 30 recapping their discussion from the previous day about the new measures put in place to prevent more complaints about his treatment. Strampel wrote the following:

1. We will have another person (resident, nurse, etc) in the room whenever we are approaching a patient to perform procedures of anything close to a sensitive area.

2. The procedure which caused the patient emotional distress because of her interpretation will be modified in the future to be sure that there is little to no skin to skin contact when in these regions. Should this be absolutely necessary, the procedure will be explained in detail with another person in the room for both the explanation and the procedure.

3. New people in our practice will be oriented to be sure they understand these requirements.

He wrapped up his note by saying he was "happy this has resolved to some exten[t] and I am happy to have you back in full practice." Nassar had temporarily stopped seeing patients when the Title IX investigation began in late May but had been back in the office for more than four weeks when Strampel sent this note. In late June, Nassar sent an email to Strampel, which was forwarded to Moore, saying that he intended to resume seeing patients on July 1 unless he was told he should wait longer. The only response he got was from

Strampel, who said to make sure someone else was in the room with him until the investigation ended.

Much like the promises he made to another medical school dean a quarter century earlier about staying out of Great Lakes Gymnastics Club, Nassar did not wait long to break these new guidelines. Before the fall semester was in full swing, Nassar was seeing young patients on his own and putting his ungloved hands inside them.

The police investigation led by Sergeant O'Brien technically remained open while Nassar continued to see patients and sexually abuse some of them. O'Brien didn't make any record of talking to Nassar again after their initial interview. The polygraph test she mentioned to him never materialized. A polygraph specialist with the police department told O'Brien it wouldn't provide any useful information.

O'Brien never asked Nassar what he was doing standing in a corner with his back turned to Thomashow. She never spoke directly to any of the four medical experts Moore interviewed for the Title IX report. There is no record that O'Brien or Moore ever spoke to the female resident who was asked to leave the room midway through Thomashow's appointment even though they sought her name from an administrator at the clinic.

In late May of 2015, nearly a full year after her interview with Nassar, O'Brien called a county prosecutor to discuss what she had uncovered. The prosecutor told her it didn't sound like she had enough for any charges but suggested that O'Brien ought to speak to a medical expert from outside the university to make sure Nassar's story checked out. There's no record she ever did.

Larry Nassar first grew interested in working with athletes in the late 1970s at North Farmington High School, where he earned a varsity letter for his work as a student athletic trainer and graduated in 1981.
Credit: North Farmington High School

Larry Nassar continued to work with gymnasts during his time as a medical student at Michigan State. He volunteered at Great Lakes Gymnastics Club, where he met coach John Geddert. This photo of Nassar at work in the Great Lakes gym in the late 1980s or early '90s was posted by Geddert on his Facebook page in 2014. It has since been removed.
Credit: Facebook

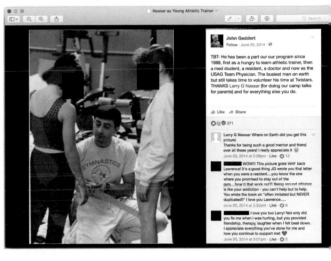

This 2016 photo shows Twistars USA Gymnastics owner John Geddert being pushed in his Corvette in the parking lot of his gym by young gymnasts, whom he routinely put through extreme conditioning drills.
Credit: Anonymous

After scoring a perfect ten on vault at the 1984 Summer Olympics in Los Angeles, gymnast Mary Lou Retton hugs her coach Bela Karolyi. *Credit: Getty Images, Bettman*

In April 1981, shortly after defecting from Romania to the United States, (from L to R) choreographer Geza Pozsar, coaches Marta Karolyi and Bela Karolyi, and an interpreter meet in Washington, DC, with Texas Rep. Bill Archer (R) to discuss methods of getting their families out of Romania. *Credit: Getty Images, Bettman*

At age seven, Jamie Dantzscher was ecstatic when her parents signed her up to train in her first gym, AV Twisters in Palmdale, CA. At eleven, Jamie left the gym to train to be an elite gymnast. *Credit: Jamie Dantzscher*

At age eleven, Rachael Denhollander convinced her parents to let her sign up for gymnastics in Kalamazoo, MI, where she trained during the late 1990s. *Credit: Rachael Denhollander*

Back and foot injuries from diligent training eventually led Rachael Denhollander to seek medical treatment from Larry Nassar at age fifteen. *Credit: Rachael Denhollander*

Atlanta, GA. July 23, 1996: Team USA gymnast Kerri Strug screams in pain at the 1996 Summer Olympics as she is carried from the floor of the Georgia Dome by a USOC athletic trainer (L) and Marta Karolyi (R) while Larry Nassar awaits to treat her injured ankle. Strug helped the US women win gold in the team competition. *Credit: IOP/AFP/Getty Images*

In late 1999, when Bela Karolyi became national team coordinator for the US women's artistic gymnastics program, the famed Karolyi ranch became the epicenter for Team USA. Gymnasts vying for the 2000 Olympic team made monthly trips to the facility for mandatory training sessions. *Credit: Authors*

Parents of national team gymnasts were not allowed to accompany their daughters during training sessions at the Karolyi ranch. *Credit: Authors*

Sydney, Australia. September 14, 2000: Bela Karolyi keeps a close eye on his athletes during a practice session at the Sydney Superdome before the start of the 2000 Summer Olympic Games. *Credit: Mike Powell/Allsport*

Anaheim, CA. December 4, 2000: John Dantzscher gets a hug from his daughter, Jamie Dantzscher, who was preparing to perform in front of an audience at The Pond during the post-Olympic tour. John was severely injured in a car accident in Sydney, Australia, while there to watch Jamie compete in the 2000 Summer Olympic Games. *Credit: Rick Loomis/Los Angeles Times via Getty Images*

Former Michigan State University president Lou Anna Simon took over as chair of the NCAA executive committee shortly after a child sex abuse scandal rocked Penn State University in November 2011. In response to the scandal, Simon said, "The right thing is saying something when you see something, and doing something after you said something." *Credit: Stephen Nowland/ NCAA Photos via Getty Images*

Kathie Klages worked with Larry Nassar for two decades, mostly as head coach of Michigan State University's women's gymnastics team, and defended his character against multiple accusations of sexually abusive behavior. *Credit: Emily Nagle/The State News*

Team USA head coach John Geddert celebrates after the US women's artistic program wins gold in the team competition at the 2012 Summer Olympic Games in London. Behind Geddert, (from L to R) gymnasts Kyla Ross, McKayla Maroney, and Jordyn Wieber celebrate. *Credit: Thomas Coex/Staff/AFP/Getty Images*

The Fierce Five: (from L to R) Jordyn Wieber, Gabby Douglas, McKayla Maroney, Aly Raisman, and Kyla Ross after winning gold at the 2012 Summer Olympic Games in London. All five women would later publicly identify as survivors of Larry Nassar's sexual abuse. *Credit: Ben Radford/Corbis via Getty Images*

The 2012 Summer Olympic Games in London were Larry Nassar's final Olympics, but he continued to treat and sexually abuse national team gymnasts, among them McKayla Maroney, whom he's seen treating at the 2013 World Championships in Antwerp, Belgium. *Credit: Thomas Schreyer*

Kyle Stephens was the first of 156 women to address Larry Nassar and the court during his Ingham County, MI, sentencing hearing in January 2018. Angela Povilaitis, the assistant attorney general who led the prosecution of Nassar and fought for the survivors' voices to be heard, looks on. Kyle told Nassar, "Little girls don't stay little forever. They grow into strong women that return to destroy your world." *Credit: Scott Olson/Getty Images*

Amanda Thomashow, who filed a police report against Larry Nassar in 2014, delivers her victim impact statement at Larry Nassar's January 2018 sentencing hearing. She cofounded a sexual assault education and advocacy organization after challenging Michigan State University for how it mishandled her complaint. *Credit: Scott Olson/Getty Images*

After her victim impact statement at Larry Nassar's January 2018 sentencing hearing, 2000 Olympic bronze medalist Jamie Dantzscher, the first former Olympian to publicly accuse Nassar of sexual abuse, rests her feet in the courthouse hallway. "I'm truly proud of myself for something I've done related to my elite gymnastics career," Jamie told the court of her decision to come forward. *Credit: Authors*

"How much is a little girl worth?" Rachael Denhollander asked in her victim impact statement. The last of 156 women to testify, Rachael's statement received a standing ovation in a court proceeding that, by then, more closely resembled a survivors' rally. *Credit: Jeff Kowalsky/AFP/Getty Images*

Judge Rosemarie Aquilina told Larry Nassar she "signed [his] death warrant" after sentencing him to up to 175 years in state prison. *Credit: Scott Olson/Getty Images*

Women from victims' advocacy groups cheer survivors as they leave the courthouse following Larry Nassar's sentencing. *Credit: Anthony Lanzilote/Getty Images*

In late May 2018, hours after being released into the general population at a federal prison in Tucson, AZ, Larry Nassar was physically attacked by other inmates. He was moved to a federal prison in central Florida where he will serve a sixty-year federal sentence for child pornography charges. *Credit: Scott Olson/Getty Images*

In a December 2018 press conference in Beverly Hills, CA, attorney John Manly and his clients (from L to R) Rachael Denhollander and former national team gymnasts Jeanette Antolin, Jordyn Wieber, and Jamie Dantzscher (not pictured) urge Congress to investigate the US Olympic Committee and USA Gymnastics for allegedly covering up Larry Nassar's abuse. *Credit: Sarah Reingewirtz, Pasadena Star-News/SCNG*

Protestors regularly attended Michigan State's monthly board of trustee meetings during the 2017–2018 academic year to urge the university to take a less combative approach to working with survivors. *Credit: Authors*

June 5, 2018: (from L to R) Rhonda Faehn, former director of the USA Gymnastics Women's Program; Steve Penny, former president and CEO of USA Gymnastics; and Lou Anna Simon, former president of Michigan State University, appear before a Senate committee investigating abuse in Olympic and amateur athletics. Penny repeatedly asserted his Fifth Amendment right, declining to answer the senators' questions. *Credit: Mark Wilson/Getty Images*

In September 2018, former USA Gymnastics president and CEO Steve Penny was indicted by a Walker County, TX, grand jury on charges of tampering with evidence, a third-degree felony. The charges stemmed from Penny's order to remove documents pertaining to Larry Nassar from the Karolyi ranch. In October 2018, Penny pleaded not guilty and was released on bail. *Credit: Walker County Sheriff's Department*

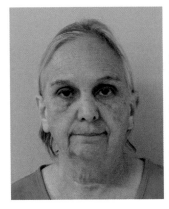

In June 2018, USA Gymnastics athletic trainer Debra "Debbie" Van Horn, Larry Nassar's longtime colleague, was indicted by a Walker County, TX, grand jury for sexual assault of a child, a second-degree felony. Prosecutors alleged she "acted as a party" by knowingly turning a blind eye to Nassar's sexual abuse of national team gymnasts at the Karolyi ranch. Van Horn pleaded not guilty in September 2018 and was released on bail. *Credit: Walker County Sheriff's Department*

September 24, 2018: (from L to R) Jamie Dantzscher; Rachael Denhollander (at podium); Marci Hamilton, CEO of CHILD USA, a think tank that works to prevent child abuse; and Sarah Klein, one of the earliest known victims of Larry Nassar's abuse, lobby Pennsylvania lawmakers to eliminate the criminal statute of limitations for child sexual abuse and extend the civil statute of limitations so victims of child sex abuse can hold abusers and the institutions that enable them accountable. *Credit: John Manly*

Chapter 19

The Cover Story

*You want to take a picture of a prototypical NGB, you take a
picture of us.... We're the No. 1 country in the world in the medals
count.... Every metric that I could provide you is going up.*
—STEVE PENNY, FORMER USAG PRESIDENT AND CEO,
SPRING 2015

It was well known among the national team gymnasts training at the
Karolyi ranch that unless you got to practice half an hour early, you
were considered late. So, it was around 8:00 a.m. one morning in early
June 2015 that a chain reaction of events began that would ultimately
bring an end to Larry Nassar's time with Team USA and send the organization he'd worked with for nearly two decades into a tailspin.

It was typical for Alyssa Baumann, seventeen, and her roommate
at the ranch, Aly Raisman, then twenty-one, to sit on the gym floor
each morning and apply heat packs or roll out stiff muscles before
practice officially began with a regimented formality known as the
lineup. Raisman, the veteran, had won gold in London three years
earlier, and Baumann, who'd been a national team member since
2013, was attempting to make her first Olympic team. Each day at
the ranch Baumann, Raisman, and the other gymnasts would
assemble at precisely 8:30 a.m. and stand shoulder-to-shoulder,
shortest to tallest, in military-style precision under the intimidating
gaze of Marta Karolyi. It was a routine reminiscent of a drill sergeant

conducting morning inspection of the troops. The half hour prior to the lineup was one of the few times in the gym that gymnasts could relax and speak freely. On this particular morning, Baumann and Raisman's teammate Maggie Nichols, who was seventeen at the time, joined the conversation. The subject turned to Larry Nassar and how uncomfortable he made them feel when he penetrated them during their sessions with him.

"Does he stick his fingers up there? Do you jump when he does that?" Baumann asked her teammates. "I think it'd be weird not to," another one added. They all agreed.

Sarah Jantzi, then thirty-five, was Nichols's personal coach from Twin City Twisters, a gymnastics club located in the northern suburbs of Minneapolis. Days later, after a practice at her club in Minnesota, she pulled her star gymnast aside to ask her about her experiences with Nassar. Nichols told Jantzi that when she went to see Nassar for her knee injury, he massaged her groin area "too close" to her vagina and that he also sent her a private message on Facebook, telling the seventeen-year-old she looked beautiful in her prom dress.

Jantzi suspected Nassar's behavior was sexual abuse and alerted Gina Nichols, Maggie's mother. On June 17, ten days after the national team camp broke, Jantzi sent a text message to Rhonda Faehn, the senior vice president of USA Gymnastics and the head of the women's program, asking if Faehn could talk on the phone. Faehn made contemporaneous notes of her conversation with Jantzi, which she later turned over to a Senate subcommittee investigating the Nassar case.

6/17—Sarah Jantzi called me @ 5:48 pm (I called her after she texted me to speak).

She notified me of her athlete having 3 uncomfortable encounters of therapy w/ trainer Larry Nassar.

She stated he massaged her on the groin area and too close to the vagina for her knee.

2013 Worlds Selection Camp 2015 Italy selection camp 3 Xs.

Also stated that he private FB messaged her that she looked beautiful in her prom dress. She just felt uncomfortable.

2 other athletes agreed about the uncomfortable factor

Simone Biles

Aly Raisman

After speaking with Jantzi, Faehn immediately called Steve Penny, relaying what Jantzi had shared. What happened in the weeks and months following that conversation would set Steve Penny's career and the organization he led on a path to ruin.

In June 2015, a little more than a year before the Rio Olympics, the women's gymnastics team looked well positioned to repeat its gold-medal-winning performance in London. Simone Biles, arguably the greatest gymnast America has ever produced, was the sport's undisputed star. She hadn't lost a meet of any kind in two years and, in October 2015, would win her third consecutive all-around title at the World Championships in Glasgow, Scotland, something no gymnast had ever done. Nassar survivors and their supporters would later conclude USA Gymnastics was driven by two goals: the pursuit of money and medals. In June 2015, both were in abundant supply. Then Penny got that phone call from Rhonda Faehn.

When Rhonda Faehn first told Steve Penny about the troubling way Nassar had conducted himself with Maggie Nichols, Penny responded "that he would handle the matter and notify the proper authorities. . . . By 'proper authorities,' Ms. Faehn understood Mr. Penny to be referring to law enforcement," according to the USOC's internal investigation.

But on June 17, 2015, Penny didn't notify the proper authorities. He didn't call law enforcement or the Department of Family and Protective Services in Texas, which the law in that state required when an allegation of child sexual abuse is made. He did what had become standard operating procedure whenever reports of sexually inappropriate behavior reached his desk in Indianapolis. He called his lawyer.

Penny says that after speaking with Faehn and Jantzi, he was given the impression "that an athlete was uncomfortable with Nassar's treatment." It was not "an unambiguous claim of sexual abuse," Penny's attorneys said in response to questions from the authors. But Penny's actions suggest he had enough concern about the report concerning Nichols that he wanted to keep it quiet. A day later, he called Nichols's mother, Gina, in Minnesota.

"I understand Maggie has some concerns," Gina Nichols recalls Penny saying as he started the conversation.

"He never once said, 'Is Maggie OK?'" Instead, Gina Nichols says, Penny told her, "We need to keep this quiet. It's very sensitive. We don't want this to get out."

Ten days later, on June 28, Penny attended a USAG board meeting, but he did not mention Nassar to the full board. After the meeting, Penny met privately with the chairman of the board, Peter Vidmar, a two-time gold medalist from the 1984 Olympics, and vice chairman Paul Parilla, a practicing attorney. Vidmar told Parilla and Penny the allegations involving Nassar "made [his] blood curl," and that Nassar "will never touch one of our athletes ever again," or words to that effect, according to the USOC's investigation.

Despite Vidmar's strong reaction, nobody from USA Gymnastics notified police or the Department of Family and Protective Services in Texas at that point either. Instead, on July 3, USAG hired Fran Sepler, a consultant and investigator in workplace harassment who had experience interviewing sexual abuse survivors but no prior experience with USAG. Over the course of the next three weeks, Sepler conducted in-person interviews with Maggie Nichols, Aly Raisman, and McKayla Maroney, in that order, and asked them about their experiences during treatment sessions with Nassar.

Nobody from USAG ever reached out to Alyssa Baumann at the time, even though Rhonda Faehn emailed Steve Penny alerting him to Baumann's concerns.

"Sarah Jantzi came to me yesterday and said she knew she wasn't supposed to talk about Larry but Maggie brought it up to her... that now Alyssa Baumann came forward apparently when the girls started talking in their rooms to say that Larry massaged her oddly as well," Faehn wrote to Penny.

Faehn would later admit in sworn testimony in a civil lawsuit and in testimony submitted to the United States Senate that in June and July 2015 nobody, to her knowledge, contacted Simone Biles either, even though Faehn, according to her own handwritten notes, was aware that Biles was also uncomfortable with Nassar's treatments. According to Biles's attorney, John Manly, Faehn and other USAG officials knew in the summer of 2015 that Biles, the reigning world champion and their top gymnast, may have been sexually abused by Nassar but nobody bothered to pick up the phone to call Biles or her parents, and neither Biles nor Baumann was interviewed during USAG's internal investigation.

Were Steve Penny and USAG attorneys in the days and weeks that followed the start of Sepler's internal investigation trying to keep a lid on a potentially explosive story? Penny only informed a handful of USAG employees about the investigation of Nassar and stressed the need to keep the matter confidential. He attempted to exclude the parents of gymnasts from interviews with Sepler. Rhonda Faehn later told Senate investigators she refused to follow Penny's directive, saying as a parent herself she would want someone to notify her if her child were involved. After Faehn raised her objections, Penny relented and said parents could be present during interviews.

In an interview with the attorneys conducting the USOC's internal investigation, Sepler said her July 11 meeting with Maggie Nichols "was inconclusive as to whether abuse or misconduct had occurred." After her second meeting with Raisman, on July 17, Sepler texted Raisman, stressing the need for discretion: "Please remember that there are risks in sharing information at this point. There is a process in place and staying clear of the process will protect you and others."

Raisman has since said she interpreted that text from Sepler as an attempt to silence her. Sepler responded that she wasn't trying to silence anyone and merely wanted to inform Raisman that an investigation was already under way. In fact, there was no police investigation going on at that point. In mid-July 2015, Fran Sepler was the only person looking into the matter.

After meeting with Sepler, Raisman called Faehn and told her she was "rattled by the interview." She went on to explain to Faehn that she neglected to mention to Sepler the troubling incident involving McKayla Maroney at the 2011 World Championships in Tokyo, when Nassar sexually assaulted Maroney in a hotel room.

"Raisman told me that Nassar would text Maroney to come to his hotel room for private treatments," Faehn wrote in her testimony to the US Senate, adding, "I told Raisman I would report Maroney's experience to Penny right away, which I immediately did."

In early to mid-July 2015, Nassar remained unaware he was the subject of an internal review by USAG. He had no idea Team USA gymnasts had even raised concerns about his behavior. That changed on July 22. The Secret US Classic, a qualifier for nationals, was scheduled in Chicago that coming Saturday, July 25, and two of the gymnasts who'd spoken to Fran Sepler, Maggie Nichols and Aly Raisman, were scheduled to compete, along with Simone Biles and other national team members. As the national team doctor, Nassar expected he would be making the trip to Chicago that weekend to treat athletes. That day he received a phone call from USAG attorneys Scott Himsel and Dan Connolly and then an email that same day from Himsel summarizing the call:

As we explained on the call, USA Gymnastics has been made aware of concerns regarding some of your therapy techniques, and that athletes are uncomfortable with certain areas of their bodies that are being treated. These concerns are being reviewed, and USA Gymnastics has decided that it is in everyone's best interest that you not attend the Secret US Classic in Illinois this weekend. As we mentioned on the phone, I am sure you can appreciate as a medical professional that in today's atmosphere, we need to address these concerns thoroughly and discreetly.

Nassar responded that he felt "horrible" that any gymnast would feel uncomfortable with his treatments. He agreed to send Himsel links to videos of his techniques, which he said he'd used "for educational purposes," and then falsely told Himsel that he had "not had any complaints in the past."

In a follow-up email, discussing how his absence from the upcoming competition in Chicago would be explained to his colleagues, Nassar proposed a solution: "Can we just say that I am sick?" he asked. Himsel agreed with Nassar's suggestion to use that cover story.

A day later, Nassar's attempts at deception only continued. He emailed Himsel again, telling him,

> **I am very disappointed in myself for not being better at explaining my treatments but I always talk to the athlete and get feedback while doing these treatments since they are in a sensitive area....There are always other people present and all is done out in the open. Actually, when you think about it, it is an amazing accomplishment to have gone 29 years on the national team without a single complaint about my treatments.**

In what would be her final interview on behalf of USA Gymnastics, Sepler met with McKayla Maroney on Friday, July 24, two days after Nassar sent his email to Himsel. The devastating details of that interview made an impact on Penny, who seemed to instantly recognize how damaging it would be if details of Maroney's experience ever saw the light of day. Penny summarized Maroney's sexual abuse in a series of graphic bullet points, noting that she saw Nassar *"100s of times"* and that, in her case, Nassar was *"rougher, more aggressive, pulling in the vaginal area....Much more troubling, she reported digital penetration three times—in Japan 2011, London 2012, Belgium 2013."* He added that Maroney *"felt no therapeutic effect but felt he [Nassar] was getting sexual gratification"* and that her session with Nassar involved *"penetration of 3 fingers for a sustained period, then Dr. Nassar stopped and breathed heavily. Thereafter Nassar began sending her gifts. He also began bringing her coffee."*

It's not clear whether Penny made those notes for his own benefit in order to inform USAG attorneys of the details of Maroney's sessions with Nassar, or in preparation for what was to come the following week. That next Monday, Penny met with three attorneys from Faegre Baker Daniels, the Indianapolis law firm that served at the time as counsel for USA Gymnastics. Later that day, he called the FBI field office in Indianapolis to set up a meeting, and a day later, Penny, USA Gymnastics vice chairman Paul Parilla, and attorney Scott Himsel finally met with the FBI to share what they knew about Nassar's treatment of Nichols, Raisman, and Maroney.

"I believed that Nassar needed to be reported to law enforcement for investigation," Penny says he'd concluded by that point. But, he adds, "no determination had been made by USA Gymnastics or me about the validity of the 'medical technique' used by Nassar."

It took Penny more than five weeks from the initial report to involve law enforcement in the Larry Nassar case. He did so only after a three-week-long internal investigation and after multiple consultations with his in-house counsel, evidence that suggests the organization's public image remained one of his chief concerns. On July 30, Penny sent an email to Jay Abbott, the special agent in charge of the FBI's Indianapolis field office. "We have a very squirmy Dr Nassar," Penny wrote to Abbott. "Our biggest concern is how we contain him from sending shockwaves [sic] through the community."

There is another explanation for Penny's delay in reaching out to the FBI. It can also be attributed to a well-established practice USAG had in place for handling reports of sexual abuse. For years, complaints about sexually inappropriate behavior by coaches at USAG-sanctioned clubs weren't referred to police, as is required by Indiana law. That was only done when the complaints were made directly by the victims themselves or, in the event the victims were minors, by their parents. Instead, the files detailing suspected abuse by coaches were tucked away in two locked cherrywood file cabinets, each four drawers high, within the executive suite inside the USAG offices in downtown Indianapolis. Steve Penny and his executive assistant, Renee Jamison, were the only ones with the keys.

That procedure of locking away a report of suspected abuse rather than making the report known to the proper authorities was followed in a different sexual abuse case, one that actually went public in the late summer of 2015. That case also involved a prominent member of the USA Gymnastics community, who was facing troubling accusations.

Chapter 20

Damage Control

In his twenty-five years working on a national level, Marvin Sharp developed a reputation as one of a handful of coaches across the country who could help elite gymnasts realize their Olympic dreams. Just as John Geddert did before him, Sharp started from humble beginnings. His first gym, housed within a warehouse in Indianapolis, opened in 2001. The success of his best athletes propelled his career and business fortunes. In 2008, Sharp coached Indiana native Bridget Sloan to a silver medal in the team competition at the Beijing Olympics. Sharp was by her side the entire time and later coached Sloan's teammate from Beijing, Samantha Peszek. In 2010, he was named USA Gymnastics Coach of the Year. A year later, he moved into a bigger, more modern location of Sharp's Gymnastics Academy, in northwest Indianapolis, a short drive from USA Gymnastics' national offices.

In August 2015, while Steve Penny and others worked to contain complaints about Larry Nassar, the gymnastics world was stunned when Sharp, then forty-eight, was arrested inside his home on charges of child molesting, sexual misconduct with a minor, and possessing and receiving child pornography. At his gym on Georgetown Road, in a room that served as a photo studio, Sharp had gymnasts as young as five sit for photo shoots in sexually suggestive poses. A fourteen-year-old gymnast told police that, starting when she was twelve, Sharp had her pose for photo shoots in her bra and panties and, at one point, in a straitjacket. He once trimmed the girl's pubic hair and touched her vagina during a photo shoot. He also fondled her during purported physical therapy sessions. The fourteen-year-old, who trained as a pre-elite gymnast, told investigators she was worried Sharp would kick her out of the gym or hurt her if she didn't cooperate with him.

When police searched Sharp's home and gym, they found locked safes with thumb drives containing thousands of images of child pornography, including minor boys engaging in oral sex and masturbation. Sharp's arrest made national news when he was led away from his home in handcuffs. For a coach so respected within the elite gymnastics community, it was a shocking fall from grace. On September 19, 2015, just after 8:00 p.m. and less than a month after his arrest, Sharp was found dead in his cell in the Marion County, Indiana, jail. His death was ruled a suicide by suffocation.

In an August 2016 exposé, the *Indianapolis Star* reported that Sharp's case was one of those instances where a complaint was buried by USA Gymnastics, locked in the cherrywood file cabinets within the USAG executive suites along with dozens of other complaint dossiers detailing the actions of allegedly abusive coaches.

The *Star* first reported how in October 2011, longtime gymnastics coach and judge Pat Warren sent an email to Steve Penny and USAG board chairman Peter Vidmar in an attempt to warn them about Sharp's disturbing behavior around minors. Warren had longstanding connections with top USAG officials. Her ex-husband, Gary Warren, was a gymnastics coach, who would go on to serve as director of the National Team Training Center (the Karolyi ranch). In her email to Penny and Vidmar, Warren described how in one instance Sharp treated a ten-year-old gymnast's hamstring injury by having her lie on her stomach as he "picked her leotard up, put it in her crack and ice massaged her hamstring."

On another occasion, Warren wrote, Sharp had a thirteen-year-old gymnast who'd pulled her groin go into his office and take her leotard off and put on a T-shirt so he could ice massage her pelvic area. When the thirteen-year-old felt uncomfortable and called her mother, the mother, according to Warren, picked her daughter up from Sharp's gym and moved her daughter to a new gymnastics facility the next day.

Warren explained in her email to Penny and Vidmar that when she was working as a gymnastics coach in Indianapolis in 2009, a number of her athletes were cheerleaders who'd left Sharp's gym because "Marvin was weird and they didn't want any part of it." Among other things, Warren wrote, Sharp would take his young gymnasts into his office, one at a time, to measure them for their leotards.

"He has a problem and should not be coaching young children," Warren wrote to Penny and Vidmar.

In October 2011, neither Penny nor Vidmar notified law enforcement or Indiana's Department of Child Protective Services about Warren's email. Years later, in August 2015, when Sharp's arrest made national news, Penny acknowledged to Indianapolis police that they'd received a warning about Sharp four years earlier. But the police never investigated Penny or Vidmar for failing to alert authorities earlier about Sharp's behavior. The two-year statute of limitations for failure to report had expired.

"I thought they would go after [Sharp] and they didn't do anything," Warren says about her attempts to warn USAG leaders, adding, "the fact that they did nothing—nothing—disgusts me to no end."

When the *Star* revealed in its August 2016 investigation that USA Gymnastics had prior knowledge of Marvin Sharp's behavior, efforts to discredit the story came from a curious source—the Indianapolis Metropolitan Police Department. Detective Bruce Smith was supervisor of the department's Child Abuse Unit at the time of the Marvin Sharp investigation in 2015. He was also friends with Steve Penny. Their daughters, the *Star* first revealed, attended the same school and were on the same gymnastics team. In an interview for this book, Smith acknowledged his personal relationship with Penny. He said the two men chatted, as parents often do, while milling about and waiting for their daughters to finish gymnastics practices and that they often carpooled to and from practices.

In August 2016, when the *Star* documented multiple instances where USA Gymnastics failed to alert authorities of suspected sexual abuse by coaches, citing the Sharp case specifically, Detective Smith took the unusual step of contacting a *Star* police-beat reporter, telling that reporter the newspaper was "barking up the wrong tree." Smith praised the way USAG handled the Sharp case, saying Sharp was reported to police on a Friday and in handcuffs and under arrest by that Sunday evening, and he told the reporter the statute of limitations had expired on prosecuting Penny or anyone else at USAG for failing to report the suspicions about Sharp that were raised in Pat Warren's 2011 email. Smith went further. He drafted what the newspaper described as a press release (it was never made public) defending USAG's handling of the 2011 complaint against Sharp. Smith says he merely provided talking points to his public information officer because he was getting so many calls from the media.

An internal affairs investigation later cleared Smith of any wrongdoing, and he denied being directed by Penny to actively defend USAG's handling of the Marvin Sharp case; however, the USOC's investigation of that incident found the text messages between Penny and Detective Smith during that period reflected "a seemingly single-minded focus on protecting USAG's public reputation."

Smith has since been promoted to lieutenant and now works in the homicide division. He says if he's guilty of anything, it's defending USA Gymnastics' handling of the Marvin Sharp case at a time when the organization was facing intense scrutiny for its mishandling of the Nassar investigation.

"It absolutely cost me. It hurt my reputation and called into question my dedication to abuse victims. Until you've sat through a child autopsy or days and days of a child describing abuse, you wouldn't understand. My daughter is in gymnastics. Do you think I would provide cover for somebody who didn't have my child's interests at heart? It's absurd," Smith said.

In late summer 2015, with the Sharp story making national news and the Olympic games a year away, the last thing Penny wanted on his watch was another sex scandal. The World Championships were approaching in October. Nassar had been instructed by USAG attorneys not to treat national team gymnasts, but he had yet to be formally terminated as the organization's national medical coordinator. While the general public didn't know about Nassar's troubling behavior, several national team gymnasts and their parents did know about it, and as the weeks dragged on, they were frustrated by the lack of answers and progress in the FBI's investigation. For the gymnasts and their families, it was impossible not to see the parallels between the Sharp case and Nassar.

In an August 27 email to Steve Penny and Rhonda Faehn, Aly Raisman's mother, Lynn, wrote,

**if the FBI needs to speak with Aly, please have them reach
out to us directly....Obviously we've read about Marvin
Sharp. In a number of news articles it is alleged the sexual
misconduct/abuse was during physical therapy sessions. The
similarity to Larry is disturbing.**

It was around this same period that Steve Penny also developed
a closer relationship with Jay Abbott, the FBI agent who was first
put in charge of the Bureau's Nassar investigation. As the two men
exchanged emails, they communicated with one another in an
increasingly more familiar tone. The emails are documented in the
USOC's internal investigation of the Nassar case and in a July 2019
United States Senate report, which details the Bureau's mishandling
of the Nassar investigation. In early October 2015, Penny and Abbott
met in Indianapolis over drinks. Penny offered to recommend
Abbott for a job he knew would soon be available, chief security officer for the United States Olympic Committee. Penny even went so
far as to email Larry Buendorf, the man who planned to step down
from that position after the Rio Olympics.

Hey Larry,

**Looking forward to seeing you in Rio. I wanted to let you know
that I found a great guy who might be the perfect fit for your
role when you decide to leave. His name is Jay Abbott and he
is the senior agent in charge at the FBI office in Indianapolis.
Let me know if you would like to speak with him.**

USAG staffers say Penny's attempts to build a relationship with
Abbott fit with his deal-making personality. Penny's attorneys say
any suggestion that he was trying to curry favor with Abbott "is

absurd. The only 'favor' that Steve wanted from Agent Abbott or anyone at the FBI was for them to promptly and thoroughly investigate Nassar."

Penny continued through the late summer and autumn months of 2015 to ask the parents of the gymnasts involved in the Nassar case to remain quiet despite no signs of any progress in the criminal investigation. On September 4, Agent Abbott emailed Penny, telling him "pertinent interviews have been completed and the results have been provided to the FBI and [United States Attorney's Office] in Michigan for appropriate action."

According to the 2019 Senate investigation, the FBI conducted a phone interview with McKayla Maroney September 4 in which she "described Nassar's explicit criminal conduct." But no action appears to have been taken by the Bureau based on that 2015 interview, and when an agent from the Los Angeles field office conducted a second interview with Maroney in 2016, there was no mention of the original September 2015 interview, nor was there any explanation of why the Bureau had failed to act on the information Maroney provided the previous year.

Because Penny told them Nassar had *already* been reported and any action on their part might jeopardize the investigation, national team gymnasts and their parents remained silent about the Nassar investigation. It wasn't until July 2016, just before the Olympic Trials and a full year after Penny says he was notified about the Nassar allegations, that Gina and Maggie Nichols received their first phone calls from an FBI agent investigating the case. By then the case had been transferred from Indianapolis first to Detroit and ultimately to the Bureau's Los Angeles field office.

"What took you so long?" Gina asked the special agent.

Aly Raisman and her mother had similar interactions with Penny in the months after Raisman initially reported Nassar's sexual abuse. Largely because of Penny's assurances that the investigation was being handled, Raisman says she didn't meet with the FBI until September 9, 2016, in Colorado Springs, Colorado, a month after serving as the captain on Team USA's gold-medal-winning team in Rio and well over a year after first reporting Nassar. Penny flew in for the interview. Raisman bristled at his presence. Penny gave her the creeps. On the flight back from Rio, Penny had texted Raisman, telling her she looked beautiful. The text made her uncomfortable enough that she shared it with her mother, who in turn told Rhonda Faehn. Raisman wouldn't allow Penny in the room when she spoke with the FBI agent investigating the case.

"Steve Penny was trying to control when I was going to be interviewed by the FBI. He was trying to control every part of it. The biggest priority was to make sure I kept it quiet so they'd have a good Olympics. It's disgusting," Raisman says.

Penny, through attorneys, disputed this account. "Nothing could be further from the truth," Penny's attorneys say. "Unfortunately, Steve should not have relied on the FBI or legal counsel as much as he did. Upon reflection, Steve believes USA Gymnastics should have encouraged the athletes and their families to contact the FBI directly versus encouraging the FBI to contact athletes."

The 2019 Senate report of the Nassar case documents several emails where Penny appeared to make efforts to check on the status of the FBI's investigation. It's not clear why the Bureau failed, for more than a year, to act on the credible information Penny and Maroney provided in 2015.

The Senate investigation concluded that the FBI "failed to pursue a course of action that would have immediately protected victims in harm's way. Instead, the FBI's investigation dragged on and was shuffled between field offices while Nassar continued to see patients at MSU."

As summer turned to fall in 2015, Nassar and USA Gymnastics were still searching for a way to explain his absence from major gymnastics competitions. USAG leaders knew if Nassar didn't attend the 2015 World Championship in Glasgow, Scotland, in late October, it would raise questions from the medical staff. By that point, Nassar had hired an attorney, Matthew Borgula, who sent USAG attorneys an email telling them Nassar would "no longer honor [USAG's] request to provide false excuses to his colleagues, the USAG staff and/or the athletes about his absences."

That missive from Borgula backed USAG's attorneys and Penny into a corner. They could have come clean at that point and publicly revealed that Nassar was relieved of his duties due to an ongoing investigation about his treatment methods. That would have alerted not only the public at large but also Michigan State University, where Nassar continued to see patients daily, that serious questions had arisen concerning Nassar's behavior with patients. It would have also been the truth. But, as USA Gymnastics' own lawyers, Scott Himsel and Dan Connolly, made clear in an email to Penny at the time, telling the truth was not the preferred option:

> We can tell the full story of what we've learned thus far. We think it is highly likely that would become a media story and prompt Larry to sue for defamation.... Neither Dr. Nassar nor USAG wants the attendant negative publicity at this time.... Our suggested alternative is this. Have us call back Dr. Nassar's lawyer. Tell him that a replacement will handle the World Championships and we can work on messaging regarding that.

Neither Connolly nor Himsel would comment about their email to Penny. In an email to the authors, Faegre Baker Daniels partner Robert Stanley said the rules of professional conduct prevented Himsel and Connolly from commenting on matters relating to their representation of USA Gymnastics.

In the summer and fall of 2015, USA Gymnastics was not the only amateur sports body aware that Larry Nassar was being investigated by the FBI. In July, Penny emailed Scott Blackmun, then CEO of the United States Olympic Committee, and Alan Ashley, chief of sport performance for the USOC, informing them that national team gymnasts had made claims of Nassar sexually abusing them during treatment sessions.

Neither Blackmun nor Ashley reported what Penny had told them to other USOC board members. Like Penny, they also neglected to inform Nassar's full-time employer, Michigan State, that Nassar was under investigation for sexually abusing young female patients. Instead, according to the USOC's internal investigation of the Nassar case, Blackmun and Ashley deleted Penny's email.

Under Blackmun, the USOC had increasingly taken a laissez-faire approach when it came to its oversight of the national governing bodies within the Olympic system. He helped construct what the USOC's investigation of the Nassar incident dubbed a "loose governance model." Blackmun was at the top of the organizational chart for the USOC, but when faced with information that a USAG doctor had sexually abused Olympians, he took a not-my-problem approach and hit delete. Blackmun and Ashley did not respond to interview requests for this book.

As it became clear to Larry Nassar that his two-decade run as the doctor to Olympic stars was about to be over, he was determined to go out on his own terms. In late September 2015, after more than two months of being barred from gymnastics events, Nassar composed a lengthy post on his Facebook page announcing his retirement from USA Gymnastics. He started by sharing a simple message in more than a dozen different languages before translating it to English.

"It is time," he wrote. "Indeed, it is time."

He went on to recount in detail his rise through the ranks of the gymnastics world, pointing out his many accomplishments and thanking the people who helped him throughout his career. He said he was looking forward to spending more time with his children and his wife. He wrote, "I am a better person for knowing all of you. Good luck everyone! Thanks for the memories!"

His Facebook page filled with messages of support, thanking him for his years of service. Nobody from USA Gymnastics at that time ever made any effort to explain the real reason for Nassar's departure. He was gone and no longer treating national team gymnasts. Problem solved.

Shortly after Nassar posted his retirement message, he ran into Trinea Gonczar, one of his closest and longest-standing patients from the gymnastics world, at a medical conference. Gonczar, who had not yet processed that she had been sexually abused by Nassar, was attending the conference for her job and remembers talking to him about his retirement. Nassar told her that he wanted to spend more time with his family and pour his remaining energy into the foundation he founded for autistic children. She viewed his reasoning at the time as "typical selfless Larry." Years later, she wonders what he planned to do while working with an even more vulnerable population of children.

While Nassar reaped well wishes and fond farewells, Amanda Thomashow's police report about her 2014 visit to Nassar's campus office collected dust somewhere inside the Ingham County prosecutor's office in Lansing. O'Brien handed what she had found in her investigation of Nassar to the prosecutor's office on the first day of July 2015.

It had been a month since O'Brien last spoke to an attorney at the prosecutor's office who suggested she find an expert in the field of pelvic manipulations who didn't have ties to Michigan State. At that point, O'Brien's investigation had relied solely on those who had either close personal or professional associations with Nassar. If she ever did make an effort to find someone without a potential conflict of interest, O'Brien made no note of it in her report.

O'Brien did not make a record of any attempt to reach out to the local high school where Nassar volunteered his time to see if his behavior there raised any red flags. She didn't note contacting anyone at USA Gymnastics at any point during her investigation. She didn't appear to know that less than one week before she turned in the evidence she collected on Thomashow's complaint, USA Gymnastics had hired its own investigator to delve into remarkably similar complaints about Nassar.

Years later, O'Brien refused to speak to investigators from the state attorney general's office during a probe into how the university handled claims about Nassar. She and other members of the police department declined interview requests for this book.

The information O'Brien did collect went untouched until the middle of December, during which time Nassar continued to prey on patients while he remained the subject of an open criminal sexual assault investigation. Three months after Nassar posted his Facebook message about his retirement, police contacted Thomashow to let her know her case was closed. No charges would be filed. The prosecutor's office suggested the police should tell her that she might want to submit a complaint to the state's licensing board so they could review the procedures Nassar needed to follow. Thomashow says she never received that message.

Thomashow's ambitions to attend medical school and study neurology had fizzled. Her love for the community where she grew up and the university in her backyard were gone. She worked a job in retail as she ping-ponged between feeling completely invisible and feeling like her entire hometown was laughing at her.

In 2016, she decided it was time for her to leave East Lansing. She and her partner at the time made plans to move to California. By the time students started spilling back onto campus with cars packed with duffel bags and dorm furniture, Thomashow was packing a car as well. The back seat of her car was full and waiting in her driveway one afternoon while she sat in the office of her veterinarian. Her last stop before heading west was to collect the paperwork she would need to register her dog when they arrived at her new home.

She had just received the vet's signatures when she felt her phone buzzing in her pocket. She recognized the area code was from East Lansing. The three digits that followed were the numbers used by most Michigan State phone lines. *What now?* she thought as she picked up the phone. She tucked it under her ear and said hello. The date was August 30, 2016.

The woman on the other end of the phone sounded a bit shaky. She introduced herself as Detective Andrea Munford of the MSU police force. Thomashow picked up on the labored breathing of someone starting an uncomfortable conversation as she listened to Munford explain the reason for her call. Thomashow still had a busy day ahead, and her patience with her alma mater had long since worn thin.

Munford told Thomashow that she'd had a long interview the previous day with a woman who filed a report about being assaulted by a doctor on campus. Munford said she remembered the doctor's name, Larry Nassar, from the complaint Thomashow had filed two years earlier. She wanted to know if Thomashow would like the police to reopen her case.

"Yes, of course," Thomashow told the detective. As the angry feelings from how her case was treated in 2014 started to bubble quickly to the surface of her consciousness, Thomashow hurried to end the phone call. Before she hung up, Munford told her she should be prepared to hear Nassar's name in the news. The other woman had spoken to reporters, and a story detailing what he did was coming soon.

Thomashow absorbed the news while a fresh wave of adrenaline and raw, familiar emotions ricocheted beneath her skin.

"Well, this is it," she said to no one in particular. "There will be hundreds."

Part III

THE WRONG ARMY

Chapter 21

Cracking Under Pressure

Larry Nassar had a slight hitch in his gait as he walked into a sparse interview room inside Michigan State's police headquarters for the second time in a little more than two years. A video camera in the corner of the room shows him entering wearing a dark polo shirt with a Holt High School logo on the left breast. His khakis stretched tight over his knees as he settled into an armless chair opposite Detective Sergeant Andrea Munford. It was 4:15 p.m. on August 30, 2016.

It had been a little more than twenty-four hours since Rachael Denhollander sat in a different room in the same building and described in painstaking detail what Nassar had done to her. Rachael told Munford that she had previously spoken to a team of investigative reporters in Indianapolis who might be publishing a story about Nassar in the near future. She explained that the reporters had received other complaints about Nassar from gymnasts she had never met. Munford, taking Rachael's story seriously, wanted to get the doctor's side of the story as soon as possible.

Just as Valerie O'Brien, now a captain and Munford's boss, had in the spring of 2014, Munford thanked Nassar for responding so quickly to her request to meet with him. She told him he was not under arrest and was free to leave at any time. He shrugged off the suggestion that he'd feel the need to cut their conversation short. Why would this time be any different?

Munford told him that she knew he and O'Brien had discussed reviewing some of the things he did when treating patients a couple years ago. "What do you recall about that investigation?" she asked.

Munford was a sergeant on the university's police force during Nassar's first visit to the interrogation room in 2014. She was part of a small group of officers selected that year to join the department's new special victims unit, which was touted at the time as one of the first SVUs at a campus police department in the country. Police Chief Jim Dunlap saw Munford, who went by the name Andrea Beasinger at the time, as a natural fit to supervise the group.

Munford graduated from Michigan State in 1996 and joined the force shortly after receiving her criminal justice degree. She worked in the bicycle unit and investigated crime scenes as she moved up the department ladder. In 2007, Dunlap tabbed her to lead the investigation of the department's only remaining unsolved murder.

The rape and murder investigation dated back thirty-seven years to 1970, years before Munford was even born. It stalled decades earlier, but after eleven months of work, Munford's group found their man by matching DNA from old evidence to a convicted felon who had died in a Florida prison years earlier.

DNA analysis wasn't the only tool Munford employed to catch sexual offenders. When she became one of the original members of the newly formed special victims unit in 2014, Munford used a style of investigating known as a victim-centered and trauma-informed approach. She embraced the philosophy that her interactions with victims should help restore a sense of control that is often taken from them during an assault. Munford's top priority was helping victims get a sense of justice in whatever legal form was best for them.

Munford positioned herself as an experienced guide to help victims through a daunting criminal justice system. She tried to take into account the complicated effects of trauma on a victim's memory when questioning them. Actions that may have caused detectives to doubt the account of a victim, such as laughing during an interview or forgetting specific details or chronology, are a normal neurological response to traumatic situations, Munford learned in training. She worked on asking questions and responding to answers in a way that wouldn't cause additional harm to victims, who often hold deeply seated fears that they won't be believed.

She helped the department secure grant money to inform local bartenders and cabdrivers to spot troubling situations and intervene before they became sexual assaults. As the university's sexual assault investigation process was being reviewed and found lacking by the federal government in 2015, Munford's tact stood out to women who reported campus assaults. One woman told the *Detroit Free Press* that the investigators who handled her Title IX case at Michigan State "didn't believe me. They kept delaying. They didn't interview all my witnesses. It constantly felt like I was under the microscope and not him." The same woman said Munford left a much different impression. "She really had an understanding of what I was going through. She really listened to me."

Munford, as one of a small group of detectives in the department who handled similar cases, had investigated dozens of sexual assault complaints and conducted hundreds of interrogations by the summer of 2016. She had seen clear examples of her approach producing results. As she sat across from Nassar in the small interview room, she was armed with the exhaustive research and documented evidence Rachael Denhollander brought her a day earlier. She also had confirmed with O'Brien that Rachael wasn't the first former patient to lodge a complaint about the renowned doctor who was now crouched over in his chair a few feet from her in the interrogation room. She was ready to make him feel uncomfortable.

She interjected with follow-up questions as Nassar, with his typical air of confidence, started to walk her through the medical purpose of his pelvic floor treatments just as he had done in the same building two years earlier. She didn't offer a sympathy laugh when he told her he had been making videos of his technique since "thirty pounds ago" and patted his stomach.

"Well, the reason I'm asking is we did have another complaint," Munford told him after several minutes of talking in general about his treatment methods.

"Really?" he said, rocking his whole body forward as he tilted his head to the side. For the first time in either of his taped interviews, Nassar began to stutter.

After a few more minutes of asking about his technique, Munford took a deep breath and told Nassar she had an awkward question she needed to pose. Nassar nodded.

"When you have young girls in there. They're athletes—" she began.

Nassar cut in: "They're usually with their parents. They're usually with their parents, that's why I explain a lot." Munford continued talking over him.

"Well, yeah," she said. "They're athletes—"

"Right," he said between her words.

She continued: "They have lovely figures—"

"Right. Right, right, right."

"They're very cute girls—"

"Right."

"Do you ever get aroused during these exams?"

"Do I ever get *aroused* during the exams?" Nassar repeated, straightening himself up in his chair. Munford got more specific and asked if he would ever have an erection during one of his exams.

"Obviously, you don't, you know what I mean. So, I, I, I..." Nassar stuttered and shook his head.

Munford's voice stayed calm and steady. "Is there a reason that you would during an exam?"

"I *shouldn't* be getting an erection during an exam," he said as he scrunched his face into an anguished look.

Munford explained to him she was asking because both the woman who lodged the new complaint and the woman's mother remembered noticing that his face was flush and his pants were bulging as he finished one of their appointments years ago. Nassar let out a guttural sigh as he searched for an explanation. Less than fifteen minutes after introducing himself to Munford, Nassar wore the look of a man who was no longer in control.

The interview continued for another half hour. Unlike in Nassar's previous interviews with police in 2004 and 2014, Munford let him know that this was not just a matter of perception or misunderstanding. She told him the description she heard a day before was significantly different from what he was telling her. He objected strongly when she told him that the woman said he penetrated her with his fingers even though he could not recall any details of the appointments from sixteen years ago. He grew more frustrated as he asked why this woman would not have said she felt uncomfortable in the moment. Munford asked him to imagine that he was a vulnerable teenager in the office of a powerful, well-known doctor and to consider the confusion that might have been filling her mind. She yielded no ground.

Munford eventually guided the conversation back toward the signs of sexual arousal he showed in the exam room.

"I mean, c'mon," he said, fidgeting in his chair. "I'm not trying to gain some type of sexual gratification out of doing that. If there was arousal it, it, it would be because of, of, whatever, I don't know. Ya know?"

"What is 'whatever'?" Munford pressed. "I don't know."

"When you're a guy sometimes you get an erection, but I don't—" Nassar said. Now it was Munford's turn to interject.

"Well, you get an erection when you're aroused," she said.

"You know, well, I don't know, I'm just saying you, you, you, uhhh, I'm not uhh..." Nassar scrambled for the right words. "How do you say this? If I had an erection, I don't understand why I'd have an erection from the treatment, from what I'm doing. And that's rather embarrassing. It would be rather embarrassing, okay? To have that happen, okay? That's not appropriate, okay? That's just not professional, you know what I mean, I don't know how else to explain. Yes, I'm a guy, and yes they're young ladies, but I'm trying my best to be professional."

Nassar tried to push their conversation back toward a clinical tone. He explained that he attempted to elicit feedback from all of his patients. Two years earlier, he had beat himself up inside the interview room. He told O'Brien he must have missed some signs and that he needed to explain himself better. Now, he was on the defensive. He did explain what he was doing to his patients, he told Munford. They must not have understood.

Munford sat calmly across from Nassar while he explained to her that he communicated with his patients throughout their treatment. He said it was his "protective mechanism" from claims like these. When something hurts them, he said, he needs the patients to tell him, and then he adjusts. Munford suggested there was a difference between feeling physical pain and the type of pain that comes with being sexually assaulted. Nassar attempted to convince her that a patient would let him know if she felt uncomfortable in any way. Munford disagreed.

She excused herself to get a business card in case he had anything else he wanted to add later. Nassar's forehead dropped into his hands as soon as Munford left the room. For several minutes, he sat in silence and pinched the bridge of his nose, never taking his eyes off the tops of his shoes. Munford returned, and they talked for a few more minutes.

"About how many times would you say you've done this procedure?" she asked him.

"It'd be thousands, you know, over the years," he said. "It's been a long time that I've been doing it."

Thousands. Nassar continued to sputter through his last attempt at an explanation as the magnitude of his career-long con started to sink in. He saw hundreds of young girls, some of them hundreds of times. Munford had one of them on record and knew of one other who had complained a couple years earlier. There can be power in numbers, she knew, when trying to build a case on a subject that is incredibly hard to prove. Finding the others, or rather having the others find her, would require a serendipitous stroke of good timing. Munford didn't know then that the puzzle pieces that would unlock the floodgates of Nassar complaints had already started falling into place nearly two months earlier in a hotel room more than two thousand miles away.

Chapter 22

Coming Forward

Dominique Moceanu, thirty-four and now two full decades removed from her time as the youngest and most promising gymnast on the 1996 gold medal squad, was in a suite at the Hilton in San Jose, California, surrounded by fellow former Olympians when she noticed a face she hadn't seen in person for years. It was Jamie Dantzscher. She was heading right toward her.

The two women had been teammates on Team USA in the mid- to late 1990s and had remained friends through the years. It was a Sunday evening, July 10, 2016. The reception, organized by USA Gymnastics, was intended to honor past Olympians and help rally support for the team headed to the Rio Olympics in August. Hours earlier and less than a mile away, the Olympic Trials had concluded at the SAP Center before a sellout crowd of more than nineteen thousand enthusiastic gymnastics fans. The team selected earlier that day to represent the United States in Rio filled the hotel room with optimism.

Led by a dominant Simone Biles and veterans Aly Raisman and Gabby Douglas, the team soon bound for Brazil also included new-comers Laurie Hernandez and Madison Kocian. Like the monikers given to previous teams, they were dubbed "The Final Five," a nod to Marta Karolyi, who would retire as national team coordinator after the Rio Olympics. The American women were the odds-on favorite to secure yet another team gold medal. Moceanu could tell by the look on Jamie's face she wasn't there to revel in any of the celebratory atmosphere.

"I need to talk to you," Jamie said as the two women met in the crowded hotel suite. Moceanu glanced around and noticed many of the other former Olympians in the room now staring at them. She pulled Jamie out onto the patio, where they could speak more privately.

Moceanu's energy and daring style in the gym made her a crowd favorite before injuries and family issues derailed her career in the late 1990s. Outside the gym, she and Jamie were two of the most high-profile gymnasts to ever break ranks and criticize the coaches and culture within their sport. Moceanu didn't spare the most powerful couple in all of gymnastics, Bela and Marta Karolyi, accusing them of physical and emotional abuse.

In a 2008 interview with HBO's *Real Sports with Bryant Gumbel* and later in her 2012 memoir, Moceanu alleged that Marta Karolyi physically abused her, grabbing her by the neck and slamming her face into a phone, and that Bela Karolyi body-shamed her, criticizing her weight and forcing her to step on a scale in front of teammates. The Karolyis denied the physical and emotional abuse. For years afterward, Moceanu had been an advocate for reforms within club and elite-level gymnastics. Although she was a household name, she, like Jamie, had turned into something of an outlier among her peers due to her outspokenness.

Just days before walking into the hotel suite in San Jose, Jamie had finally begun to process her childhood experiences with Larry Nassar. She'd been coaching at a gymnastics camp in Concord, California, when a friend asked Jamie to inquire at the camp about a coach. The friend said this coach molested her years earlier. In the course of asking questions on behalf of her friend, Jamie confronted a reality she'd buried for more than sixteen years.

This is what Larry Nassar used to do to me, she thought to herself at the time.

Jamie knew she needed to tell somebody about her experiences. But who? She knew about the upcoming reunion for former Olympians that weekend after the Trials and decided to seek out Moceanu. Jamie dreaded such events. She couldn't stand the thought of seeing anyone from USA Gymnastics. She'd been largely alienated by those people since her own public criticism of Bela Karolyi during the 2000 Sydney Olympics. Once outside on the patio with Moceanu, away from the crowded room, Jamie blurted out what she'd kept buried for so many years.

"Hey, did Nassar ever stick his fingers up in you?" Moceanu recalls Jamie asking her.

"Whoa, whoa, whoa!" Moceanu replied, stunned by what she'd heard. "Hold on a second. Jamie, this is not okay. Does anybody else know about this? You have to report this!"

Jamie and Moceanu had no idea that more than a year earlier USA Gymnastics had launched its own investigation of Nassar's sexual abuse. They didn't know that the FBI had been informed of Nassar's behavior nearly a year earlier.

As Jamie shared her most painful memories that Sunday evening in San Jose, Moceanu couldn't help but be reminded of something another friend and fellow gymnast had shared with her years earlier about Nassar. Moceanu was in New York City at that time for a commercial appearance when she met up with Jessica Howard, a former national champion in rhythmic gymnastics. The two old friends met at Moceanu's hotel to catch up. At one point, their conversation turned to the state of gymnastics and the number of people within the sport who had deep character flaws. It was then that Howard mentioned Nassar.

"The way he massages you is weird, just creepy," she told Moceanu that day. Moceanu never pressed Howard for details at the time. She, too, had been massaged by Nassar during her time with the national team but had never experienced anything inappropriate. She filed the conversation with Howard away in her memory. The day after Jamie confided in Moceanu about Nassar's behavior, Moceanu reached back out to Howard. She didn't waste time when she got her old friend on the phone.

"Did Larry Nassar ever assault you?" Moceanu asked bluntly. There was silence. Then she heard crying and sniffling on the other end of the line.

"Dominique, I've never told anyone, not even my therapist," Howard responded.

Moceanu's heart sank. "Jess, you have to report it," she told her.

Moceanu spent the following weeks working behind the scenes with both Howard and Jamie in an effort to bring their stories to light. She put Jamie in touch with Katherine Starr, who was also a former Olympian. Starr and Moceanu had first met years earlier, in 2012, not long after Starr launched Safe4Athletes, an advocacy group aimed at providing athletes a safe outlet to report abusive behavior within their sports. The daughter of British immigrants, Starr had competed as a swimmer for Great Britain under her birth name, Annabelle Cripps, and went on to become an All-American at the University of Texas. In 1982, at fourteen, she was raped by Great Britain's national team coach. Feeling powerless and alone, with no adults to turn to for help, Starr remained silent about the sexual assault for years.

Starr had worked previously with attorney John Manly as a consultant on child sex abuse cases. When Jamie first met Manly in early August 2016 inside an Oakland airport conference room, it was

Starr who set up the meeting, providing Jamie a safe place to tell her story.

Around the same time that Jamie met Starr and Manly inside a tiny room in Oakland, the *Indianapolis Star* filled its front page with an unrelated, damning report detailing how claims of sexual misconduct were handled by USA Gymnastics, whose national headquarters sit just a few blocks north of the *Star*'s newsroom. Three investigative reporters—Marisa Kwiatkowski, Mark Alesia, and Tim Evans—spent months poring through public documents and visited ten different states to uncover what happened when gymnastics coaches were accused of abusing their athletes. The resulting story, which was published August 4, 2016, said that the organization's policy of not reporting all complaints to law enforcement officials "enabled predators to abuse gymnasts long after USA Gymnastics had received warnings." The article ended with a small note letting readers know how to get in touch with the reporting team if they had additional information to share.

Rachael found the story online the day it was published. She was working then in Louisville, Kentucky, while raising three young children and getting ready for Jacob to return to school for his doctorate. She didn't know anything about Amanda Thomashow's police report or the FBI investigation or Jamie's recent revelation to Moceanu. Since her heartbreak on her twenty-fifth birthday, Rachael had placed Nassar's sexual abuse on the backburner of a busy life. When she read the article, though, she saw a new chance to expose him. She emailed the *Star* reporters almost immediately.

The reporting team was interested in Rachael's story, but they would need more than one woman's word to publish an article accusing Nassar, a physician with a publicly unblemished record, of heinous crimes. A little more than a week later, a second tip arrived. This one came from Manly, who saw the August 4 article when doing gymnastics research after his meeting with Jamie. He asked the reporters if they had heard of Nassar and told them he was preparing a lawsuit on Jamie's behalf to be filed under the name "Jane Doe."

Two complaints made on the public record—one by an anonymous Olympian and another by a woman willing to share her identity with readers—was enough of a start to give the reporters reason to dig further. Kwiatkowski, Alesia, and Evans learned as much as they could about pelvic floor treatments and the career of Larry Nassar. As tips and comments related to their original gymnastics story continued to trickle into their inboxes, they kept an eye peeled for anything related to the Olympic doctor.

The note that kicked their story into a new gear came from Jessica Howard. By late August 2016, at Moceanu's urging, Howard decided to share her story with the *Star* as well. After speaking with Howard, Alesia sent an email to his colleagues and his editor:

> **Dr. Nassar asked her to wear shorts without underwear. No gloves (as with Rachael). He massaged inner thighs and buttocks and then penetrated her vagina. It happened five or six times....She thought it must be part of therapy.**

Three women, in three different states, had now shared a strikingly similar story with the newspaper. All three women would eventually share that same story with John Manly, who'd represent them in civil lawsuits. Nassar had penetrated them as minors, without the consent of adults, without gloves, and without any medical chaperone in the room. Alesia signed off on his emails to his colleagues and editor by emphasizing his sense of urgency in capital letters.

"WE ARE ONTO SOMETHING HERE THAT IS BEYOND F'D UP," he wrote.

"We have to do whatever it takes to report the truth about what's going on."

On August 31, a day after his flustered interview with Andrea Munford and two days after Rachael Denhollander first reported him, Larry Nassar was once again banned from seeing patients or showing up at the MSU Sports Medicine Clinic. Uncomfortably idle, he channeled his energy into trying to quash the latest attempt to expose him.

He contacted the attorney who helped him sort out his USA Gymnastics departure a year earlier. He composed a long email to William Strampel, the dean of the College of Osteopathic Medicine, to suggest some things he could do to "earn his keep" while he was away from the clinic during the police investigation. The list included teaching more classes and perhaps laying the groundwork for a sports medicine department at the university. He ended the letter by saying that "as a result of all that has happened," he was considering giving up the manual manipulation treatments that had made him famous.

He logged on to Facebook and started to privately reach out to parts of the vast network of friends he had developed in the gymnastics community in search of support. That weekend, old friends, gymnasts he first met in his makeshift training room behind the heavy, brown doors of the Great Lakes Gymnastics Club, visited him at his home. He described what he knew about the allegations made against him and stated unequivocally he was innocent.

Nassar didn't yet know the name John Manly. He had no idea about Manly's meetings with Jamie or the lawsuit they were preparing. He didn't yet know that a team of reporters in Indianapolis was digging deep into his career. He didn't know they had spoken to Jamie Dantzscher, Jessica Howard, and Rachael Denhollander. He didn't know how long this investigation would last, how public it would become, or where it would all lead. Nonetheless, he prepared to battle in more significant ways than he had against Amanda Thomashow in 2014 or the trio of accusations from national team members in 2015. He was unnerved.

Nassar received an email on Tuesday, September 6, from Tim Evans. The subject line read, "Questions from a newspaper reporter." Evans explained to Nassar that he and his colleagues were reporting on how USA Gymnastics handled claims of sexual assault and had received multiple tips accusing him of misconduct. He wanted to give Nassar a chance to share his side of the story.

Nassar forwarded the note to Strampel early the next morning to get his boss's thoughts on how to proceed. He said he had talked to a personal attorney but also wanted legal advice from the university, if they could offer any. Strampel said he would look into it. The university's general counsel instead suggested to Strampel that he should contact the university's communications department for advice on how to handle the impending *Indianapolis Star* article. As the university's police department geared up to investigate the renowned doctor, some of the most powerful people on campus made sure he was getting good public relations advice.

Strampel passed along three potential courses of action from one of the university's top spokesmen:

1) Do not answer at all.

2) Answer the questions and be very aware not to take the tone of "blaming the victim" in your responses.

3) Answer the questions in writing being very specific about what you do is science based and has helped 100s if not 1000s of people.

Nassar thanked him for the advice and told him that he was working with his own attorney to try to set up a meeting with the reporters for early the following week. He said he was still hoping to keep the story from being published and that he would send along more updates when he had them. Strampel responded just a few minutes later, making his allegiances clear.

"OK, Good luck," the dean wrote. "Keep me informed as much as you want. I am on your side."

Chapter 23

Breaking News

Tim Evans parked his car outside a law office in the busy down-town area of Grand Rapids, Michigan, on a Monday morning in the middle of September almost one week after his initial email to Larry Nassar. The veteran investigative reporter was nervous. After thousands of interviews over the course of forty years as a journal-ist, there weren't many assignments that gave him butterflies. As he would recall in a first-person account of that day published in the *Indianapolis Star* years later, he had them now.

Back in Indianapolis, his colleagues were putting the finishing touches on another draft of their story. Rachael Denhollander's interview with the reporters had been completed weeks ago. John Manly assured them he had filed a civil lawsuit on behalf of Jamie days earlier. It was only a matter of time before it was processed through the California judicial system and appeared for the pub-lic to see on the court's online database. Jessica Howard wasn't yet ready for her story to appear in a newspaper, but she shared enough background information with the *Star* team to corroborate the other complaints. They knew now that as soon as Jamie's lawsuit was filed as a public court document, they would have what they needed to move forward.

Evans's job that day was to get Nassar's side of the story. He arrived to find Nassar and attorney Matthew Borgula waiting for him in a conference room of the law office in Grand Rapids. The table in front of them was stacked with materials that Nassar said would help explain his techniques and shed light on how his patients misunderstood his intentions. He clearly held out hope that he could convince Evans that there was no story worth writing. A laptop, textbooks, and medical journals sat on the table in front of them when Evans entered the room and introduced himself.

Nassar asked if he could show Evans a short video before the reporter turned on his recorder. He pulled up the file on the laptop and hit play. A zoomed-in image of a girl's backside filled the screen. Nassar's hands massaged the insides of her thighs on the tape as he started to explain to Evans the science behind his method.

He spoke in a confident, clinical tone that made the potentially troubling video seem professional. He told Evans he made the video for training purposes. To Evans, who wrote about the experience in his first-person account, Nassar sounded rehearsed, as if he had walked others through these same questions in the past. Nassar's hands in the video worked their way up the young girl's thighs. He spoke to the camera as he explained the procedure he was performing.

Evans's phone buzzed in his pocket. He looked down to see a text from his colleagues back in the newsroom. Jamie's lawsuit had just popped up on the court's website. Evans let Nassar and his lawyer know there was another legal issue brewing and asked if they wanted to review the lawsuit before continuing.

Borgula and Nassar stepped out of the conference room and skimmed through the forty-three-page filing. The document laid out a similar story to the one that Denhollander had told Michigan State police two weeks earlier. Nassar read that an Olympic medalist from the 2000 Sydney games was accusing him of assaulting, harassing, and molesting her.

Jamie's name didn't appear in the lawsuit, but the details in its pages—her age, her home state of California, the description of her well-decorated career in gymnastics—made clear to Nassar right away who "Jane JD Doe" really was. He appeared flabbergasted. He told Evans a thank-you note that Jamie had sent him after the 2000 Olympic games still hung in his office a little more than an hour down the road in East Lansing. In light of the new lawsuit, Borgula told Evans, Nassar wasn't going to answer any more questions.

The confident, borderline-arrogant doctor Evans met when he first arrived in Grand Rapids that morning was gone by the time he packed his things to leave a short while later. Nassar pleaded with him not to write the story, offering to give him dirt on other gymnastics officials instead.

As Evans headed for the door, Nassar's eyes started to fill with tears. He traveled from his home in Holt to Grand Rapids that morning in the hopes of convincing Evans the allegations made against him didn't warrant a story in the newspaper. It was now clear he wasn't going to succeed in that effort. Nassar pleaded with the reporter to be fair as Evans prepared to walk out of the office. As Evans reached out to shake Nassar's hand, he noticed it was trembling.

Borgula provided Evans with a prepared statement to use in their story. After talking to his client, the attorney told Evans that Nassar denied all the allegations made against him and that no law enforcement agency or USA Gymnastics official had ever made allegations like these in the past.

Borgula didn't talk to reporters again after that statement. It's not clear why he and Nassar parted ways, but shortly after those statements were issued—statements in which the doctor lied—Nassar hired new representation.

Rachael Denhollander's phone rang a few hours later. The story, she was told, would be posted shortly on the *Indianapolis Star*'s website.

Finally, she thought.

The past weekend had been torture for Rachael and her husband Jacob. They knew the *Star* reporters planned to hold off on publishing the story until they had a copy of the California lawsuit. The suit was supposed to be filed the previous Thursday. By Friday night, no update had arrived, and Rachael was nervous that the civil attorneys in California might have reached some type of settlement. A settlement would mean no lawsuit, which would probably mean no newspaper story, which would mean Rachael and her police report would be all alone in a long-shot legal battle.

She and Jacob spent their Friday night at a cookout thrown by the Southern Baptist Theological Seminary to celebrate the start of a new school year. Jacob was beginning his first semester of doctoral work at the seminary the following week. As they traded pleasantries with acquaintances and strangers, they silently worried that the past month of dredging up painful memories was about to become a waste of time.

The phone call from Alesia once again sent Rachael's emotions spinning in opposing directions. She was elated that her work would not be in vain and hopeful that the impending story would encourage others to speak up. She also knew that the truly difficult work was only just beginning. She braced herself for the backlash.

As Rachael and Jacob waited for her picture to appear on the front page of newspapers, the general public was not yet lining up to heap praise on the courage of outspoken survivors of sexual abuse. The "Me Too" movement, initially hatched by Tarana Burke a decade earlier in 2006, wouldn't hit its much louder second life as a hashtag and social media phenomenon that encouraged thousands to speak up and millions more to start listening until a year after Rachael came forward. Rachael's biggest fear in those interminable weeks waiting for the story to be published wasn't a reaction of anger but one of apathy.

She worried her story would disappear, lost amid a sea of head-lines during the final months of a particularly contentious presidential election. She worried that she had just ripped loose psychological scabs that had taken her years to build, and that the general public and the institutions associated with Nassar would shake their fists or act shocked for a couple days and then move on without changing anything.

After her call with the *Star* team, Rachael texted Jacob to let him know the story was coming. He waited at work—hanging cabinets in a stranger's kitchen as part of his carpentry job—for the story to appear online. Rachael refreshed the browser on her laptop at home until at last she saw the story pop up. She clicked on the link and saw a picture of herself staring back at her.

Nassar's name appeared in the third paragraph. Rachael's name, in the caption of a video of her explaining that she was sexually abused, was several inches above it. The video at the top of the online story begins with Rachael on a couch in her home.

"I was very embarrassed," she says to the camera. "And I was very confused, trying to reconcile what was happening with the person he was supposed to be."

The investigative team included another note at the bottom of the story that said they intended to continue investigating Nassar. The note provided a phone number and an email address for anyone else who had tips about the Olympic doctor.

Within hours, their phones started to ring and their inbox started to fill with messages. The story spread on gymnastics-related mes-sage boards and was passed among friends. The *Star*'s story rippled through the Lansing area and out to gymnasts from coast to coast. Women who had long felt alone or uncertain about how to classify the ugly feelings they had about their appointments with Nassar scrolled through the story with their limbs shaking and tears

forming in their eyes. For some, the repressed memories were devastating and led to physical manifestations such as panic attacks,
rashes, and depression. It would take weeks and months to process
their emotions and come forward. Others found a small silver lining
of hope when they reached the contact information at the bottom of
the page. By the following day, sixteen other people had contacted
the reporting team with similar concerns about Nassar.

The number would have seemed validating for Rachael and
Jamie, perhaps even damning for Nassar, if not for the many more
who responded differently. Nassar's lifetime of building goodwill
paid off in the initial aftermath of the *Star*'s story. Jamie's anonymity
did not last long in gymnastics circles. She and Rachael were called
liars, "sluts," and worse on social media and message boards. At one
point, a USA Gymnastics attorney contacted one of Jamie's old boy-
friends to ask about her personal life. Nassar's inbox, meanwhile,
filled with messages of support.

On Monday, September 12, hours after the news that he was being
sued by "Jane JD Doe" derailed Nassar's meeting with Evans, he
called his friend and protégé Brooke Lemmen to ask for a favor. At
Nassar's instruction, Lemmen went to the MSU Sports Medicine
Clinic in the evening and located the large, four-drawer filing cabi-
net that contained files from Nassar's patients that dated back to the
beginning of his time as a medical student. She stuffed them into a
pair of boxes and hauled them down the hallway to his office.

She then walked into his exam room, and for the next hour
worked her way from one side to the other gently pulling photographs, autographed posters, and thank-you notes from the walls.
The stack of smiling faces she piled together would have been inches
high, freeze frames from the most memorable moments of America's quarter-century rise to gymnastics dominance.

Lemmen would later tell police that she realized while she drove home from the office that night that Nassar shouldn't have access to the files she had just collected. She said she decided not to deliver them to his house the next morning and instead returned them to the clinic for safekeeping. She took pictures with her phone of some of the thank-you notes and autographed pictures she collected and sent those along to Nassar instead.

Chapter 24

Fallout Begins

Larry Nassar's friends in gymnastics were at their loudest and most supportive in the week after the *Indianapolis Star*'s story first revealed the allegations against him. He received sympathy from colleagues and dozens of former gymnasts, some of whom had been sexually abused by him and not yet realized it. Michigan State coach Kathie Klages gathered her team on campus and gave a teary-eyed speech proclaiming that she believed Nassar was innocent. She asked the gymnasts, young women who in most cases had been inside Nassar's training room for years, to sign a greeting card letting him know they were thinking of him.

Nassar told one of his superiors, Dean William Strampel, that head coaches at other universities reached out to say they were trying to figure out how they could support him through the legal process. One coach, he said, called during her vacation in Costa Rica to say she was starting a fund to help him pay for attorneys. He said others were putting together an affidavit to attest to his good character and were hoping to collect one thousand signatures from people in the gymnastics community.

Nassar knew not every voice would be supportive. Shortly before 7:00 p.m. on September 15—three days after the first story published in the *Indianapolis Star*—he emailed Strampel to say he was "trying to make sure I take advantage of this time before the 'Me Toos' come out in the media and the second media blitz occurs." He said he expected the *Star* "will make their next crucifixion of me on Monday."

Four hours later, Nassar followed up with another note. It's not clear what changed in the interim, but his confidence had unraveled quickly. He wrote, "This is not right. I am meeting at 6:30 a.m. with my new attorney that I had to call to help me with this emergency. I thought I better let you know. I knew the media blitz was going to create more people to call in accusations about me but this is absurd. I have not been charged with any crime. I don't understand why this is happening. This is not right.... This is not right."

Strampel told him the next morning that more people had come forward with claims that he hadn't followed the guidelines they had established for him after the 2014 complaint. Things were moving outside of his control, the dean said. That afternoon, Nassar received a letter informing him the university was starting the process of terminating his employment.

Nassar had turned fifty-three years old a month earlier. He had arrived on Michigan State's campus as a twenty-five-year-old medical student. More than half a lifetime later, his time at the school was done.

The news of Larry Nassar's dismissal from Michigan State left Steve Penny in a panic.

Just as when Nassar's abusive behavior was first reported to USA Gymnastics in June 2015, Penny's correspondence and actions in the weeks and months following Nassar's termination from Michigan State reflect those of a man more concerned with self-preservation and messaging than the mental health and well-being of the athletes he was charged with protecting. The story was spiraling out of Penny's control. For a man with a background in public relations and marketing, few things could have left him feeling more helpless.

On September 21, 2016, a day after Nassar's termination from MSU, Penny reached out to Jay Abbott, the FBI agent in Indianapolis, with whom he'd established a personal connection months earlier.

"Will call you shortly if that's okay. Am I in trouble?" Penny wrote.

"No . . . and no worries," Abbott responded.

Penny was no doubt concerned about how he and other USA Gymnastics officials had gone about reporting Nassar to the FBI in July 2015. When it was revealed that USAG had parted ways with Nassar more than a year earlier, the organization initially said it reported the allegations about Nassar "immediately" to law enforcement. After media inquiries, USAG was forced to acknowledge that it had reported Nassar only after a five-week internal investigation.

Questions had also arisen about whether Nassar had sexually assaulted other members of the US national team. At that point, Jamie, known then by her pseudonym "Jane JD Doe," was the only former Olympian to have publicly accused Nassar of sexual abuse.

What the public didn't know at that time was that attorneys for USA Gymnastics had been working for months on a negotiation to keep the details of another former Olympian's abuse by Nassar from ever seeing the light of day. In the summer of 2016, weeks before the Nassar story broke, Penny received a letter from attorney Gloria Allred.

Known for her involvement in court cases that attract media attention, Allred has a history of representing women who take on powerful men and institutions. In recent years, she's represented dozens of women who've sued actor Bill Cosby and President Donald Trump in relation to alleged sexual misconduct. A rape victim herself, Allred is also known for representing "Jane Roe," or Norma McCorvey, in the landmark 1973 Supreme Court case *Roe v. Wade*, which legalized abortion nationwide.

Allred added "Fierce Five" gold medalist McKayla Maroney to her client list in 2016. She wrote a letter to Penny on Maroney's behalf that outlined Nassar's sexual abuse and offered USA Gymnastics the chance to settle the matter quietly, out of court and away from the public eye where it might cast a dark shadow on the lead-up to the Rio Olympics that summer.

"Dr. Nassar told McKayla that she was one of his 'favorites' and that she needed his 'special adjustment,'" Allred wrote. "She has become a mere shell of who she used to be and is left with chronic fatigue and thoughts of suicide from severe depression and anxiety. We are writing this letter to provide you with a singular opportunity to resolve Ms. Maroney's claims through a confidential mediation process."

Allred ended her letter to Penny by requesting that USAG attorneys respond by June 2, 2016. The two sides negotiated for months. Eventually, USAG struck an agreement with Maroney in late November 2016, paying her $1.25 million, according to the *Wall Street Journal,* to resolve any claims she had against Nassar and USAG. In return, she agreed to remain silent about the sexual assaults she'd suffered on hundreds of occasions.

Chapter 25

Trash Day

One day after Rachael and Jamie's story appeared on the *Indianapolis Star*'s website, it was also published on the front page of the *Lansing State Journal*, which was owned by the same parent company, Gannett. Nassar's picture filled most of the top half of the page that morning, atop a big, bold headline spelled out in all capital letters: MSU DOCTOR ACCUSED OF ABUSE.

The phone calls that helped to speed the end of his time at Michigan State started pouring into the MSU police department that morning. Nassar's photo alone was enough to launch some former patients back into deep and dark memories of their appointments with him. Gymnasts and other Michigan State athletes traded messages with friends linking to the story and asking urgent questions. "OMG did you see this??" or "Is this the guy you told me about?"

Parents who had sat in the exam room or dropped their daughters off dozens of times at Nassar's office or his home texted and called to see if anything like this had happened to them. A few women had been waiting for an opportunity to speak up for years and quickly started searching for ways to share their stories with police. By 11:00 a.m. on September 13 in California, John Manly had fielded calls from five women who had seen his name in the *Star* article. He recommended they start by contacting the police.

Trash Day

Andrea Munford took her second phone report on Nassar, the first since her meeting with Rachael Denhollander, in the middle of the afternoon. It was 11:00 p.m. when she got her last voicemail of the day and called back shortly after. The woman told her she had been "waiting for this to happen" and that she tried two years earlier to report Nassar but was told the statute of limitations had expired. She said reading the descriptions of what happened to Denhollander in the *Indianapolis Star*'s story was like seeing a script ripped "from a textbook" of how she was sexually abused.

Munford and the rest of the MSU police ramped up the resources devoted to their investigation the following morning. While more reports continued to arrive, Munford and a handful of other officers went to work building their case. Munford called the physical therapist Denhollander saw after being treated by Nassar to corroborate part of her interview. The therapist told her that 99 percent of the work she does is external. In the rare cases that she would do internal pelvic work, she always wore gloves, she wanted to make the procedure as quick as possible, and she would never perform it on a woman who is a virgin, she said. She also made clear that there "is no reason for thrusting down there."

Munford visited Nassar again the following day, this time at his home in Holt. She met two officers from the local sheriff's department and an officer from Michigan's Children's Protective Services agency in a nearby parking lot before knocking on his door together. They spoke to Nassar and his wife about some of the accusations they had received in the past few days. They told him he would not be allowed to stay in his home with his children that night and waited until he departed for a hotel.

The next morning, a pair of MSU police officers visited Nassar's old office to confiscate his work computer. Officer Kim Parviainen called Dr. Suzanne Thomashow, Amanda's mother, to follow up on her daughter's report the same day. Two other officers interviewed the risk administrator for the university's health care system to make sure the evidence they were going to collect from Nassar's office was complete and unaltered. By the end of the week, just four days after a newspaper report started to crack the dam of complaints about Nassar, Munford's team had removed him from his home, secured the detailed records of his interactions with patients, and spoken to at least two medical experts about the legitimacy of internal osteopathic treatments. Parviainen would find a third medical source to add to the list early next week.

Munford was also working fast to piece together enough probable cause for a search warrant that would allow her back into Nassar's home as soon as possible. Hard evidence—anything that could be used to help corroborate the stories Munford and her colleagues were hearing on a daily basis—would be crucial to give those claims a fighting chance in court. Nassar had deftly talked his way out of charges two years earlier. Munford knew she had flustered him during their interview, but that wouldn't be enough. A more prepared interaction with the help of an attorney would likely help Nassar hold the upper hand if a judge had to decide between the word of a purported medical expert and a handful of women with similar complaints.

The case moved fast inside the walls of the MSU police department. It sped forward outside as well. Nassar was no longer allowed in his office as of the end of the day Monday, September 19. The university was planning to announce his termination the following day. When his name hit the papers again with this news, Nassar's reputation, which had served as his shield, was sure to take another hit. Munford knew desperation would be setting in soon. She cranked away at her keyboard as Monday drew to a close. Her search warrant was ready. The next morning, she would bring it to a judge in hopes they had collected enough troubling information from callers to get inside Nassar's house.

Tuesday morning was trash collection day in the pleasant, winding subdivision of Holt, Michigan. Sometime early that morning, the wheels of a brown Granger trash bin would rumble down the short driveway in front of the Nassars' split-level ranch. The police vehicles that wound their way through the neighborhood to Nassar's home on Tuesday, September 20, had to be careful to avoid the big bin as they pulled up in front of his house.

Magistrate Mark Blumer had not hesitated to sign Munford's warrant that morning. When Munford arrived around 11:00 a.m. to knock on Nassar's door, no one was home. She called Nassar's new attorney, Matt Newburg, to let him know that if someone wanted to be present for the search—and if Nassar preferred an intact front door—he needed to get home soon with the keys. Newburg said Nassar was with him at his office. They would be right over.

Their team, now ten detectives and officers in total, split up once they were inside to cover every inch of the fifteen-hundred-square-foot home as efficiently and thoroughly as possible. They found a hoarder's trove of medical records, documents, and other items while they moved from room to room. Munford would later tell Matt Mencarini of the *Lansing State Journal*, "it appeared he never threw anything out."

There was a stack of records lying on the floor of the master bedroom beside the night table. Another stack piled up against the wall of a basement hallway. Officers made their way to the southeast corner of the basement where they found Nassar's training table, his various bottles of lotions, and dozens of small rolls of tape.

The drawers in his makeshift home office were stuffed with files, CDs, videotapes, and more. The detectives didn't bother to sort through them at the house. They grabbed them all and hauled them up the steps to the driveway.

One detective logged and labeled each new piece before it was placed inside one of the vehicles. Anything that could hold information was deemed worthy of confiscating. There were a pair of laptops, two flash drives, five SD cards with various amounts of memory, three 8-millimeter camcorder tapes, a couple dozen VHS tapes, more than one hundred CDs and DVDs, a stack of floppy disks, a couple cell phones, an iPod Touch, an Amazon Kindle, and a large box stuffed full of Olympic memorabilia.

Detective Erin Held made her way through the house with a camera around her neck. She snapped photos of the evidence they collected and recorded videos of the search in progress. When she got back outside, she trained her eyes on the large brown trash bin still sitting on the curb. She decided it was worth a look. She flipped the lid open to find it was still full. The trash collectors had taken their time getting to the bins on Nassar's street on September 20. Held pulled three large bags out of the bin and stuck those in with the rest of the evidence.

The afternoon was nearly over by the time the team returned to the police station on the southern edge of campus. The investigators loaded a cart with the storage devices and Olympic memorabilia to be wheeled into the building. Two of them drew the unenviable task of searching for relevant material in Nassar's week-old trash. As one detective tagged the items and secured them in the on-site evidence room, two others picked their way through the garbage.

One of them pulled an unusually heavy grocery bag out of one of the piles. Inside they found three different external hard drives. Two of the three sleek silver boxes were neatly labeled, leaving no doubt who used to own them: "USA Gymnastics, Larry Nassar, MSU Sports

Medicine" and "Dr. Larry Nassar USA Gymnastics." He brought the hard drives over to the evidence room just a few minutes after his colleague had finished logging and locking up the other items they had collected. They reopened the room at 4:55 p.m. and added the three new items to their substantial pile.

It took nearly a week for the officers to make their way through all of the material they collected from Nassar's house to search for anything that might be useful. They added an additional laptop—a work computer Nassar had returned to Michigan State earlier that week—to the pile of evidence the day after searching his house. When the Digital Forensics and Cyber Crime Unit opened the work laptop, they found its hard drive had been wiped completely clean.

As her coworkers combed through the evidence they had collected, Munford continued her interviews and delved further into the medical nuances of pelvic floor manipulations. Experts told her that Nassar's habit of not wearing gloves and performing the exams without another medical professional in the room were red flags, but they also said internal manipulations weren't an automatic indication that what he was doing was a crime. There was a chance Nassar could explain away the troubling patterns, pitting the word of a famous physician up against a small group of mostly anonymous women. A prosecutor might shy away from a case with that much uncertainty or, if his case did end up in court, allow Nassar to accept a plea deal for much less significant but easier to prove charges.

The detectives hoped to find something more to strengthen their case. They collected Nassar's personnel files from the university. They sent warrants to Google and Facebook to get the two tech companies to provide data about Nassar's online habits. They had made their way through most of the items from his home and office without unearthing any proverbial smoking guns. Finally, one of the members of the staff's Computer Forensics Unit made his way through the external drives they found in the garbage.

The first few images he found on the drive made his jaw drop. He stopped his search to loop in his bosses. Eventually, MSU police would team up with the FBI to review the contents of the drive. Within the next few days, the investigators uncovered thirty-seven thousand images and videos of child pornography. Some of the images showed children younger than twelve years old.

Police traced the metadata of the images to discover that a large portion of the material was downloaded to Nassar's hard drive during a four-month stretch in late 2004. The period of activity began September 18, 2004—one day after Brianne Randall-Gay uttered Larry Nassar's name inside a police station for the very first time and about a week before her mother met with Nassar and got the sense he believed he had been "put on the radar screen."

The descriptions of Nassar's treatments were murky enough that he might be able to convince the world that he had been upholding his Hippocratic oath even if he was working in a questionable gray area of medicine. The images found inside his curbside trash bin were unambiguous. They made it hard to see Nassar's explanations as anything but a sinister cover story. One month after Rachael Denhollander and her husband nervously set foot in the MSU police department, Nassar's shield was crumbling.

Chapter 26

Victim-Centered

Sexual misconduct and abuses of power dominated the nation's headlines in the first few weeks of October 2016. America, and much of the rest of the world, was paying close attention to the contentious spectacle of a presidential race that was winding its way toward a particularly ugly final month.

During the first week of October, the *Washington Post* uncovered decade-old audio recordings of Republican nominee Donald Trump making lewd comments about being able to grope and kiss women without asking because "when you're a star, they let you do it." The revelation of the *Access Hollywood* tape spurred more than a dozen additional women to publicly accuse Trump of harassing or assaulting them at some point during the previous forty years. The allegations became a central focus of the campaign during early October. New reports came on nearly a daily basis. They were followed quickly by denials from Trump, who on several occasions included disparaging remarks about the women making the accusations.

The many women who were coming to grips with reporting Nassar found it nearly impossible to escape the reminders and parallels of their own trauma. Most followed any updates about Nassar that appeared and waited, impatiently and skeptically, to see if his crimes would be taken seriously.

By the start of October, Andrea Munford was ready to lay out to prosecutors what she and her team had discovered. She was eager to present what she had found to the county attorney in hopes that they might take the next step, issuing a warrant for Nassar's arrest. She and police chief Jim Dunlap scheduled a meeting with the Ingham County Prosecutor's Office for the first Tuesday of the month. The discovery of Nassar's pornography stash added a new layer of strength to their case. Sixteen women had filed police complaints that showed a clear pattern of behavior, and several others with connections to Nassar had also called to outline their concerns.

Gretchen Whitmer was four months into her stint as the acting prosecuting attorney in Ingham County when she sat across the table from Munford and Dunlap inside the police station to review their work. Her predecessor, Stuart Dunnings III, resigned from office the previous spring when he was arrested on charges of paying multiple women for sex and using his position of power to "make life a little easier" for those women if they had issues with the law.

Whitmer's résumé made her a welcome replacement in the wake of Dunnings's crimes. She was the first woman to lead a party caucus in Michigan's state Senate when she took over as the Democratic minority leader after serving for a decade as a state politician. When her term limit expired, she taught classes about women's issues and the law at Michigan State and served as the spokeswoman and advisor for a women's health nonprofit. She was only a few months away from becoming the first major candidate to officially announce her plans to run for governor in the 2018 election. Whitmer's background painted the picture of an advocate who would attack an alleged serial child molester with vigor, but few politically minded public officials pick fights they aren't certain they can win.

The exact nature of their conversation at the police station remains in dispute. Dunlap would later tell a reporter from the *Detroit News* that Whitmer proposed moving forward with charges on child pornography possession because they would be "relatively easy to convict on." Dunlap said Whitmer did not want to pursue sexual assault charges against Nassar because they would be far harder to prove at trial. Whitmer told the *Detroit News* in the midst of what turned out to be a successful campaign to become governor that Dunlap's memory of the meeting was "patently false."

In either case, within hours of their disappointing meeting with Whitmer, Chief Dunlap placed a call to Michigan's attorney general in hopes that the statewide agency might take on the case instead. Police can send requests for arrest warrants to county, state, or federal prosecutors. Deciding which cases end up where is typically dictated by which laws were allegedly broken, the level of interest any of those three entities would have in pursuing the case, and the amount of resources they have available at a given moment in time.

Child pornography charges in the hands of either local or federal prosecutors might have been enough to strip Nassar of his medical license and keep him behind bars for a while. For Munford, that wasn't enough. Her experience with trauma victims led her to see this case through the eyes of Nassar's survivors. She knew from her extensive training that feeling heard and acknowledged was an important part of the healing process for many of the women who had been calling her with heartbreaking stories over the last several weeks. She didn't want those stories to be cast aside because it would be easier for the prosecutor's office to declare victory by pursuing different charges. She wanted Nassar's survivors to be the ones declaring victory.

Dunlap had his detective's back. A nearly five-decade veteran of the department, he had helped create the special victims unit and encouraged the victim-first philosophy. He called to gauge the interest of Attorney General Bill Schuette in pursuing assault charges shortly after Whitmer left his office. He followed up with an email that afternoon.

"These cases...and these victim/survivors deserve a review," Dunlap said. "I am hopeful now they will get an advocate."

Whitmer sent Dunlap a note Wednesday morning that said she believed they shared the same goals, but her office wasn't yet ready to sign an arrest warrant. By then, Dunlap was already making plans to meet with a different prosecutor the next morning.

Munford had seen the tall, blond woman with a professionally stern face before. Angela Povilaitis, in her capacity as an assistant attorney general, taught seminars to law enforcement officials on the best ways to interact with victims of sexual abuse and how to interpret some of the unintuitive responses trauma can elicit in victims. She was one of several experts interviewed in a training video for first responders that explained the neurobiological reasons why someone reporting sexual abuse might have disjointed memories or have been frozen by fear during an attack where investigators might wonder why they didn't attempt to flee.

Povilaitis said on the tape that while it may be natural for most to view a confusing, illogical story as a problem for victims, she considered it to be evidence that something truly traumatic had occurred. She said she believed that a good investigator, usually the first person a victim encounters on the trip through the justice system, can have a major impact on how much that victim trusts the rest of the process and how willing they will be to continue pursuing charges. The video was published in November 2014, just as Munford and her new special victims unit at Michigan State University were getting up to speed.

Povilaitis, a 2000 graduate of Wayne State's law school, seemed on paper to be a custom fit for the Larry Nassar case, the type of prosecutor who would dedicate the time and possess the expertise needed to hold him fully accountable. At the start of her career, she prosecuted child abuse and sex abuse crimes in the largest county in Michigan. For four years, she served on the board of a nonprofit dedicated to raising awareness about child abuse and neglect. In 2012, she was hired by Michigan's attorney general to lead a special group of lawyers that focused on prosecuting complex, multivictim sexual assault cases that were often decades old. Four years later, when Schuette received an email from Chief Dunlap, he sent Povilaitis to East Lansing to learn a bit more about the case.

Munford, Dunlap, and Valerie O'Brien all gathered in the chief's office at the police station to greet Povilaitis and fill her in on what they knew about Nassar. Povilaitis had read some of the initial news reports about the gymnastics doctor and was eager to hear what type of case the police were trying to build. Later, Munford would describe to the *Lansing State Journal* how she sized up Povilaitis as they all greeted one another and settled in to discuss the case.

She held out hope that Povilaitis would want to aggressively pursue criminal charges, but she also knew it was hard to find a prosecutor willing to take on a case that didn't yet look like a sure thing. Munford was prepared to give the best combination of sales pitch and pep talk she could muster.

Povilaitis, though, started talking first. She launched into a story about a particular case she steered to a successful guilty plea seven months earlier. The defendant was a former Catholic priest named James Rapp. The priest taught at a Michigan high school in the 1980s and sexually abused some of his male students. He was seventy-five years old when he appeared in court in 2016 and was already in the middle of serving decades in an Oklahoma prison for separate molestation crimes.

Povilaitis explained that keeping the old man behind bars for the rest of his life wasn't her only motivation in pursuing the case. She wanted to give his former victims a chance to feel justice. She wanted to give them a voice. She made sure that as a part of Rapp's guilty plea, each of the men he abused would get a chance to share their story in court. She collected photos of each of them from the time when they were sexually abused and displayed them while each came forward to provide victim impact statements at Rapp's sentencing. She said she saw value in giving the men a chance to be heard where they were believed.

Munford struggled to contain her excitement as Povilaitis continued to talk. She realized she wasn't going to have to do any convincing. Povilaitis was the one giving the sales pitch, and her approach to how she wanted to move the case forward sounded exactly like what Munford had in mind. She had found the right prosecutor. The detective decided she could no longer hide her feelings.

"Is it inappropriate to high-five right now?" she asked. Povilaitis didn't think it was.

They didn't leave time for any more of a celebration. Both women knew they had a daunting mountain of work ahead of them if they were going to find a way to provide Nassar's survivors with the same moment of redemption that Father Rapp's survivors received. They made the short walk from Dunlap's office down the hall to Munford's glass-walled office. The new partners were eager to dive in.

Povilaitis and Munford waded through the growing list of allegations the detective had been collecting. Munford's phone continued to ring steadily with Nassar-related calls through late September and into October. She conducted interviews during work hours. On nights and weekends, she caught up transcribing interview notes and filing formal reports. The growing stack of complaints now reached well into double digits.

The first few weeks of reports provided a clear picture of how Nassar operated. Munford and Povilaitis could now piece together the patterns to see how he won the trust of patients and their parents with flattery and gifts, how he disguised what he was doing and confused the women and girls who had concerns.

There was no guarantee that a judge would allow Nassar's pornography collection to be entered as evidence in a sexual assault case. The case was shaping up to be a debate about the interpretation of a doctor's touch and the fine distinctions that separated sexual abuse and legitimate medical treatment. Even if Nassar's habit of using his bare hands and not fully explaining his methods made him guilty of medical malpractice, Povilaitis knew it might not be enough to prove his sinister, sexual motives.

A skilled defense attorney might argue Nassar broke convention and pushed boundaries but did so in the search for innovative ways to help his patients. A wily litigator might bog down a jury's minds with the same medical jargon Nassar had used to skate free in the past, planting the same seeds of doubt that had convinced dozens of his patients that their instinct to recoil was wrong. How could a doctor be so brazen if he knew what he was doing was sexual assault?

The child pornography case, which had been sent to the office of the US attorney general because the federal courts would allow for harsher punishment, was a good start toward keeping Nassar away from children in the future. But Munford and Povilaitis were determined to hold Nassar accountable for his sexual assaults as well. They understood the psychological healing benefits victims could receive from hearing that what happened to them was a crime and that Nassar was responsible. Povilaitis knew she could build a case against him, but she also knew it would take time. Both women wanted to remove, as fast as possible, any opportunity for Nassar to hurt another child.

They needed to find a way to separate the complicated medical arguments and Nassar's professional reputation from what they now saw as his clear pattern of abuse. Munford thought she might have a solution. In late September, she spoke with a young woman whose story didn't fit with the others. The young woman wasn't an athlete. She wasn't even a former patient. She had waited more than a decade for a chance to share her story with someone who could help her, and now the chance had arrived for Kyle Stephens.

Chapter 27

Critical Testimony

Angela Povilaitis read through Kyle's police report about hide-and-seek games in the Nassar family basement and failed attempts to convince her parents that their friend was abusing her. She thought Nassar's defense team might try to raise doubts about Kyle's story by asking why she had not come to the police earlier, a frequently used tactic to cast sexual abuse victims as pile-on opportunists making up lies. Munford showed her an interview police had done with Kyle's former boyfriend, who said she told him about Nassar's abuse years ago. She had also tracked down medical records from the therapists Kyle saw throughout high school and college that indicated she had disclosed sexual abuse. Munford's team had already done the work needed to show that Kyle's story had remained consistent for years.

Povilaitis was impressed. Her new partner knew what she was doing. Povilaitis wanted to learn more, though. Before using Kyle's story as the basis to arrest Nassar, she needed to know that Kyle as a witness would be strong enough to stand alone under cross-examination during a preliminary hearing. Many assault cases wither on the vine when victims aren't mentally ready to relive their trauma in a public setting. In those instances, charging an offender can dredge up bad memories without getting results, causing more harm than good for the victim. Povilaitis decided she needed to meet Kyle if they were going to move forward.

Povilaitis and Munford were still relative strangers when they settled into a pair of airplane seats for a short flight from Detroit to Chicago on a brisk fall morning in the middle of October.

Once on the ground, they hailed a cab to Chicago's affluent Gold Coast neighborhood. Stepping out onto the curb on Dearborn Street, they peered up at a recently restored, six-story stone edifice. The once-abandoned building was purchased a year earlier by the owners of Restoration Hardware. The posh renovations included a Parisian-style courtyard café, a rooftop garden, and a pastry shop mixed in with floors full of upscale furniture and home finishings for sale.

Kyle waited for them in the pastry shop. The twenty-four-year-old young professional had taken the train from her modest apartment to meet Povilaitis and Munford for the first time. She picked the spot.

"This is going to be a shitty day," she told them. "Let's at least go someplace pretty."

They talked about lighter topics, slowly getting comfortable with each other, as they ate breakfast on the first floor. After an hour or two, they wandered through the showrooms of furniture until they found a quiet place to talk in detail.

Kyle told them about growing up in Holt, Michigan, and the busy lives both of her parents lived as medical professionals. She explained that Sundays were a time to relax for them, and they almost always spent that time with the Nassars. She vaguely remembered visiting them at an apartment when she was very young, but most of her memories of their old family friends were set in the basement of the white, split-level ranch where Nassar, his wife, Stefanie, and their three children still lived.

Kyle described the times Nassar would bumble from room to room in the basement during their games of hide-and-seek before masturbating in front of her. She told Povilaitis and Munford she could still recall the smell of the lotion he used. Her hands shook when she told them that it still made her gag whenever she caught a whiff of the same scent.

Critical Testimony

The detective and the prosecutor asked her to sketch out a diagram of the basement on a sheet of paper. They sat in the showroom and laughed at the idea that another shopper might have imagined the three women crowded around the paper were planning the details of some soon-to-be stylish living room. The tension and doubt Kyle felt leaving her apartment that morning had melted away.

Kyle told them the sexual abuse continued for years and described how Nassar grew bolder. She relived the night she told her parents, the odd meetings with Dr. Gary Stollak, and the heartbreaking decision to give up on convincing her father after a painful year. She said she never stopped allowing her mind to dream up ways she might prove herself right. In middle school, Kyle fantasized about hiding a recorder in her pockets and trapping Nassar into providing a confession.

She choked back tears sitting on the couch in the fake family room where she sat with two relative strangers as she described the fractured relationship she had with her father for all of her teenage years. Every few months, an argument prompted Kyle's father to remind her that she was a liar and she still owed their friend a proper apology. By the time Kyle started high school, her parents decided she would babysit the Nassar children and help Stefanie when Nassar was traveling for one of the endless gymnastics trips. She said Nassar never attempted to assault her after she spoke up, but through an occasional comment, a lingering look, or even standing a little too close, he continued to find ways to make her feel small and defeated.

Kyle found purpose in caring for his three kids. She decided if she couldn't get Nassar in trouble for what he had done to her, she would do everything in her power to keep his own kids from harm. She told Munford and Povilaitis her only reservation in coming forward was the fear of how it would impact them. She remembers worrying about the other girls too. She could vividly see herself standing in the Nassar family's kitchen washing dishes in the summer of 2012 while

249

highlights from a gold medal performance were broadcast around the country. She wondered how much time Nassar spent alone with the young, pretty gymnasts who were becoming national heroes.

Less than a year later, Kyle stopped looking after Nassar's children and submitted an anonymous complaint about him to the Children's Protective Services office in Michigan. She says she laid out in detail how Nassar sexually abused her and explained she was concerned for the safety of his children and all the other children and young women he interacted with on a regular basis. Her call did not prompt any type of CPS investigation, according to Kyle, who says years later police helped her check to see what became of the anonymous complaint. A spokesman for CPS said the organization does not comment on specific cases, but indicated that in a situation like the one Kyle described the organization normally would launch an investigation.

The money Kyle made from babysitting the Nassar children helped offset the cost of the years of therapy she paid for on her own throughout high school and college. Kyle applied for grants in high school to cover most of the medical bills her parents wouldn't acknowledge. She silently allowed them to believe she had lied to them about Nassar throughout high school, but she played the details of what really happened in the basement over and over again in her head to make sure she never lost the truth.

Finally, in the weeks before leaving home for college, she decided she would try once more to convince her father she was not a liar. In a month, she would be at school and out of her parents' house. She felt she had nothing to lose. Kyle found her dad in the family room on an early August day and sat beside him.

"I wasn't lying about Larry, Dad," she told him.

His eyes snapped to hers and his voice dropped to a menacing growl.

"What did you just say?"

"I wasn't lying," she said, her resolve growing stronger.

His big hand shot out and grabbed her at the collar. He pinned her back against the chair and repeated his question. Kyle struggled away from her father's hand and choked out the words.

"I. Was. Not. Lying."

The hand at her throat went limp. Her father's face crumpled in pain. The rest of his body followed suit. Whether it was the realization that his daughter no longer had any reason to hold on to a lie or the determination in her eyes when she repeated herself, he finally believed the truth no father wants to fathom. He shrank backward into the couch and stared into space. Kyle felt like minutes of silence passed before he gathered himself enough to speak. "What happened?" he asked.

"I am *not* ready to talk to you about that," she told him.

In the furniture showroom, Munford and Povilaitis fought to maintain their own composure. They leaned forward in the showroom and listened intently. Kyle's body shook as she spoke, but she didn't break down. She pressed on with her story.

She described the remorse her father felt and the arduous path they tried to take toward building a new relationship. He apologized and accepted that Kyle wouldn't be able to forgive him easily. He told her he didn't understand how he misread the signs or how he'd overlooked her obvious pain. Kyle told Munford and Povilaitis how she moved to Chicago and started to create a new life for herself. She said that over the years, she reached a level of peace with her father but that neither of them was fully restored.

The chronic pain issues that hampered Kyle's father continued, as did his steady use of prescription medication. He struggled on for several more years, but his desire to fight was gone the day he accepted the reality of what happened to Kyle. He eventually told his only daughter that he no longer felt as if he deserved to be alive. On March 30, 2016, less than six months before Rachael Denhollander's story came out in the *Indianapolis Star*, Kyle's father died by suicide.

*　　*　　*

A friend who knew Kyle's family's connection to Nassar sent her a link to the story in September. She read the first few paragraphs before collapsing in tears on her bathroom floor. Another friend, a lawyer back in Lansing, called the police department on her behalf and found out how to connect Kyle and Munford. Kyle's first conversation with Munford came on the phone as she was driving to dinner with her boyfriend. They spoke again the following day for nearly two hours.

"For me, it was always that I was never supported," Kyle says. "So, I felt that if even one person ever came forward, and I got wind of it, I would come forward. I was going to do whatever I had to do."

Munford and Povilaitis could see that determination written on her face as she reached the end of her emotional story inside the furniture store in the swanky Chicago neighborhood. Some of Kyle's mental wounds were still raw, but they told her they had no doubt she was strong enough to tell her story in court and withstand cross-examination.

Kyle returned home to her apartment and sank into bed. Povilaitis and Munford made their way back to the airport. They were exhausted, but their trip had been a success. They had earned Kyle's trust. A full day in the trenches together had also cemented their trust in one another.

The medical cases against Nassar might take months to build. They knew now that they wouldn't have to wait. Kyle's story was different, and it was enough to file charges. As they flew back across Lake Michigan, Munford and Povilaitis felt confident they had what they needed to arrest Larry Nassar. This realization also came with a heightened sense of urgency. Nassar no longer had access to young women and girls through his medical practice, but Kyle's story confirmed he was still a threat. If Nassar had molested someone like Kyle Stephens, a six-year-old family friend, in his home, were other children still at risk? They would need to move quickly.

Chapter 28

Defensive Posture

While Munford and Povilaitis made their short trip to visit Kyle Stephens in October, Michigan State's top leaders were looking to Chicago for help as well. The university had not yet been named in a lawsuit. None of its employees beyond Nassar were named in a criminal investigation. Nonetheless, Michigan State president Lou Anna Simon and her board of trustees could see the crisis developing on their horizon. Simon surveyed the options in front of her and weighed her responsibilities to the massive fifty-thousand-student institution she steered. She decided to start by playing defense.

On October 10, 2016, Simon and her trustees hired Chicago-based attorneys from one of the largest law firms in the country. The group from Skadden, Arps, Slate, Meagher & Flom included one of its most famous partners, Patrick Fitzgerald.

Fitzgerald's track record during his time as a federal prosecutor before joining the firm garnered comparisons to giant-slaying investigators of another era that inspired Hollywood films. Fitzgerald convicted two former Illinois governors during his time as a US attorney and worked on high-profile cases such as prosecuting the men who conspired to attack the United States with a plan that included the 1993 World Trade Center bombing.

His role at Michigan State started out with much less fanfare. University leaders made no public mention of their decision to hire

Skadden until four months later. At that point, board chairman Brian Breslin said that Fitzgerald and his team would conduct "a factual review necessary to address the allegations being made and to assess Nassar's former work at the university."

Breslin's words led many to believe that the firm's main role would be to spearhead an internal investigation that would assess Michigan State's past actions related to Nassar and share them publicly, much like the investigation done by former FBI director Louis Freeh in the wake of the Jerry Sandusky sex abuse scandal at Penn State University. Fitzgerald and his team, though, had no intention or directive to produce a public report or share findings that would hold anyone at the university accountable for missing warning signs about Nassar. Breslin decided not to say anything about the last section of the contract the two parties signed in October 2016, which said Skadden would also provide "assistance in anticipation of and with respect to any civil litigation that may arise."

Fitzgerald and his group weren't hired merely to investigate the circumstances of Nassar's misconduct at Michigan State. They were defense attorneys hunting for the university's liabilities. When the inevitable civil lawsuits did come, everything that the law firm uncovered in its investigation was all considered privileged information between an attorney and their client, protected from law enforcement and the public.

Simon's reaction in the first few months after Michigan State fired Nassar set the tone for the university's response. Her analytical mind saw the vulnerabilities and played out the scenarios that could unfold. The math did not look pretty for the institution she had elevated through her life's work. She plotted a course forward with the fear of watching her legacy crumble serving as her compass.

A week after the contract with Skadden was signed, Michigan State's lawyers began interviewing the employees who had worked most closely with Nassar. No one from the university attempted to contact Rachael Denhollander or any of the other women coming forward to learn more about their stories or provide a show of support. No one from the athletic department or Nassar's old clinic reached out to his old patients to inform them of the allegations against him or to let them know whom to contact if they had a similar experience. Simon, who had trumpeted the importance and the simplicity of speaking up years earlier in the wake of Penn State's scandal, stayed conspicuously silent. Her counterparts at USA Gymnastics adopted a similar approach.

On November 8, 2016, two Texas investigators made the lonely trek down the dirt road that leads to the Karolyi ranch. Their visit was unannounced. By then, Tom Bean, a detective with the Walker County Sheriff's Department, and Steven Jeter, a sergeant with the Texas Rangers (a statewide investigative law enforcement group), had already interviewed several former national team gymnasts who said they were sexually assaulted at the ranch by Larry Nassar. Bean and Jeter wanted to get their hands on documents that might indicate who else Nassar had treated. They were hoping to take a look around the Olympic training site and see the so-called end room, where several gymnasts say Nassar penetrated them during treatment sessions. At that point, Nassar was already being investigated by Michigan State University police and the FBI. Bean and Jeter hoped to add more charges to the sprawling criminal case. They barely made it past the front gate.

Amy White, the national team travel manager, was at the ranch that day working with the acrobatic gymnastics program and greeted the two men. Rather than allow them to search the property, White called her boss, Steve Penny, for instructions. Eventually, Ranger Jeter spoke directly with Penny, who told him that they were not to search the ranch and that if they wanted to do so in the future, they'd need a warrant. Frustrated and visibly upset, Detective Bean and Ranger Jeter left determined to return with a search warrant.

As Bean and Jeter drove away from the ranch that day, through the dense forest of east Texas, Penny immediately took steps to remove some of the evidence the investigators were seeking, according to testimony White provided as part of the USOC's investigation of the Nassar case. On November 8, White said, she and Gary Warren, a director who helped run camps at the ranch, were ordered by Penny to remove documents. Penny specifically told White to immediately bring "anything that has Nassar's name on it" to the USAG offices in Indianapolis, according to White's interview with the USOC's investigators. White proposed shipping the materials via FedEx and told Penny she didn't have a big enough suitcase for all the paperwork to fit.

An agitated Penny told White to buy a bigger suitcase if she had to and insisted she bring the documents herself. So, White then purchased a suitcase from a nearby Target and, with Warren's help, packed up the documents and then paid the extra baggage fee to fly the overweight suitcase from Houston to Indianapolis. Medical forms. Waiver forms. Emails. Rooming lists. Flash drives. Anything with Nassar's name on it or anything that appeared related to his work was packed in that suitcase bound for Indianapolis.

The next day, warrant in hand, Bean and Jeter returned to the Karolyi ranch to find White and everyone else, outside of a few staffers, gone. The few documents they were able to retrieve on that second visit appeared incomplete and provided nothing revealing about Nassar's medical treatment of gymnasts at the ranch.

"I just knew the documentation we were getting wasn't what we were looking for," Bean says. Neither Bean nor Jeter would ever see the missing documents.

Rachael Denhollander did her best that autumn to continue to fill the void of information coming from USA Gymnastics and Michigan State. To keep pressure on the entities pursuing Nassar, she knew it was important to keep the story in the news. She also felt the pressure of knowing that the only way to be sure he wasn't molesting other children was to get him behind bars. The responses from the big institutions she was pitted against thus far had inspired no confidence that they would hold Nassar and his enablers accountable.

Rachael remained the lone public face for the burgeoning case for almost all of 2016. Interview requests flooded in, and she reviewed past work from each publication and journalist before deciding how to respond. She believed outside pressure would be crucial to continue to keep the case moving forward. She was also wary of any misinformation cementing in the public's mind through reporters who didn't understand the nuances of Nassar's abuse. Much of the community around East Lansing and in the gymnastics world still wanted to believe Nassar's deeds could not have been as devious as Rachael described.

Life for the Denhollanders during that time unfolded with a degree of chaos that outpaced the usual bedlam for a family with three young children. Rachael's two daughters were teething. Her son, a toddler, suffered from a neurological issue that doctors had trouble diagnosing. Overnight stays in hospitals to help find the problem often meant she and Jacob subsisted on cat naps rather than full nights of sleep. Jacob remained a full-time carpenter while slogging through his first semester of doctoral studies.

Other than her family, Rachael remained largely isolated as she strained to keep momentum for her case headed in the right direction. As the only woman to share her name with the public at that point, she received the brunt of criticism from the large crowd that believed Nassar was being unjustly persecuted.

She couldn't connect with other survivors because their conversations could be construed as collusion by defense attorneys if they sounded too similar. Munford and the rest of the police department weren't able to provide frequent updates either. Rachael didn't meet Povilaitis in person until many months later. The fear of any detail or step in the process going wrong consumed the Denhollanders' minds on a daily basis. Keeping up with all these developments while continuing to navigate the other parts of their busy lives was exhausting but unavoidable. The meticulous attorney in Rachael struggled with having to trust others to handle the investigation properly. In the first few months after reporting, Rachael frequently learned about updates in the process she started when she read about them in the news or received a phone call from a reporter. She was in the middle of changing a diaper in mid-November when a reporter called to ask if she had heard anything about Nassar being arrested. Charges were coming soon.

Larry Nassar was filling the tires of his car with air at a Belle Tire auto shop a few miles from the university the Monday morning of Thanksgiving week, 2016. He was wearing jeans, a red sweater, and a large, black winter coat when he was approached by MSU officers in an unmarked car. They informed him they had a warrant for his arrest, handcuffed him, and drove him back to the station on the edge of campus.

Nassar made small talk with the arresting officers as they worked their way through a forty-five-minute intake process. He asked where he would go next while they took mugshot photos and finger-prints and swabbed his mouth for a DNA sample. They chatted about the Spartan football team's close loss to Ohio State a few days earlier while he waited for someone to drive him to the county jail.

Rachael learned he was in custody that same afternoon. Kyle Ste-phens heard from Munford while Nassar was still in the back of the police car. The warrant for his arrest included three charges of sex-ual assault related to the story Kyle had told Munford and Povilaitis a month earlier. On Tuesday afternoon, the state's attorney general held a press conference to announce Nassar's arrest and let people know that the three charges against him were "just the tip of the iceberg." More than fifty women had reported Nassar to the police, but the majority of the charges against him were still months away from being filed.

Kyle smiled, thinking about the way the week would unfold for Nassar. She knew Thanksgiving had always been his favorite holiday.

Nassar returned home on bond after his arrest, but his freedom would be short-lived. Less than a month later, federal prosecutors were ready to unveil what police had found in the large brown trash can at Nassar's curb in September. He was arrested again on Decem-ber 16 on charges of possessing child pornography. His mugshot was printed at the top of the front page of the *Lansing State Journal* the next morning. This time, he would be denied bail.

The news of Nassar's pornography collection raced through the gymnastics community in the final weeks of 2016. The façade Nassar curated for a quarter century shattered for hundreds, if not thousands, of people who had defended him and minimized the allegations against him. Women who previously believed Nassar had spent years treating them in good faith suddenly saw the warm, friendly man through an entirely different lens. For many of them, the rest of the pieces fell into place quickly. They realized the things he had done to them on his training table weren't innovative healing techniques. The man they had been defending had sexually abused them too.

Nassar's closest supporters clung to the last shreds of hope that they had not so wildly misjudged their friend. Kathie Klages, who not long before broke down in tears and had her Spartan gymnasts sign a sympathy card for him, now searched for a way to make sense of the new charges. In a conversation with Christy Lemke-Akeo, whose daughter Lindsey competed for Twistars and Michigan State during her gymnastics career, Lemke-Akeo says Klages suggested that perhaps the hard drives found at the foot of Nassar's driveway had been planted there by police who were trying to make their case stronger.

Other Michigan State employees, who had known Nassar for decades, reckoned with their misperceptions or racked their imaginations for an innocent explanation. Coworkers who knew the cheery side of Nassar struggled to digest the news in late December that FBI agents had discovered thirty-seven thousand pornographic images and videos, including videos that showed children engaged in sexual acts. In some of the files recovered, an agent told the court, Nassar appeared to record himself fondling a child in his backyard pool.

Sally Nogle, the veteran head athletic trainer for the Michigan State sports teams, emailed that afternoon with Tracey Covassin, who ran the undergraduate athletic trainer education program on campus.

"It is so hard to believe, but what we are seeing is so awful I am now believing it," Nogle wrote. "Just too much info from what I am reading. How could he fool us and so many others?"

Covassin responded hours later: "Can I still hold out hope? I have never seen him do anything inappropriate and have not heard of anything inappropriate....Is there any chance that the photos were of him doing procedures?"

Their emails came as Michigan State's athletic department was thrust into turmoil by new revelations. On December 21, 2016, with attorney John Manly by her side at a conference room table in Southern California, Tiffany Thomas Lopez told a room full of reporters that she had filed a civil lawsuit against Nassar and others at Michigan State who had ignored her cries for help.

Months earlier, Thomas Lopez had returned home from a trip to the grocery store to see Nassar's face on the nightly news. She tearfully relived her attempts to raise warnings about Nassar more than fifteen years earlier. She remembered the responses she got from athletic trainers Lianna Hadden and Destiny Teachnor-Hauk. After calling police back in Michigan to share her story, she read more about the case in news reports and learned that Manly and his law office were not far from her home in California. A few days before Christmas, she became the first former Spartan athlete to come forward as a survivor of Nassar's sexual abuse. She shared her name and sat for interviews. Rachael Denhollander was no longer alone in the public eye. More reinforcements would be arriving shortly.

As the calendar year drew to a close in East Lansing, Covassin emailed her staff to let them know how to handle any questions about the unfolding case. She wrapped up her note to Nogle by telling her that she ought to let Destiny Teachnor-Hauk know that she should consider hiring her own attorney. The attorneys hired to protect Michigan State months earlier would be ramping up their internal review and would be asking questions to protect the university, not its individual employees.

Covassin signed off by wishing Nogle "Happy Holidays!!!" December was coming to a close, and on Michigan State's campus and in USA Gymnastics centers around the country, many were only just beginning to grasp the size of the public reckoning that would consume both institutions in the year to follow.

Chapter 29

The National Spotlight

It is perhaps indicative of the anguish sexual assault victims experience when wrestling with the decision to share their stories publicly that for more than five months after the Larry Nassar story broke in the *Indianapolis Star*, not a single gymnast from the US national team, current or former, stepped forward to identify themselves by name as one of his victims. The national team gymnasts who'd filed civil lawsuits to that point had done so anonymously. That all changed on a Sunday evening in late February 2017. Jamie Dantzscher, Jeanette Antolin, and Jessica Howard agreed to appear on CBS's *60 Minutes* to speak publicly for the first time about Nassar's years of sexual abuse.

Steve Penny knew the interview was coming. He'd known it for weeks. He knew the national broadcast would be damning and raise questions about why, for decades, Nassar was allowed access to young women alone in their rooms at the Karolyi ranch and at international competitions. Penny knew the report would also bring further scrutiny to how USA Gymnastics, and how he as president and CEO, first reported Nassar to authorities.

Two days before the broadcast, Penny once again reached out to Jay Abbott, the FBI special agent in Indianapolis to whom he'd first reported Nassar in July 2015, forwarding Abbott an email with the job posting for the USOC chief of security position.

Abbott responded to thank him and added, "I'm also aware of your timeline reporting and will be happy to discuss further tomorrow morning."

That same day, Penny wrote Abbott back: "This is getting much worse for me."

A savvy marketer at heart, Penny understood the power of public perception, so it is not surprising that in the days before the *60 Minutes* broadcast, he reached out to anyone who could help provide him with public relations cover. It was around this time that he decided to reach out to Tasha Schwikert, a former national team member and bronze medalist from the 2000 Sydney Olympics. Schwikert was a week away from taking the bar exam in Nevada. She was caring for her one-year-old daughter, while her husband was overseas in Europe playing professional basketball. She already felt stressed and overwhelmed, and she was surprised to pick up the phone and hear Steve Penny's voice on the line.

"We're in some deep shit," he told her.

Penny never called Schwikert before now when he needed her help. She hadn't had any meaningful interactions with him in years. She was close to becoming a licensed attorney but still felt intimidated by Penny, still clung to a sense of indebtedness to USAG. Mindful of the upcoming *60 Minutes* interview, Penny asked Schwikert if she would be willing to put out a statement in support of USA Gymnastics and Larry Nassar. Then Penny proceeded to ask her point-blank if Nassar had ever abused her.

Schwikert froze. Then she panicked, fumbling for an answer.

"No," she replied, knowing full well as the word left her lips that it was a lie.

She didn't reveal to Penny that in the run-up to the 2000 Olympics, Nassar sexually abused her three to four times a day after she tore a tendon in her groin. Schwikert didn't reveal that more than a year after those Olympics, as a seventeen-year-old, she flew to Michigan, alone, and stayed in a guest room in Nassar's home for a week, where he abused her by sticking his fingers in her vagina as she lay on her bed and on a training table in his basement. At that point, Nassar was treating her Achilles tendon. He'd told her there was a pressure point in her vagina that would increase blood flow to the tissue in her heel. Schwikert never questioned him. She and her mother trusted Nassar completely and were grateful he'd cleared out a week of his schedule to treat her in his own home. "It was almost like going to an uncle's house. It was like family," Schwikert says about her trip to Michigan.

While Schwikert hadn't yet allowed herself to process the extent to which she was sexually assaulted by Nassar, and while she remained unprepared mentally to go public with her story, by February 2017 she understood the overwhelming evidence mounting against her former doctor. At that point, more than eighty women had come forward to say Nassar had sexually assaulted them. After some consideration of Penny's request, Schwikert refused to make any statement about Nassar, agreeing instead to release a more general comment about her medical treatment while on the national team. Her statement was posted on the official USAG Twitter account hours before the *60 Minutes* broadcast:

As a member of the national team from 1999–2004, I firmly believe USA Gymnastics always had my health and well-being top of mind. The program provided me with the resources and experiences that helped me achieve my goals.

Penny's feeble effort to control the message backfired. The *60 Minutes* interview finally gave faces to the stories national team members had shared anonymously for months, faces to women who not only had been sexually assaulted by Nassar but also women who'd been failed by the glaring lack of oversight within the system that enabled him. The extent of Nassar's sexual abuse was finally becoming clear to a large national audience.

Jamie Dantzscher, Jeanette Antolin, and Jessica Howard became in-demand guests, appearing on a series of national broadcasts. Orchestrated by John Manly and his media advisors, the appearances had the dual goal of raising awareness of abuses within the sport and pressuring USA Gymnastics and Michigan State University to resolve ongoing civil litigation.

On March 15, less than a month after appearing on *60 Minutes*, Howard wrote an editorial for the *New York Times* detailing her abuse by Nassar. Among other things, she described her time serving as a board member for USA Gymnastics and the meetings where the issue of alleged sexual abuse by coaches was periodically part of the agenda.

"The meetings seemed to revolve around two things: money and medals. When a sexual abuse case came up during my time on the board, the concern was about the reputation of the coach—not the accusation of the athlete," Howard wrote.

A day after Howard's editorial, Steve Penny, bowing to mounting public pressure, resigned as president and CEO of USA Gymnastics. The *Wall Street Journal* later reported that he received a $1 million payout.

While cathartic, the experience of going public forced Jamie, Antolin, and Howard to confront how much work they still had to do as individuals in order to fully heal. Jamie and Antolin had spent five years together on the national team and would go on to win three NCAA national championships together at UCLA. By any measure, their gymnastics careers were a resounding success. But when they reconnected after coming forward as survivors of Nassar, they discovered they'd each spent years engaging in self-sabotaging behavior. They'd suffered from eating disorders and gone through a series of abusive relationships.

"We both had achieved success as gymnasts and our lives seemed like a shit show. In our conversation, we're rehashing all this stuff and crying, coming to the realization that a lot of our issues had stemmed from us being sexually abused as kids and not even knowing it," Antolin says.

Jessica Howard was a three-time national champion in rhythmic gymnastics. She was thirty-three at the time of her *60 Minutes* interview, and yet she was still terrified at the thought of publicly criticizing USA Gymnastics. Like other national team gymnasts, her sense of self-worth was tied in part to how well she was regarded by those at the national governing body. She not only had buried what happened with Nassar, she'd buried what she endured training under her personal coach, Efrossina Anguelova. All of that bubbled to the surface.

When Howard was twelve or thirteen, she says, the Bulgarian-born Anguelova would poke her in the buttocks and tell her she "looked like an elephant" or "like a sack of potatoes." Howard was rail thin, stood five foot four, and weighed less than ninety pounds. But Anguelova's words cut deep. Howard started starving herself to remain thin. Her grandmother would bake her three dozen chocolate chip cookies every Sunday in the hopes Howard would eat something during the week. On most days, Howard would pull the tiny cookies apart, eat only the chocolate chips, and feed the rest to her dogs.

As a twelve-year-old, Howard practiced five to six hours a day, six days a week, in an un-air-conditioned gym in Jacksonville, Florida, in temperatures that were often dangerously high. There was one fan in the gym, but in rhythmic gymnastics, gymnasts use ribbons and balls in their routines, and because the fan interfered, it frequently had to be turned off.

The mat that covered the old YMCA basketball court where Howard practiced became so slick from the sweat pouring off of her body, she was convinced she'd one day slip and tear a muscle or ligament. She remembers Anguelova making her do split leaps, a basic but physically demanding skill where gymnasts run across the floor and leap into the air into an exaggerated split with their legs. After one or two passes of split leaps, Jessica would typically be breathing heavily. Anguelova had her do split leaps for more than an hour, without water. It got to the point during those sessions that Jessica's chest burned. She'd lose feeling in her feet. If she stumbled or failed to execute the split leap to perfection, Jessica remembers Anguelova's feedback was brutal.

"She would tell us we were 'idiots, morons.' We were 'pieces of shit.' Like, how could we think we were ever gonna be gymnasts if we couldn't even do a split leap?" Anguelova did not respond to requests for comment for this book.

At fifteen, after the 1999 World Championships, Howard's hips hurt so badly she had difficulty walking, let alone practicing and competing. That's when USA Gymnastics suggested she go to the Karolyi ranch for a week to see Larry Nassar for treatment.

Howard was initially thrilled to get a chance to see Nassar. It was a break from the grueling routine of practices with Anguelova. Prior to her first treatment session, Nassar told her to wear loose-fitting shorts and no underwear. As he'd done with so many others, Nassar massaged her legs, worked his way to her inner thighs, and then penetrated her vagina with his fingers. Uncomfortable and confused, Howard remembers her body going rigid. Nobody else other than Nassar was in the training room at the time.

After the first session, Howard used a pay phone at the ranch to call her mother. Unsure of what had just happened to her and in a soft voice, she remembers framing everything she said to her mother that day as if it were a question. "I think I might have been molested?" she said. "I might have been? Maybe?"

After speaking for several minutes, they agreed Howard must have misunderstood the nature of Nassar's treatment methods. She continued to see him throughout the week until the final day that she was scheduled for "treatment." Howard remembers sitting balled up on the floor of her cabin that day in the narrow gap between the bed and the wall, her knees pulled up to her chest and arms wrapped tightly around them.

"I don't want to go back," she told the other gymnasts, who were sharing the cabin with her.

"Yeah, he touches you funny," they agreed.

When Howard didn't show up for her session, Nassar came to her cabin, took a few steps into the room, and tried to coax her to come out.

"Come on. Come to treatment," he said, repeatedly.

"No, I don't really feel good. I'm just going to skip the last session," Howard said, holding her ground.

Like many elite-level gymnasts, the far more serious self-harm for Howard came after she was done competing. In 2004, as a favor to her former coach, she made a trip to Bulgaria to help an aspiring Olympian with her training. Howard hadn't competed for years, and something about the experience of being back in that gymnastics environment served as a trigger. Howard didn't stay in a hotel during her trip to Bulgaria but rather in a small room off of the gym, with bleak, white walls. That's where she cut herself for the first time. Using a safety pin and scissors, Howard carved a small hole in her forehead, just above the middle of her eyebrows.

"The physical pain focused something away from other thoughts," Howard says, recalling the incident.

Howard went on to cut herself for the next six years, mostly on her chest, where the wounds could be easily hidden with clothing. She'd stick a safety pin into her skin on her chest and pull it right through. She'd cut herself until the amount of blood became so alarming, she had to stop. The cutting was by no means the only self-destructive behavior. Howard suffered from bulimia so severe it started to erode her esophagus. She struggled with relationships, substance abuse, and suicidal thoughts.

The childhood trauma Jessica Howard, Jamie Dantzscher, and Jeanette Antolin experienced didn't just go away or get wiped clean after a round of national media interviews. Far from it.

"This lasts your entire freaking life," Howard says. "It absolutely changes the trajectory of your ability to have and maintain every single kind of relationship and has side effects that could be life threatening."

Chapter 30

Uncivil Actions

While the new wave of national media exposure focused attention on Larry Nassar's criminal charges playing out in public, an equally ugly legal battle was being waged behind closed doors. In a series of depositions, resulting from attorney John Manly's civil lawsuits filed in California, coaches and administrators within USA Gymnastics revealed not only a stunning lack of oversight of Nassar but also the national governing body's ineffective and long-standing practice of not reporting sexual assault complaints.

Steve Penny; Ron Galimore, USAG's chief operating officer; Marta Karolyi; and Rhonda Faehn all acknowledged in sworn testimony in cases filed by gymnasts Aly Raisman and Jamie Dantzscher that it was a violation of USAG policy for any adult to be alone with gymnasts, particularly in the gymnasts' hotel rooms, and yet they all said they had no idea Nassar had access to the athletes in their cabins at the Karolyi ranch or in their hotel rooms at competitions.

Renee Jamison, Steve Penny's former executive assistant and the woman who for years had the keys to the cabinets at USAG headquarters where dozens of secret dossiers detailing sexual abuse allegations against coaches were filed away, explained to lawyers conducting the deposition how sexual abuse complaints were routinely handled by USAG.

Q: "So when you received a complaint about a coach that had engaged in—or that you suspected had engaged in criminal conduct, your job was to immediately call the police; is that right?"

A: "I was told to forward all such matters to our legal counsel."

Q: "So your first reaction wasn't to call the police, it was to refer it to a lawyer for USA Gymnastics?"

A: "Yes."

In his June 2017 deposition, Bob Colarossi, the former USA Gymnastics president and CEO who preceded Penny, explained how sexual abuse complaints were only taken seriously and investigated by USAG if the complaint came from someone who actually witnessed the abusive conduct:

COLAROSSI: "It had to be someone with firsthand knowledge."

MANLY: "What does firsthand knowledge mean?"

COLAROSSI: "They either witnessed what happened—well, it would have to be—they would have to have witnessed what happened."

MANLY: "How many sexual abuse cases are you aware of where the abuser abuses the victim in front of another person?"

COLAROSSI: "I'm not aware of any."

During an afternoon break in Colarossi's often heated deposition, Paul Parilla, an attorney for USA Gymnastics and vice chairman of the USAG Board, walked into the lobby of Manly's Irvine, California, law firm and could no longer contain his dislike for the attorney, who'd been questioning Colarossi, by that point, for more than four hours, calling him a "dickhead," as was later captured in the deposition.

MR. MANLY: "Your client walked by my secretary—my recep-
tionist, who is standing right there as he was walking out of
the room and yelled, 'Fucking dickhead.' She heard it. Is that
right, Caroline?"

MS. AKHAVAIN: "Yes."

"If you say anything like that again, you want to call me a name,
you call it to my face," Manly told Parilla that day.

The contentious atmosphere did not bode well when mediation
talks began again in earnest in late October 2017. John Manly and
the other attorneys representing the girls and women suing Larry
Nassar, Michigan State University, Twistars Gymnastics, and USA
Gymnastics had set aside a week, beginning on Monday, October
30, to attempt to resolve the cases outside of the courtroom. Attorneys from the United States Olympic Committee declined to attend
the mediation talks even though the USOC was named at the time
as a defendant in multiple lawsuits. By that point, more than 130
women had come forward identifying themselves as victims of
Larry Nassar's sexual abuse. They ranged from minors as young as
fourteen to women as old as fifty-seven years of age.

The referee chosen by all parties to mediate the cases was Jon
Muth, a respected Grand Rapids attorney who'd handled well over
a thousand mediations in his career. This would be one of his most
challenging. Muth took the job while battling a life-threatening illness. In the summer of 2014, he was diagnosed with idiopathic pul-
monary fibrosis, a rare disease that, for unknown reasons, results in
scarring of the lung tissue, making it hard for those affected to take
in a breath and get enough oxygen. Muth had never smoked and was
an avid cyclist who averaged more than three thousand miles a year.

Doctors told him he had a 10 percent chance of living beyond five years and that his disease was incurable, untreatable, and progressive. Undeterred, Muth continued working beyond his retirement, taking on mediation clients on a contract basis as his health allowed.

In a typical mediation, there are three rooms—one for the plaintiffs and their lawyers; one for the defendants and their lawyers; and then a third, neutral room. It's the role of the mediator to float back and forth between the rooms, relaying messages and offers to the opposing sides and then bringing parties into the neutral room so they can engage directly with one another in order to reach a settlement.

By late October, John Manly had partnered with Grand Rapids attorney Stephen Drew and Okemos, Michigan–based attorney Jamie White to represent the largest group of Nassar victims. Okemos attorneys Mick Grewal and his associate David Mittleman were in another room at the mediation with a group that included at least a dozen of their clients and the family members of clients. There were attorneys in attendance from Michigan State University, who served as the school's in-house counsel; attorneys from the school's insurance company; and the insurance company's adjuster. There were so many attorneys representing so many different interests— perhaps twenty that Muth can recall—that Muth, a man with 35 percent lung capacity, kept an oxygen tank with him to catch his breath as he constantly floated between five different rooms.

The mediation took place at the Dominican Center at Marywood, a former boarding school for the Dominican Sisters of Grand Rapids. The irony was not lost on Manly, the product of a Catholic school education whose firm by that point had won settlements or judgments in excess of $1 billion suing the Catholic Church in priest abuse cases.

The various attorneys set aside the first few days of mediation to deal with those plaintiffs who'd filed claims against Michigan State. Thursday was scheduled to address lawsuits filed against Geddert and his Twistars USA Gymnastics Club, and Friday was the day attorneys planned to deal with lawsuits filed against USA Gymnastics. They never made it to Thursday.

Muth and the attorneys involved are ethically prohibited from speaking about what transpired in those first few days of mediation, but according to people with direct knowledge, the talks broke down when Michigan State's lawyers indicated the school would pay no more than $20 million to settle all claims. It was an insultingly low offer. Privately, those close to the case estimated that any settlement would likely run into hundreds of millions of dollars. As a reference point, more than $100 million had been paid by Penn State University to settle claims by at least thirty-five people who accused assistant football coach Jerry Sandusky of sexual abuse. When talks stalled in Grand Rapids, a lengthy legal battle appeared inevitable.

The girls and women suing Michigan State at that time faced a challenging legal hurdle. The vast majority of their claims were well outside the existing statute of limitations. Back then in the state of Michigan, victims of sexual assault had up to three years from the date of the incident or, if the assault happened when they were a child, until their nineteenth birthday to file a lawsuit. There was also a law on the books in Michigan granting sovereign immunity to state entities like Michigan State. The well-intentioned law, by no means unique to Michigan, was designed to prevent massive lawsuits from financially crippling publicly funded institutions. While a half dozen exceptions to the sovereign immunity law existed, none provided solid legal ground for the attorneys representing Nassar's victims to make a stand in their cases against MSU, and the university's attorneys knew it.

Laws, however, can change. Around the time of the first failed mediation talks, Jamie White, one of the Michigan-based attorneys who'd joined forces with John Manly in the case, began spearheading an aggressive lobbying effort to change the laws in Michigan in order to make them more favorable to sex abuse survivors.

Nassar's survivors were now waging an increasingly public fight on multiple fronts. Rachael put her experience and connections in the state legislature in Lansing to work. She and Sterling Riethman, a twenty-five-year-old former diver who was also sexually abused by Nassar, worked with state politicians starting in the fall of 2017 to draft a proposal for laws that would make it easier to hold predators and the institutions that harbored them responsible. The proposals, which included changing the statute of limitations and the protections received under sovereign immunity, were informed by a better understanding of how long it takes some victims of sexual abuse to feel comfortable sharing their stories.

Jamie and her former Olympic teammates, meanwhile, were using their notoriety to make progress in the court of public opinion. The *60 Minutes* episode and subsequent interviews set up by the well-oiled media arm of John Manly's law firm brought more attention to the case and, more importantly, emboldened other national team gymnasts to come forward. In October 2017, McKayla Maroney, then twenty-one, defied the confidentiality agreement she'd signed months earlier and revealed in a lengthy Twitter post that Nassar had sexually assaulted her starting when she was thirteen.

"Our silence has given the wrong people power for too long, and it's time to take our power back," Maroney wrote.

A month later, Maroney's teammate in London in 2012, Aly Raisman, revealed during a *60 Minutes* interview and in her autobiography, *Fierce*, that Nassar had also sexually assaulted her. Raisman, the captain of gold-medal-winning teams from London and Rio, was the highest-profile former national team member yet to come forward as a survivor. USA Gymnastics, Michigan State, and leaders at both institutions were sent reeling by the news. The media spotlight burned with greater intensity as the criminal case against the man responsible for it was only weeks away from its scheduled start.

Chapter 31

Striking a Deal

The sun was shining on a warm autumn day in Louisville, Kentucky. Rachael Denhollander was enjoying a few minutes of peace while grocery shopping with her children when the phone rang. The name Angela Povilaitis lit up Rachael's screen. The two women had developed a strong, mutual respect by November 2017, but as the date for a trial crept closer, any phone call from the attorney general's office brought with it a new wave of stress.

Nassar and his defense team—now composed of Matt Newburg and Shannon Smith, a Detroit-based attorney with a history of defending sexual offenders—were holding tight to their argument that all of Nassar's alleged instances of sexual abuses were in fact legitimate medical procedures. Nassar's claim of innocence was one of principle more than anything else. Nassar's wife, Stefanie, had divorced him earlier that year. His chances of working with gymnasts or practicing medicine in the future were gone. Months earlier, in July, he pleaded guilty to child pornography charges in federal court. While his sentence for those crimes was not yet set in stone, the fifty-four-year-old man was likely staring at multiple decades in prison no matter how his criminal sexual conduct cases in state court concluded. Still, he clung to the idea that he had not sexually assaulted the more than a hundred women who had filed complaints against him.

Jury selection in Ingham County was scheduled to begin December 4. The trial would be presided over by Judge Rosemarie Aquilina, who had recently decided the child pornography charges against Nassar would not be allowed as evidence because it would unfairly impact a jury's perception of the defendant.

Rachael and her fellow survivors were nervously unsure of what to expect from Aquilina. Born in Germany, the fifty-nine-year-old judge had previously worked in politics, in private practice, and as the first female judge advocate general in the Michigan National Guard, where her aggressive style earned her the nickname "Barracuda Aquilina." She continued to stand out after she was elected to sit on the bench of the Thirtieth Circuit Court in Ingham County in 2008. She kept a streak of magenta-dyed hair tucked into her black pompadour. Her second crime novel—titled *Triple Cross Killer* and featuring a blood-spattered cover with the tagline "A Little Naughty Can Get You Killed"—was due to be published in December around the same time as Nassar's trial.

Six months earlier, in April 2017, Aquilina rankled Nassar's survivors when she issued a gag order to prevent any who were involved in the criminal case from speaking publicly about their experiences with Nassar before his trial. Judge Janet Neff, the federal court justice who presided over Nassar's child pornography case, called Aquilina's gag order "unconstitutionally vague." Neff said the order limited the survivors' free speech and ability to heal, which could "prevent new victims from coming forward." Aquilina issued a new order with more specific language to address some of the negative feedback but held to her belief that some type of restraint was necessary to provide a fair trial and avoid a "carnival atmosphere."

The gag order remained in place in November as Aquilina put plans in motion to summon a jury pool of eight hundred citizens. She cast a wide net in hopes of finding twelve people in the greater

Lansing area who had not heard of Larry Nassar, his federal child pornography crimes, or any of the other harrowing stories of his past.

Opening arguments were expected to begin in early January. The deadline for any type of plea deal that could preempt a lengthy, costly trial—December 1—was just weeks away.

Rachael pressed the phone to her ear, and Povilaitis delivered some unexpected good news. Nassar's attorneys called earlier that day to explore the potential of a plea deal. There were no guarantees the two sides would find an agreeable middle ground, but Povilaitis wanted to know what kind of punishment the women she represented would find acceptable.

Povilaitis and her team set about informing and gathering input from each of the 125 women and girls who had lodged criminal complaints about Nassar at that point. She knew from the start she wasn't going to agree to any terms of a plea deal without their blessing. Rachael remained skeptical. She wasn't sure Nassar's narcissistic tendencies would ever allow him to admit he wasn't helping his patients. She wouldn't accept a plea unless Nassar was forced to admit his actions were solely for his own sexual pleasure. Rachael and Povilaitis weren't even completely convinced that a plea deal was the right way to proceed.

A guilty plea could lead to a softer sentence and a chance that he would outlive his time in prison. They didn't know yet how long his federal sentence for the child pornography charges would be. A trial would allow Povilaitis to lay out, in painstaking detail, the depths of Nassar's crimes and the long-term effects they had on the women he abused. A trial would remove any doubt about the damage he had done.

A trial would also mean Rachael and others would have to take the witness stand and relive their trauma in a public setting. They would face questions from attorneys who would try to cast them as liars and opportunists. It would also be a humongous gamble. If a jury found Nassar not guilty of sexual assault, he could live the rest of his life claiming to never have harmed a patient, even with the child pornography crimes on his record. In the fall of 2017, Povilaitis needed no reminder of the risks that come with throwing a case into the hands of a jury of twelve random citizens.

Weeks earlier, Povilaitis had stood in front of a jury in western Michigan as confident as she had ever been. She laid out her closing arguments against a long-haul trucker who had been accused of raping eleven women in four different states during a thirty-year time span. The defendant admitted to having sex with several of the women but argued the sex was consensual.

He told jurors that the women were angry with him and that through his terribly bad luck, this group of strangers, separated by hundreds of miles and more than a decade of time, had all decided to take out their anger in the same way: by telling police he was a rapist. Povilaitis was confident the jury wouldn't buy that defense, and yet after a day of deliberation, jurors rendered their verdict: not guilty. All trials are gambles.

"Do whatever is best for everyone else," Rachael told Povilaitis over the phone. "If people feel like they need to go to trial, I'm willing to do that. If there are people who really feel like they don't want to do a trial, I'm good with that too."

The two women talked about the details of what they thought would make a fair plea deal. They discussed the sentencing range, how many crimes Nassar would need to admit to, and who would get a chance to address him in court. The last point was not negotiable for Povilaitis.

Foregoing a trial would mean giving up the chance to enter all of Nassar's crimes into evidence. It would mean the court would not rule on every charge against him. Povilaitis decided from her very first days on the case that every woman and girl who filed a complaint needed at least the opportunity to share her story with the court and confront Nassar in person. With a plea deal, their chance to do that would come through victim impact statements at a sentencing hearing. Povilaitis assured Rachael that unless everyone who wanted to speak was guaranteed that chance by Nassar's attorneys and the judge, there would be no deal.

Victim impact statements were not a part of sentencing procedures in Michigan until 1985 when new laws were adopted as part of a nationwide movement to give victims a voice in the justice system. The previous year in a California courtroom—just a few hours north of where Mary Lou Retton would win gold that summer—the mother of Hollywood star Sharon Tate provided that state's first victim impact statement at a parole hearing for one of the members of the Manson family cult who murdered her daughter in 1969. Tate's statement, which helped lead to a denial of parole, is often cited as a high-profile benchmark for the court's changing attitude toward victims.

In the earliest days of a formal American justice system, victims were responsible for building their own cases against a defendant. Victims remained front and center in legal proceedings throughout the 1800s. It wasn't until roughly the turn of the twentieth century that they started to be pushed, literally and metaphorically, further back in the courtroom. By the late 1960s, most states gave both prosecutors and defense attorneys the right to keep victims out of the courtroom during a trial other than when they were on the stand to testify.

An unlikely marriage of law-and-order conservatives (who believed defendants were receiving an unfair advantage in criminal battles) and a growing group of feminist activists (who wanted victims to have a bigger voice) spawned the victims' rights movement in the mid-1970s. Task forces were formed, and President Ronald Reagan threw his weight behind their cause not long after moving into the White House in 1981. One of the early victories of the movement came as a wave of new laws and amended state constitutions throughout the 1980s made the allowance of victim impact statements nearly ubiquitous in state courts.

The legal argument for the benefit of impact statements is threefold, according to Meg Garvin, executive director of the National Crime Victim Law Institute. First, they help the judge understand all the ramifications of a crime directly from the aggrieved party prior to deciding what type of punishment is in order. Second, they help the victim regain a sense of autonomy that can often be lost in the course of a crime and again when lawyers and investigators pick apart details of a crime's aftermath. The opportunity to speak directly to the person who wronged them can often provide moments of closure, its own form of justice. Finally, impact statements help the community by providing citizens an active role in the legal process and a belief that order has been restored. Victims have been found to be more likely to report crimes to law enforcement if they believe the legal system operates with their best interests in mind.

Other legal scholars argue that the widespread use of victim impact statements stretches and contorts the legal limits of the court and has some potentially negative consequences. Putting too much stock in impact statements for sentencing, they say, can lead juries or judges to choose the severity of a punishment based on how likeable or emotionally compelling the victim is when presenting a statement.

Povilaitis, seeing far more benefits than problems, made victim impact statements a central part of several of the plea deals she struck in her role as a prosecutor. In this case, as in many other sexual assault cases she had tried in the past, she was going to make sure victims were heard.

She and Nassar's attorneys traded phone calls and emails to work out the terms. Nassar, they agreed, would soon plead guilty to seven counts of criminal sexual conduct in Ingham County, where he lived and where he saw patients at the MSU Sports Medicine Clinic. Then he would plead guilty to three other counts of criminal sexual conduct in Eaton County, where he visited Twistars on a weekly basis. Povilaitis worked with the survivors of Nassar's abuse and kept them updated while she negotiated the exact details of the pleas with his attorneys.

On November 21, exactly one year from the day that Munford and other officers arrested Nassar outside the Belle Tire auto shop, Povilaitis called Rachael Denhollander to let her know she was putting the finishing touches on a deal. Rachael read through the terms a final time. It was almost perfect. Almost.

Nassar was prepared to admit he put his fingers inside his patients, to admit to repeated acts of first-degree sexual assault. But the draft of the plea deal did not explicitly state that Nassar's actions were done for his sexual gratification rather than any type of legitimate medical purpose. Justice, in Rachael's mind, would not be served unless he admitted his true intentions on the record. She did not want to give him the sliver of ambiguity to claim his "treatments" turned out to be criminal even though he did them in an effort to provide medical care.

She pulled open her laptop and set to work in hopes of finding language in the legal statutes that would force such an admission. She and Povilaitis ran through their options. It was well past sunset when they found what they needed. As part of the plea, Nassar would have to waive "any and all defenses he may have asserted at trial, including any defense that the conduct for which he pleads guilty was for a legitimate medical purpose."

Nassar's attorneys saw little reason to derail a deal so close to their deadline over a technicality. They signed off, and the next morning everyone met in court.

On November 22, 2017, Nassar stood silently in an orange prison jumpsuit and a white, long-sleeved undershirt in the center of Judge Rosemarie Aquilina's courtroom for nearly twenty minutes while Povilaitis rattled off all the charges against him. The jury box was populated by roughly a dozen reporters and camera operators. The first few rows of the gallery at the back of the room were filled with attorneys and their clients, the former gymnasts and patients who had been fighting for years for the admission that would soon follow. The half-filled room buzzed with tense, hopeful whispers.

Aquilina thumbed through the signed document in front of her before looking up to ask Nassar, "How do you plead?"

"I plead guilty as stated, your honor," he said.

She walked through each of the seven charges one by one as Nassar entered his pleas onto the record. She confirmed with him that he knew each charge came with a recommended minimum prison sentence of twenty-five to forty years, but if she wanted to, she could extend that time even further. She confirmed that he knew Povilaitis had brokered a deal that would allow all of his victims—not just the ones he pleaded guilty to assaulting—a chance to make statements in court before she decided his sentence.

She asked him if he was coerced into a plea, and she asked if he was in a proper state of mind to declare himself guilty. Then she asked if he used ungloved hands when he treated his patients.

"Yes," Nassar said meekly.

"And it was not for any medical purposes, is that correct?"

He exhaled audibly, dropped his head, and closed his eyes. "Yes."

"It was for your own purpose, is that correct?"

"Yes."

"And in fact it was against medical protocol, is that correct?"

"Yes."

Aquilina then asked if the prosecutors had any further questions.

"No, thank you," Povilaitis said. "We are satisfied, your honor."

Chapter 32

Armed and Ready

Kyle Stephens stepped around a large folding table covered in smooth, black stones. She had spent the weekend with her mother and boyfriend back home in Michigan, and now they walked together into a meeting room at the Hannah Community Center just north of Michigan State's campus on Monday night, January 15, 2018. Kyle had read about the growing number of gymnasts and other women who said her old family friend had sexually abused them too, but until now she had not met any of them.

Most of the stones on the table in front of her were no more than a couple inches in diameter, small enough to be rolled and rubbed inside the palm of a hand. Angela Olson, a victims' rights advocate, had organized a few of her coworkers to paint words like "Strong" and "You Matter" and "Believe" on their polished surfaces. She laid out 150 of them on the folding table inside the meeting hall in hopes of giving the women who were starting to file through the doors a "worry stone," somewhere to channel their nervous energy that night and for the coming days.

Weeks earlier, Povilaitis and the rest of her team of attorneys and advocates had informed every person who submitted a complaint about Nassar that they were welcome to provide impact statements in Ingham County. Eighty-eight of them were signed up to speak at the start of the hearing. The scope of Nassar's hearing was already unprecedented for any of the attorneys and advocates working the case. They did not know how many days the sentencing hearing would last or what might be said, but they knew it would be stressful for everyone involved. Povilaitis, Munford, and their team had invited the women who would provide impact statements to gather that evening on Martin Luther King Jr. Day to try to set expectations, quell fears, and start building a support network.

Dozens of women and girls filtered into the meeting hall. Eyes darted from face to face wondering if they would see old teammates or friends or neighbors. Some of those present had kept their secrets about Nassar to themselves for decades. Others had just recently come to realize what had happened to them. Grown women with children of their own looked across the room at teenagers and felt wrenched with guilt. Some of them had been abused years before the younger girls were even born. The women and girls smiled politely at one another and tried to bury their nervous feelings. Many stopped at the table of worry stones and selected one or two for themselves.

With the table picked over and as most of the survivors had settled into seats, someone jokingly pointed out to Olson what she had done. A room full of angry Davids sat here on the eve of their final showdown with Goliath, and the well-meaning advocates had just filled their pockets with little weapons small enough to conceal in a hand and imperceptible to the metal detectors at the front entrance to the courthouse.

"Please don't throw your stones," Olson announced to the room. Everyone laughed. For a moment, the room felt light.

Their meeting lasted for a couple hours. The women ate pizza and chatted with one another at round tables spread throughout the room. They traded contact information and connected on social media. For many, these were the first discussions they had ever had with someone who could truly understand how they felt.

Povilaitis and her staff walked the group through some of the logistics of how the week's massive hearing was expected to unfold. None of them had ever coordinated an undertaking like this. After giving instructions, they told the large group they would see them in the morning. Then they all went their separate ways for a restless night alone.

Kyle stayed in a hotel near the courthouse the night before the hearing began. She likes to be in bed early, but trying to sleep was fighting a losing battle. She was scheduled to be the first speaker the following morning, and as the clock crept toward midnight, she was still cobbling together her thoughts and trying to put the finishing touches on what she would say.

For the better part of the previous year, Kyle had kept a running collection of her thoughts while she contemplated what she would tell the world about Larry Nassar and what she would tell Larry Nassar about her world. Munford planted the seed long ago that this chance might come at some point. So, anytime a strong memory struck and her emotions swelled, Kyle opened the same document on her computer and wrote. She figured if and when the time came, she would use her makeshift journal to organize her thoughts.

Kyle shut the door to the hotel bathroom so she could be completely alone with her thoughts. She turned on the shower and let the sound of the water drown out any last traces of the outside world. She scanned through her notes to try to find the missing pieces of what she wanted to say.

She scrolled past a passage she wrote furiously months earlier when she realized that at the time Nassar masturbated in front of her, she, like most six-year-olds, still had baby teeth and her favorite television show was *Clifford the Big Red Dog*. That was going in her statement. She wanted people to see who she was then rather than the grown woman standing in front of them in the courtroom. She found another entry where she recalled not being concerned the first time she used a tampon because her hymen had been broken years earlier by the fingers of a grown man. She was going to say that, too, while looking directly at him. She wanted to spare no detail in order to shame him.

Something was still missing. Her final words to him had to pack a punch. She wanted him to know that he had stolen many years of her life but that she was ready to turn the tables. She had suffered enough. It was his turn now. She jotted down a couple lines. She practiced saying them out loud in front of the foggy bathroom mirror. Those would have to do for now. It was nearly 1:00 a.m., and tomorrow, she knew, would be a long day.

The line for the metal detector in the lobby of the Veterans Memorial Courthouse stretched through the small glass entry and out into the bitterly cold, dark morning. Attorneys, survivors, supporters, and reporters lined up in the predawn grayness and waited for guards to unlock the doors on Tuesday, January 16. They huddled against the wind, traded polite nods, and talked quietly with one another.

Up on the third floor, the six rows of gallery benches in Judge Rosemarie Aquilina's corner courtroom filled quickly. The jury box was stuffed with cameras on long-legged tripods and journalists hunched over laptops. Others who arrived later were directed to a room down the hall where they could watch the proceedings on television screens. Povilaitis, Munford, and their team shuffled through stacks of papers at a large table on the right side of the room facing the judge's bench. Nassar's defense attorneys, Shannon Smith and Matt Newburg, sat at an identical table on the left side of the room waiting for their client. Between the two tables and ten feet in front of them stood an empty lectern.

At 9:22 a.m., Nassar shuffled into a courtroom that had already been sitting in anticipation for several minutes. Conversations stopped. Wearing an orange jumpsuit and handcuffs, Nassar made his way across the room escorted by a bailiff and into the witness box next to Aquilina's bench. Days before, the judge conferred with Nassar's attorneys and the prosecution team to decide the hearing's layout. They decided Nassar would sit in the witness stand next to Aquilina rather than at the defense table to give the women who were going to speak a chance to address him directly without turning their backs to the judge to see him.

Kyle Stephens and Rachael Denhollander sat with their significant others in the first row of the gallery behind the prosecutor's table and watched Nassar adjust his glasses and settle into his chair. Kyle shifted her weight from side to side and shook out her hands. She sat beside her boyfriend, who had turned her into a UFC fan during their time dating each other. He told her now she looked like a fighter walking toward the Octagon, the eight-sided, chain-link cage where UFC fights take place. She laughed, forcing some of the buzzing energy inside her to the surface. She felt like she had her fingers curled around the chain-link cage, rattling it as she waited for her chance to begin.

At 9:24 a.m., Povilaitis introduced Kyle to Judge Aquilina and the rest of the room. She heard one last UFC joke as she stepped from the gallery, and a smile filled her face as she approached the lectern. She looked directly at Nassar sitting beside the judge. She rubbed her palms together, leaned into the microphone, and began. "Good morning," she said. "My name is Kyle Stephens." It was the first time she had spoken her name publicly in the case.

Kyle described how difficult the legal process had been for her. She mentioned how her favorite show was *Clifford the Big Red Dog* and that she still had her baby teeth when Nassar started sexually abusing her. She told the world the graphic details of what Nassar had done to her in his basement. A camera operator winced and pulled away from his eyepiece to gather himself. The lens remained trained on the calm, collected woman in the center of the room.

She explained the rift he caused in her family. Her mother stood behind her, fighting back tears. She explained why her father wasn't there to support her as well.

"Larry Nassar's actions had already caused me significant anguish," Kyle told a silent courtroom. "But I hurt worse as I watched my father realize what he had put me through. My father and I did our best to patch up our tattered relationship before he committed suicide in 2016."

She described her own bouts with depression, eating disorders, and other ailments before turning her attention directly to Nassar. She stared him down as she told him she had been coming for him for years, and at last she was going to follow the advice he had given her in the days after she had first told her parents. She was going to tell someone. She was going to tell the whole world.

"Perhaps you have figured it out by now, but little girls don't stay little forever," Kyle told him. "They grow into strong women that return to destroy your world."

The words echoed inside the heads of dozens of other girls and women in the courtroom and around the country. Some who weren't in Lansing listened to a livestream online as Kyle spoke. They read her message as it skipped and rippled across the internet in the hours that followed. They decided they, too, wanted to be heard. They wanted to stand in front of their former tormentor and let him know they were now in control. The public destruction of Larry Nassar's world was just getting started.

Chapter 33

Expanding Ranks

News about the remarkable victim impact statements taking place in Judge Rosemarie Aquilina's courtroom traveled fast and far. By the third day of the sentencing hearing, reporters were crammed around the edges of the courtroom and had spilled into an auxiliary room down the hall. They came from as far away as France, Ireland, and Brazil. The BBC carried daily updates to other areas of Europe. America's largest networks shared video clips of the impact statements on a nightly basis. The tragic stories some of these women had been telling for more than sixteen months were finally getting the attention they warranted.

Nassar grew more hollow and his face more vacant by the day. He scribbled notes at times on the first day as he listened to the women in front of him describe their pasts. He held his forehead in the palms of his hands while a woman named Donna Markham described her daughter's depression and eventual suicide, a downward spiral that began with Nassar's sexual abuse. He shook his head at times and nodded along at others while women quoted scripture in their statements.

When Jennifer Rood Bedford finished passionately recalling her volleyball career, and her failed attempt to raise warnings and the confusion, anger, fear, and sadness that followed, Nassar removed his glasses and wiped tears from his eyes.

The women he abused grew stronger. The number who would deliver impact statements rose from the original 88 to 101 by the start of the second day. Some who had planned to remain anonymous when they spoke decided they no longer wanted to be known as "Jane Doe" and put their names on the record. Others who'd planned to submit a letter to the judge with their thoughts decided they wanted to stand in front of Nassar and the rest of the courtroom and deliver their words in person.

Jamie Dantzscher's chance to speak came on the third day of the hearings. She wore a white blazer with sharp edges and stood with the posture of a woman who had long ago learned how to project confidence. John Manly flanked her, a few feet behind, wearing an orange tie, a white pocket square, and a solemn expression. The adrenaline rush that used to precede big competitions during her gymnastics career surged inside Jamie again. She was once again on a stage with the world watching.

Extra rows of chairs had been added to the gallery at the back of the courtroom, and all of them were full when Jamie stood in front of the microphone and introduced herself. She briefly described her career and her bronze medal victory in 2000. She described Nassar's sexual abuse in her hotel rooms around the globe and in the small cabin at the Karolyi ranch in Texas. She recounted the vitriol she faced when she filed her lawsuit in 2016 from people she once considered friends who didn't believe her. Then she turned her attention to the man seated in front of her.

"Who do they believe now, Larry? I remember your obnoxious laugh and how loud it was and then you would slurp the drool off your lip. I don't see you laughing now."

Her words carried the tension of tautly restrained rage, the power of a racehorse trying to pull free of its harness. Then Jamie let loose the reins of her fury.

"How dare you ask any of us for forgiveness? How dare you act like you care for a second about our healing? How fucking dare you say sorry about everything you've done and all the lives you destroyed. We all see right through your bullshit now. You're a pathetic monster that is only sorry you got caught."

She told him his day of reckoning had come. She told him soon he would only be able to see the inside of a prison cell, and he would only be able to feel powerless.

"And now," she said, "I can finally say that I'm truly proud of myself for something I've done related to my elite gymnastics career."

Povilaitis read a letter submitted by Olympic champion McKayla Maroney before introducing her next speaker. Lindsey Lemke, the former Michigan State gymnastics team captain and Twistars gymnast, didn't plan to speak for herself when the week began. Her mother addressed the court on her behalf during the first day of the hearing. But Lemke decided after two days of watching that she wanted to add her own voice to the growing chorus. Judge Aquilina had no objections.

Lemke explained to the judge and to Nassar that months earlier she had quit gymnastics, foregoing her senior year of college because her back pain had become too much. She wondered if she would still be competing if she had seen a different doctor instead of spending countless nights in Nassar's basement and office seeking help. Lemke ripped into the people that missed opportunities to stop him. She called John Geddert a coward. She called Kathie Klages a coward. She admonished Lou Anna Simon for her cold, half-hearted response during the previous year.

"Guess what?" she said in hopes that Simon was listening elsewhere. "You're a coward too."

She told Nassar his apology was far too late for her to accept. His fate was sealed, and now it was time for his enablers to be held accountable as well.

"Larry," she said, "I hope you, Lou Anna Simon, Kathie Klages, John Geddert, and all of USAG are scared. Because you have pissed off the wrong army of women."

She leaned back from the microphone and exhaled loudly. The room stood silent for another second before a wave of applause started to build in the gallery behind her. The clapping was tentative at first. The room full of frayed nerves and bloodshot eyes didn't know the proper response for the feelings welling inside them. The noise built, though, and Lemke covered her face in her hands and held back tears. Aquilina did nothing to discourage the show of support usually forbidden in courtrooms.

"I'd be proud to fight any battle with you as my leader," the judge said. The gallery laughed. "You are safe now. I'm so proud of you and your voice. I give every victim in my courtroom, every survivor an opportunity to speak, but I've never heard such a mass of strong women speak their minds in such a powerful way. What you are saying is going to make change."

The impact of their statements spread quickly beyond Nassar's fate and started to reach the individuals and organizations who had enabled him. On the eve of the first day of the sentencing hearing, in a Twitter post with the hashtag #MeToo, America's top gymnast, Simone Biles, revealed that she, too, was a Nassar survivor.

"It is impossibly difficult to relive these experiences and it breaks my heart even more to think that as I work towards my dream of competing in Tokyo in 2020, I will have to continually return to the same training facility where I was abused," Biles wrote.

Days after Biles's revelation, USA Gymnastics announced that it planned to cut ties with the Karolyi ranch. National team gymnasts would no longer have to report to the remote Texas outpost for mandatory training.

The organization suspended Geddert the following day. He waited through the weekend before circulating a letter to the current gymnasts at Twistars to let them know he was retiring. He wrote that he had always planned to retire when he hit sixty years old and "60 has arrived." Most saw the letter from Geddert as little more than a face-saving maneuver by the man who for too long had coached through fear and intimidation.

Geddert's suspension came the same day his most accomplished gymnast, Jordyn Wieber, publicly revealed for the first time Nassar had also sexually abused her. Wieber and Aly Raisman delivered victim impact statements at the end of the first week of the hearing. For Wieber, the most famous gymnast to emerge from the Lansing area, walking past the gauntlet of media and fellow survivors felt eerie. All eyes were locked on her and Raisman as they entered the courtroom. Wieber seldom, if ever, cried. As an elite-level gymnast, she trained herself not to lose her composure. She knew it could get her kicked out of the gym. But as she confronted Nassar in open court, the emotion of the moment overwhelmed her.

"My parents trusted USA Gymnastics and Larry Nassar to take care of me," she said, wiping away tears, "and we were betrayed by both."

Raisman directly addressed USAG CEO and president Kerry Perry, Steve Penny's replacement, who appeared in court in person to hear the victim impact statements.

"I have never met you and I know you weren't around for most of this.... Unfortunately, you have taken on an organization that I feel is rotting from the inside," Raisman told her.

By the end of January, the entire USA Gymnastics board of directors would resign en masse. All of them left under the threat that if they didn't, the US Olympic Committee would decertify the organization. USOC CEO Scott Blackmun lasted another month before he, too, stepped down due to health issues.

The same morning Jamie spoke in court, Michigan State's student newspaper, *The State News*, called for Lou Anna Simon to resign on its front page and in a letter written by its editorial board. The student government declared later that day that it had lost faith in the university administration's ability to maintain a safe campus. A half dozen state politicians joined the chorus of those publicly saying Simon must go.

Simon attended one session of the victim impact statements earlier in the week. She told reporters in the courtroom she did not know the names of Nassar's victims until listening to their statements on a livestream of the proceedings during the first few days of the hearing. Lindsey Lemke, who happened to be standing nearby, told her while cameras rolled that it was hard to imagine the university president didn't know the names of the women criticizing and suing Michigan State. Simon did not return to the courtroom for the remainder of the hearings.

Outspoken and long-standing trustee Joel Ferguson joined a sports talk radio show to defend Simon at the start of the second week of statements. He cited all the money she had raised and the shiny, new addition to the school's basketball arena while arguing that there was much more going on at Michigan State than just "this Nassar thing." He was adamant that Simon would not be "run out of" her job. He scoffed, laughing aloud, at the idea that the NCAA might investigate the university because of Nassar's role with the Spartan sports teams. Hours later, the NCAA sent a letter to the athletic department declaring its plans to investigate.

While Larissa Boyce, formerly Larissa Michell, was preparing to provide her impact statement on the Friday afternoon of the first week of Nassar's hearing, Ferguson, Simon, and the rest of Michigan State's board were wrapping up a five-hour, closed-door meeting. Several trustees arrived on the fourth floor of the university's administration building that morning with plans to remove Simon from office. She battled back.

The board announced that afternoon that Simon maintained their unanimous support as the school's leader, but within twenty-four hours, her support on the board eroded further as trustees started to break ranks and join the public calls for Simon to leave. Simon's white-knuckled grip on the university she had transformed was starting to loosen as wave after wave of empowered women continued to speak in a courtroom just four miles away.

Chapter 34

A Rare Gift

The last word belonged to Rachael Denhollander. Through six gut-wrenching, visceral days, Rachael sat in the front row of Judge Aquilina's courtroom and absorbed a familiar, paradoxical swirl of emotions. She felt pride as the world-changing moment she helped to create gathered momentum around her. She felt the vindication and empowerment that coursed through the room as more women found confidence and felt supported. She had learned long ago that those good feelings ought not to be trusted, lest they be used against you.

Rachael and Jacob drove their minivan to the court each morning from her parents' house in Kalamazoo, where they were staying for the week. She told her three children that Mommy had "business meetings" to attend. She made the hour-plus drive to Lansing and sat quietly day after day on the long, wooden bench a few feet behind Povilaitis, Munford, and the rest of the prosecution team. She patiently waded through interview requests during breaks and doled out hugs after emotional statements.

She listened to Sarah Klein recall with haunting calm, nearly thirty years later, the bathtub and the experiments in Nassar's old apartment. Rachael listened as Klein asked Nassar if she was his first victim or if he even remembered who was the first. Rachael listened while Larissa Boyce asked Nassar if he remembered defending himself against her complaints twenty years earlier. She listened as Amanda Thomashow and many others asked why Nassar wasn't stopped sooner.

Rachael listened to parents crushed by the guilt of not protecting their daughters. To some of them, she explained her own mother had been in the room for her abuse. To ease their pains, she reminded them that parents had been groomed by Nassar as effectively as their children. She listened to some of the women who doubted and derided her when she first spoke up only to realize later that they, too, were victims of Nassar.

She was thrilled to be heard and believed. She was moved by the growing rounds of applause in the courtroom and the empathy pouring in from around the world. All of that joy, though, was tethered to the weight of what lay ahead. Rachael had lived with the certainty she had been sexually abused for sixteen years, nearly half her lifetime. She had learned that storybook endings don't exist.

She celebrated the community of survivors that sprouted during the sentencing hearing and the strength it created. But she also sat through those six days and silently mourned the thought that even though a network of support would continue to exist in the future, it would never be as strong or present as it was on the third floor of the Veterans Memorial Courthouse.

She knew for many of the women still coming to grips with Nassar's abuse there would be dark and lonely days ahead. There would be therapy sessions, medication, looping nightmares, flashbacks, and anxiety manifested in myriad physical and mental ways. When the hearing ended and the world was no longer watching, life and its challenges were going to keep coming. Proclaiming yourself a survivor, she knew, was only the very first step of surviving.

After six days of quietly working to reconcile the emotions inside her, it was Rachael's turn to speak. She would be the 156th person to address the court—nearly double the amount expected to provide statements when the hearing began with Kyle Stephens a week earlier.

The sky was still a dark, predawn blue when Rachael walked hand in hand with Jacob past the icy flagpole and through the cement-covered courtyard to the front doors of the courthouse. Her white overcoat was cinched tight as they waited in line to pass through metal detectors and ride the elevator upstairs to the courtroom. She kept a thin manila folder tucked against her side.

Two others, soon-to-be-mother Sterling Riethman and high school senior Kaylee Lorincz, spoke before Rachael was introduced. Rachael spoke softly at first. Aquilina reminded her to be loud and speak directly into the microphone in front of her. She didn't need the booming voice of a roaring lion to echo off the walls and grab attention this time. The courtroom, and the thousands of others watching elsewhere, were silent. They leaned in, eager to listen.

Rachael spoke with a hushed intensity as she pleaded her case for Aquilina to deliver a maximum sentence. She castigated Michigan State for its failure to listen to complaints decades ago and for playing "word games" to avoid taking responsibility during the previous sixteen months. She told Nassar that she pitied him. She explained to him that the women who stood in front of him during the past week had, at one point, truly loved him and admired him.

"You could have had everything you pretended to be," she said.

She asked her rapt audience to remember the painful stories they had heard during the past seven days.

"This is what it looks like when someone chooses to put their selfish desire above the safety and love for those around them. Let it be a warning to us all, and moving forward as a society, this is what it looks like when the adults in authority do not respond properly to disclosures of sexual assault."

Her voice and pace crescendoed toward a climax. Each word of her refrain crashed down with the emphasis of a banging gavel.

"This is what it looks like when institutions create a culture where a predator can flourish, unafraid and unabated. And this is what it looks like when people in authority refuse to listen, put friendships in front of the truth, fail to create or enforce proper policy, and fail to hold enablers accountable. This. Is. What. It. Looks. Like."

Rachael asked once more for Aquilina to consider giving Nassar the stiffest penalty she could and thanked her for her time. As she stepped back toward the gallery, the room rose to its feet to thank her. They continued clapping as she hugged Povilaitis, Munford, and Kyle and made her way back toward her seat. She closed her eyes as she and Jacob wrapped each other in a long, tight embrace. The full gallery remained standing until she let go.

Aquilina called for a brief recess before the attorneys made their closing arguments and she revealed Nassar's sentence. Povilaitis didn't have much need to state their case for a long sentence in her allotted time. Instead, she used it to reflect on the sentencing hearings and the momentous shift she witnessed in the courtroom that week. She said she hoped this would be a turning point, that she would see more women shedding the stigma of sexual abuse and being lauded for their courage in the process.

"These have been important narratives to hear and witness and listen to," Povilaitis said. "They will be the words that burn down cultural stereotypes and cultural myths. And I have a few takeaways and lessons I hope anyone watching these past seven days has learned and will take away with them. The first is that we must start by believing."

Seven long days of airing truths and taking back control had come to an end. The time had arrived for Nassar to stand and hear his punishment. Aquilina told Nassar, a packed courtroom, and hundreds of thousands more who were watching from home that the disgraced doctor was sentenced to a maximum of 175 years in state prison, a full 50 years longer than the prosecutors had requested.

The terms of the plea deal stipulated that Nassar's minimum sentence—the time before he would be eligible for early release—should be somewhere between twenty-five and forty years. Nassar was already scheduled to spend the next sixty years in federal prison for his child pornography charges. Aquilina set his minimum at forty years, which meant that even if the federal sentence fell apart on some type of appeal, Nassar would be well into his nineties before he had any hope of parole.

"I just signed your death warrant," the judge told him from the bench.

Nassar's face showed no emotion as Aquilina spoke. He was silent as he shuffled out of the courtroom. As the door closed behind him, the room erupted with cheers and applause. Women who had only met each other days earlier held each other in long, satisfying hugs. Tears spilled as a week of adrenaline dissipated and exhaustion sank in.

The crowd thinned out during the next half hour. Bailiffs started to remove the extra chairs from Aquilina's courtroom as people snapped pictures and exchanged contact information to stay in touch. Povilaitis and Munford soaked in the moment with the rest of their team. They rehashed bits of the final day's statements and Aquilina's ruling. They packed thick files back into their wheeled cases. They were finding a moment to exhale when one of the victims' advocates who had helped organize the logistics of this past week's unprecedented hearing swung open the double doors. She approached the table of lawyers and police.

"You really should come see this," she said.

The group followed her into the third-floor hallway where large windows overlooked the cement courtyard by the building's entrance. As they approached the window, their hands covered their mouths in disbelief. They draped their arms around each other's shoulders and leaned toward the glass, choking back tears.

Below, a new crowd had gathered in a semicircle outside the building. They wore winter hats and thick gloves, braving the frozen temperatures for a chance to say "thank you" to the women leaving the courthouse. They carried large poster-board signs as if they were headed toward a sporting event.

We Believe You was written in teal marker on one of them. Others carried similar messages. *Heard, Thank You! We honor your bravery.* Dozens of complete strangers lined the sidewalk to shout thanks and hand out hugs to the group of survivors leaving court. One had a collection of imitation gold medals dangling from her arm. She handed them to the women as they walked out of the building.

Rachael smiled as she walked outside. She stood once again with a manila folder tucked under her arm and her husband by her side as a local news crew approached.

"I'm grateful," she said into the camera. "This is a gift that most victims don't get."

Epilogue

On the night Larry Nassar was handed an effective life sentence, Rachael Denhollander strode down a curving walkway with a hope of brokering peace. Cowles House was among the first structures built on Michigan State's campus. The earth used to form its brick walls was dredged from the Red Cedar River more than 150 years earlier. Since 1941, it had served as the formal residence of the university's president. While Lou Anna Simon never actually moved into the building during her thirteen-year tenure as president, that's where she chose to meet Rachael.

Jacob Denhollander and John Manly waited in the car on Abbot Road trying to wrap their heads around the week that was still only half over, like ocean swimmers gasping for a quick breath before the next wave crashed down. Clips of Rachael's impact statement and Aquilina's dramatic sentencing aired throughout the United States and internationally. Rachael still needed to put her finishing touches on an editorial she was writing for the *New York Times* the following day. In the morning, she would be in New York City to appear on *The Today Show* alongside Kyle Stephens and former national team gymnast Maggie Nichols.

More media engagements would fill the gap between the end of the Ingham County sentencing hearing and the beginning of Nassar's sentencing in Eaton County, where Judge Janice Cunningham would open her courtroom in much the same way Aquilina did and add another fifty voices to the growing army of survivors. Cunningham sentenced Nassar to 40 to 125 years in prison for the crimes he committed in Eaton County, where John Geddert's Twistars is located. The attorney general would appoint a special investigator and begin a top-to-bottom investigation into Michigan State as the Eaton County hearing unfolded. Manly and a battalion of other civil attorneys continued to press for a settlement to their civil lawsuits.

First, though, Rachael rang the bell outside Cowles House and stepped inside to meet Simon. She arrived with an offer in mind. She wanted to ask the president to show contrition, to take responsibility, and to start on a list of tangible steps to change the culture on Michigan State's campus. In exchange, Rachael was prepared to tell Simon she would stand by her side and tell the public that Simon was still the right woman to repair the university she had spent a lifetime shaping. Rachael never got the chance to present her offer.

Simon started their confidential meeting that night—a face-to-face arranged with the assistance of the state's lieutenant governor—by telling Rachael that she had served her final day as Michigan State's president. She passed Rachael a copy of the resignation letter that was about to be posted to the university's website. Manly and Jacob would read the breaking news of Simon's ouster on social media as they sat outside in the car.

"As tragedies are politicized, blame is inevitable," Simon wrote in her letter. "As president, it is only natural that I am the focus of this anger. I understand, and that is why I have limited my personal statements. Throughout my career, I have worked very hard to put Team MSU first."

She remained unwilling, to the very end, to take ownership of her administration's missteps. She noted that the review led by attorney Patrick Fitzgerald found no evidence of a cover-up. She overlooked that repeated failures by university employees to listen to and believe Larry Nassar's victims kept him on campus for decades. Simon also never conceded that the school's tone-deaf response under her leadership during the previous sixteen months had compounded the pain and trauma of many of Nassar's survivors.

The board of trustees remained intact and, in a week's time, selected John Engler to succeed Simon on an interim basis. Engler, a former three-term Michigan governor, had a well-earned reputation as a political brawler and bully during his prominent career in the Republican Party. Board members hoped Engler still held enough political clout to thwart the threats coming from the state legislature. His mission was to plow through the remaining fallout from the Nassar scandal and resolve the hundreds of civil lawsuits threatening the school's financial future.

The political climate did not favor Engler. Buoyed by the media coverage of Nassar's sentencing hearing, attorney Jamie White continued his lobbying campaign to make it possible for the victims of Nassar to file lawsuits even years after their sexual abuse occurred. By May 2018, White and his lobbyist had already scored major victories at the state capitol. A bill to reform the statute of limitations laws for child sex abuse cases passed the Senate. If signed into law, it would allow sexual abuse victims to file civil lawsuits for up to thirty years past their eighteenth birthdays and was retroactive to 1997, the first year Nassar was reported. More importantly, it provided a window of ninety days from the time of the governor's signature for any Nassar victim to file a lawsuit.

After the Senate bill passed, an angry John Engler stormed in and out of offices at the state capitol, at one point slamming the door of the speaker of the house.

"We got their attention," White told John Manly.

While the political battle raged in Lansing, Manly and the other attorneys representing Nassar survivors were engaged in yet another tense round of mediation talks in Los Angeles with attorneys from Michigan State and the school's insurance companies. By mid-May

2018, 333 people—including two young men—had filed lawsuits claiming that they had been sexually assaulted by Nassar.

At the time of those mediation talks, the political battleground for Jamie White had shifted to Michigan's House of Representatives and its Judiciary Committee. The Committee had approved reforms to the state's statute of limitations laws, but that wasn't the only hurdle facing the plaintiffs. White was most concerned about the apparent lack of support for reforms he was seeking to the state's sovereign immunity law, which shielded public entities like Michigan State from lawsuits. White was concerned enough about the Judiciary Committee's pending vote on sovereign immunity that he left the Los Angeles mediation talks to fly back to Lansing to help his lobbyist count votes.

It was nearing 5:00 p.m. on Tuesday, May 13, when White called Manly, who, at the time, was locked in settlement negotiations in Los Angeles with lawyers from Michigan State.

"Man, you got to get this deal done. We're going to lose [on sovereign] immunity," White told him. "You need to settle this case."

What followed was the most anxious ninety minutes of Jamie White's life. A staggering offer of $500 million was on the table for consideration to settle the lawsuits of 333 Nassar victims who were suing MSU as well as any future claims, but it was all in danger of going away if the news out of Lansing spread to Los Angeles and MSU attorneys tried to use a political victory on sovereign immunity as leverage.

Manly and the other plaintiffs' attorneys agreed to accept the $500 million settlement, but the wait to see if that massive settlement figure would also be approved by Michigan State's board of trustees felt excruciatingly long. As the minutes ticked by, White nervously paced back and forth inside his home just outside of East Lansing. He couldn't bring himself to sit down.

Then the phone rang. It was one of White's associates.

"They settled it for $500 million," he told White.

White collapsed.

"We did it. We did it. It's done," he told his wife.

Of the $500 million from Michigan State, $425 million was divided among those initial 333 plaintiffs. Another $75 million was reserved for Nassar victims who had yet to come forward. The list of plaintiffs eventually grew to more than 500 people who say Nassar sexually abused them. For the survivors, the settlement felt like only a partial victory. It was the largest settlement ever in a sexual misconduct case involving a university, but it came with no admission of wrongdoing by the school and little hope for meaningful policy changes. A more complete reckoning was still to come as those who enabled Nassar over the decades would face criminal charges of their own.

Nassar's former boss William Strampel, dean of the College of Osteopathic Medicine, was arrested in March 2018 on charges of criminal sexual conduct related to his treatment of four female students and his failure to provide oversight of Nassar after the 2014 criminal and Title IX investigation of Nassar's sexual assault of Amanda Thomashow. On his work computer, investigators found nude and semi-nude photos of women who had Michigan State tattoos or were wearing university-branded clothing. One former student alleged Strampel hinted that she could exchange sex or naked pictures for academic help. Two others alleged Strampel groped them. Strampel's performance reviews included complaints dating back to 2005 about his inappropriate sexual comments. He resigned from his post as dean one month before Nassar's sentencing hearing and retired from his faculty duties in June 2018.

In June 2019, Strampel was sentenced to spend one year in prison on charges of misconduct in office and willful neglect of duty. Jurors found he displayed "complete indifference" regarding Nassar's procedures after Thomashow filed her sexual assault complaint. Neither Strampel nor anyone else at MSU ever bothered to check to see if Nassar was following the protocols Strampel instructed him to abide by while treating female patients. Strampel was acquitted on charges of criminal sexual conduct. Strampel's former supervisor, Michigan State provost June Youatt, resigned in September 2019 on the same day that the US Department of Education fined the school a record $4.5 million for its failures in handling complaints about Nassar and Strampel.

In June 2018, Nassar's longtime colleague on the Team USA medical staff, athletic trainer Debbie Van Horn, was indicted by a Walker County, Texas, grand jury on charges of sexual assault of a child. Prosecutors accused Van Horn of acting as a party during Nassar's sexual assault of at least one former national team gymnast. She was arrested in early September while getting off a plane in the Houston airport and later pleaded not guilty.

In August 2018, former MSU gymnastics coach Kathie Klages was charged with two counts of lying to police. She told investigators she wasn't aware of Nassar's sexual misconduct prior to 2016, even though Larissa Boyce and another gymnast both say they reported Nassar's sexually inappropriate conduct to Klages in 1997. Klages has pleaded not guilty.

In November 2018, former MSU president Lou Anna Simon was also charged with lying to police. Simon, who has since pleaded not guilty, told investigators from the attorney general's office that she was "not aware of the nature of the complaint" that led to Amanda Thomashow's 2014 Title IX investigation. She denied knowing it involved Larry Nassar specifically and claimed she was only aware "there was a sport medicine doc who was subject to a review." Simon's public protests rang hollow to many who knew her as an administrator with a fanatical attention to detail. Simon retired in

Epilogue

August 2019 with the understanding she would receive $2.45 million in severance pay over the course of the next three years. Her criminal case was pending at the time of her retirement.

Valerie O'Brien of the MSU police was promoted to Assistant Chief after the Nassar hearings. She was later suspended for undisclosed reasons and remained on paid leave at press time.

In September 2018, the US Department of Justice Office of the Inspector General announced it was investigating the FBI's failure to promptly investigate the reports of Nassar's sexual abuse of national team gymnasts. Jay Abbott, the former special agent in charge of the FBI's Indianapolis field office, who at one time corresponded in such a familiar tone about a USOC security job with USAG CEO Steve Penny, retired from the Bureau after more than thirty years of service. The FBI and Abbott declined to answer questions for this book.

The reckoning for Penny came in October 2018 when a group of armored US marshals from the Smoky Mountain Fugitive Task Force stormed a cabin in Gatlinburg, Tennessee, where he'd been vacationing with his wife and three children. A month earlier, a Walker County, Texas, grand jury had indicted Penny on charges of tampering with evidence, charges that were related to his order to remove documents from the Karolyi ranch in November 2016. Penny pleaded not guilty.

USA Gymnastics, the organization Penny ran for nearly a dozen years, had been in turmoil for months. One public relations gaffe after another led to the resignations of the two CEOs who followed Penny in the span of just two months. In November 2018, the USOC took steps to decertify USA Gymnastics, essentially stripping the national governing body of its power to control the sport. A month later, USAG filed for bankruptcy.

As of press time for this book, Scott Blackmun, the former CEO of the USOC (the organization has since been renamed the USOPC to include Paralympic athletes), was the target of a criminal investigation by the Department of Justice and FBI that began after two senators accused him of lying to Congress.

In July 2019, the USOPC disclosed in tax documents that Blackmun was given a $2.4 million buyout when he resigned in February 2018 citing health reasons. His resignation, one month after Nassar's sentencing, also came amid mounting public criticism for his inaction after learning about reports of Nassar's abuse.

In the months after Nassar's sentencing, interim MSU president John Engler's combative style continued to hurt more than help a school desperately trying to repair its reputation. Publicly, he suggested Nassar survivors were "enjoying" their time in the spotlight; privately, he suggested Rachael Denhollander was receiving kickbacks from John Manly for recruiting clients. During one highly publicized incident, he reportedly remarked upon seeing the teal cover of an alumni magazine dedicated to the Nassar incident, "Get that teal shit out of here." Nassar survivors had taken to wearing teal, the color used to raise awareness of sexual assault, as a show of support and solidarity. In January 2019, Engler was forced to resign.

A month later, the Michigan attorney general's office announced it was taking over an investigation into John Geddert's allegedly abusive behavior. If charged, Geddert would become the sixth person caught in the criminal ripple effect of Larry Nassar's downfall.

In April 2019, roughly two hundred girls and young women who say they were sexually assaulted by Nassar agreed to settle their outstanding civil lawsuits with Geddert and his Twistars USA Gymnastics Club. Geddert wouldn't comment on the $2.125 million settlement, which was the maximum allowed under his insurance policy. As of press time for this book, claims against the US Olympic Committee and USA Gymnastics remained unresolved.

Epilogue

Within hours of being released into the general population of the federal penitentiary in Tucson, Arizona, Nassar was physically attacked. After that July 2018 attack, Nassar unsuccessfully appealed his prison sentences and has since been moved to the high-security Coleman II US Penitentiary outside of Orlando, Florida, where he's refused dozens of requests to share more details about his crimes, what others knew about them, and how he avoided detection for so long.

Three months after the Nassar case concluded, Angela Povilaitis left her post as a state prosecutor to focus her efforts even more on helping victims of sexual abuse. She accepted a job as a staff attorney for the Michigan Domestic and Sexual Violence Treatment and Prevention Board. Part of her duties in the new role includes training law enforcement officials on the best ways to pursue justice in criminal investigations involving sexual assault.

She has presented her experience at conferences around the country along with one of her most trusted colleagues and friends, Andrea Munford. Detective Lt. Munford moved to a new office down the hall from her old one in the summer of 2018. The steady stream of requests for her to teach the victim-centered, trauma-informed investigation techniques that brought Nassar to justice led Chief Jim Dunlap to create a new department within the MSU police department to train officers and agents around the country.

The events of 2017 and 2018 also reshaped the personal and professional lives of many of Nassar's survivors. Several became activists and advocates fighting for tougher laws, increased education, and better support networks for victims. Jessica Howard testified before the Senate Judiciary Committee, detailing the abuses and the lack of oversight within her sport that enabled Nassar for decades. Jamie Dantzscher, Jeanette Antolin, Mattie Larson, and Dominique Moceanu were all on hand when California senator Dianne

Feinstein announced new federal legislation requiring the national governing bodies of amateur sports to immediately report sex abuse allegations to law enforcement. It passed the Senate unanimously and was signed into law in February 2019.

In Michigan, Brianne Randall-Gay agreed to help the Meridian Township Police, who had dismissed her claim in 2004, to rethink the way they handle sexual assault cases.

Amanda Thomashow took a job with the state of Michigan as a campus sexual assault response and prevention coordinator. Her office in Lansing was down the hallway from Povilaitis. She left that position in 2019 to join Trinea Gonczar in starting their own education and advocacy group called Survivor Strong.

Sarah Klein, one of the earliest known Nassar survivors, had worked primarily as a business consultant when she was thrust into the national spotlight because of the Nassar scandal. She has since joined a Delaware law firm where she now represents victims of child sex abuse. She's successfully lobbied legislatures in multiple states to put more victim-friendly child sex abuse laws on the books.

John Manly and his firm continue to represent sexual assault survivors in some of the country's most high-profile cases. He took on the cases of the two men featured in the HBO documentary *Leaving Neverland*, who said the late pop star Michael Jackson sexually abused them for years when they were children.

The bonds formed during those life-altering weeks in the winter of 2018 carried forward as the survivors returned to their homes throughout the country. Most of them fell back into the rhythms of their daily lives. In dark periods, they leaned on one another, while still processing the trauma of their abuse.

Six months after Larry Nassar shuffled out of a courtroom for the final time, Jamie Dantzscher and more than 140 of the women who spoke at Nassar's sentencing hearing gathered again, this time in the sunshine and glitz of Southern California. They donned formal gowns, and a small group of them walked the red carpet into the Microsoft Theater in downtown Los Angeles alongside Hollywood celebrities and the biggest names in professional sports.

The survivors were there to accept ESPN's Arthur Ashe Courage Award, given annually to a recipient whose perseverance and courage in the face of adversity transcend the sporting world. Jamie patiently waited backstage for the award to be presented, while celebrities and athletes including actress Jennifer Garner, NFL wide receiver Odell Beckham Jr., and Seattle Seahawks quarterback Russell Wilson and his wife, recording artist Ciara, dropped into the packed greenroom to greet survivors. Never one to impress easily, Jamie stayed mostly on the periphery while the starstruck crowd flocked around the celebrities to take pictures.

Sarah Klein, Tiffany Thomas Lopez, and Aly Raisman accepted the award that night on behalf of the group of survivors, who stood shoulder-to-shoulder behind them in an impressive display of solidarity, and told the room and the rest of the world watching on television that sharing their stories over and over was grueling and painful yet necessary to create change. They presented themselves as "a portrait of survival, a new vision of courage." It was a moment of triumph. But the moment was missing one thing—the first woman who stood alone in front of the world asking for Larry Nassar to be held accountable.

In the months since her meeting with Lou Anna Simon, Rachael Denhollander had traveled the country as a speaker, an advocate for new laws, and an author sharing a message about the need to listen to and believe survivors. She carried the weight of sharing her story.

That night in July, though, Rachael watched on television while Jamie held hands with her former teammate from Team USA and

UCLA, Jeanette Antolin, and while Larissa Boyce, who first reported Nassar in 1997, locked hands with former MSU gymnast Lindsey Lemke. She saw the cameras pan through the audience where Judge Rosemarie Aquilina, Andrea Munford, Angela Povilaitis, and John Manly all sat beaming with pride and admiration. More than two thousand miles away from the bright lights of Los Angeles, Rachael and Jacob lounged next to one another on the couch in their modest home in Louisville, Kentucky. Rachael's doctors had prohibited her from flying across the country to join the rest of the survivors.

Two days later, Jacob helped Rachael to the family minivan and rushed her to the hospital, where she was filled with an emotion she hadn't always associated with a doctor's office: Hope. Rachael delivered her fourth child on July 20, 2018, into a world she helped to reshape for little girls everywhere. She and Jacob named their daughter Elora Renee Joy Denhollander. Elora, which means "to God belongs the victory," and Renee, in honor of Detective Lt. Andrea *Renee* Munford, the first adult in a position of authority to believe.

Acknowledgments

We were several hours into one of multiple interviews with just one of the many Larry Nassar survivors who helped make this book possible when the depths of the debt of gratitude we owe all of them fully hit home. We were discussing some of the difficulties of publicly revealing a traumatic sexual assault, and this particular woman was explaining that she had vivid nightmares and trouble sleeping on days when she spoke about Nassar's sexual abuse—whether it was in court, as an advocate for change, or in an interview with a reporter. She saw the gears turning and nodded to confirm that, yes, she was taking part in this conversation knowing full well that it would lead to another horrible night ahead.

The survivors of Nassar's abuse educated and inspired many people, including us, during the last several years. The sacrifice it took to tell their stories again and again is not lost on us, and so first and foremost we thank all of them for their courage and persistence. We hope we've shared their stories in a way that will add a small bit to the massive progress they've made in how society views and reacts to reports of sexual assault. To those who were interviewed for this book, thank you for your openness and patience. To those we've met during the course of our reporting who did not appear in this book, thank you for the time you spent helping us understand the wider scope of the story.

Acknowledgments

We are not the first to explore in book form the abusive culture within club and elite-level gymnastics. Joan Ryan's *Little Girls in Pretty Boxes* did that in 1995 and set an incredibly high standard. Former national champion gymnast Jennifer Sey's 2008 *Chalked Up* and former Olympic gold medalist Dominique Moceanu's 2012 memoir *Off Balance* added powerful personal accounts to Ryan's groundbreaking book. All three women were supportive of this project, and for that we are grateful.

We are also indebted to the many parents, doctors, law enforcement officials, coaches, and attorneys who added their expertise and their experience to our reporting. They, too, were gracious beyond reason with the time and information they were willing to share with us. Attorneys and staffers at several law firms assisted in our reporting. The staff at Manly, Stewart & Finaldi was of particular help, notably Stu Mollrich, Sean Simko, Kathy Frederiksen, Annie Guthrie, and Alex Cunny. Thanks also to Michigan-based attorneys Mick Grewal and David Mittleman.

Start by Believing isn't just the title of our book. Since 2011, it's been the name of a public awareness campaign, first envisioned by Joanne Archambault, a retired sergeant with the San Diego Police Department's Sex Crimes Unit, who went on to become founder and CEO of End Violence Against Women International. The organization launched the Start by Believing campaign because she saw firsthand the damage that occurs when victims of sexual assault are met with skepticism by law enforcement, family members, and society at large. We'd like to thank her for graciously embracing the title of our book and also thank Kimberly Lonsway, the director of research for End Violence Against Women International, for deepening our understanding of the effects of sexual assault.

The journalists who covered this story locally and nationally share a unique bond. Nobody emerged from the courtroom in

Acknowledgments

Lansing after days of searing victim statements without being profoundly impacted. Many fellow reporters set aside concerns about competition in the interests of helping us produce a more complete historical record. We'd like to single out Matt Mencarini, formerly of the *Lansing State Journal*, whose exceptional work on the Nassar story helped him land at the *Louisville Courier Journal*, and Alexandra Ilitch, who left WLNS to start Veracity, a website dedicated to investigative journalism, where she continues to break important news on the Nassar case. Scott Reid, of the *Orange County Register*, who has been exposing abuses in amateur sports since long before the Nassar scandal ever broke, was also of great help.

Our story would have amounted to nothing more than good intentions and an idea if not for the early guidance of literary agent Eric Lupfer of Fletcher & Company. Thank you, Eric, for shepherding two first-time authors through the process and having the vision to bring the story we wanted to tell into sharper focus. Much the same could and should be said of Paul Whitlatch, executive editor at Hachette Books. He also took on two rookies and provided the guidance and thoughtful revision we would need to see the project through to its end. Eric and Paul both believed from the beginning that it was important to tell this story in a respectful, nonexploitative way. We're thankful they both trusted us to do that and helped us accomplish our goals to that end. Thanks also to Brant Rumble, Mollie Weisenfeld, and the entire team at Hachette Books.

Our reporting on this subject didn't start with the idea of writing a book. We spent more than a year and a half reporting this story for ESPN before realizing there was more to say. The time and advice we received from our company and colleagues gave us the foundation for this book. We'd like to specifically thank Dwayne Bray and Chris Buckle for their leadership and support in coordinating a lengthy, complicated endeavor.

Acknowledgments

Paula Lavigne and Nicole Noren's tenacious reporting for ESPN was an integral part of exposing Michigan State's shortcomings in handling sexual assault claims. They've both contributed tireless and often thankless work on campus sexual assault issues at Michigan State and beyond. Paula's knowledge, insight, and ninja-like public records skills were an irreplaceable part of bringing this story to light. More importantly, these colleagues and many others were priceless sources of wisdom and encouragement. They are the friends you want in any foxhole, and we're proud to work with them.

Our manuscript benefited from several people who agreed to offer notes as it was rounded into shape. Thank you to our colleague Tonya Malinowski for her sharp editor's eye, and to Jessica O'Beirne, host of the popular *GymCastic* podcast, for helping us fill the gaps in our budding gymnastics knowledge, and for her editing suggestions and assistance with the reporting. Thank you to Paula Lavigne (again), Mark Fainaru-Wada, and John U. Bacon for walking us through some of the early steps of getting this project off the ground, and thanks to Charlotte Gibson for making sure we had our facts straight.

Finally, our deep appreciation goes out to the friends and family who put up with us through long nights and nonexistent weekends.

Dan

I would like to say a special thank-you to my new bride, Meredith. From the nights you greeted me at the door with a glass of whiskey and a stress-relieving golden retriever after twelve-hour days of harrowing impact statements during Nassar's sentencing hearings to the way you took on planning a wedding and keeping our lives on track so I could (almost) hit deadlines, you have been the driving force keeping me moving forward. You pushed me to start a daunting challenge, and you pushed me when I needed help getting across

Acknowledgments

the finish line. Any good that comes from my contributions here starts with you. To Kath, Babu, Cathy, Scott, Ed, Lia, Colleen, Matt, Tim, Nicole, and Sean, you're all swell as well. And to John, who let a guy who was new to this level of reporting tag along at the very start of what turned out to be a life-changing story and taught him some good tricks along the way, I don't think I'll ever be able to repay you. But the next round's on me.

John

I would especially like to thank my kids, Jack and Krystyna, who, like everyone else these past several months, grew weary of hearing about "the book." I'm the fifth generation in my family to enter the journalism business. It is my hope this work stands as a proud moment in the family history. To my mother, father, and Gail, your encouragement carried me as did the support of a collection of loyal friends: Greg Amante, Andy Lockett, Lou Papathanasakis, Jim Spyropoulos, John Anglim, Jim Cleave, Matt Moresco, Drew Pompilio, and the entire Whiskey roster (the hockey team, not the alcoholic beverages), and, of course, Delaware County's favorite son, Jimmy Griesser. Finally, to Dan Murphy, this started as your idea. Couldn't imagine a better copilot.

Index

Index

Index

Index

Index

Index

Index

Index

Index

Index

Index

Index

Index